INSTEAD OF THE SAME SKI TRIP AS EVERY

TOM, DICK AND HARRY,

TAKE THE SAME SKI TRIP AS EVERY

PIERRE, HANS AND ANTONIO.

ALPINE EXPERIENCE. SKI, SLEEP, FLY EUROPE STARTING AT $774. This year, while the Joneses and the Smiths snowplow the Rockies, you can schuss a glacier or even ski from one country to another – for the same price. From only $774* per person, choose from 90 hotels, 17 resorts in Switzerland, Italy, France, Austria and Germany. Including round-trip Economy Class air, 7 nights accommodations, transfers, breakfast daily and often dinner. Plus, the undying admiration of every average Joe. Call your travel agent or **1-800-662-0021**, ext. 34 for a free Alpine Experience brochure.

swissair +
the refreshing airline
www.swissair.com

*Package costs are per person based on double occupancy and airfare from New York, Newark or Boston. Surcharges from other gateways apply. Fees, taxes and airport charges of up to $53 not included. Price of $774 is for destination Kitzbuehel. Certain conditions and restrictions apply.

Partner in the Delta Air Lines, Midwest Express Airlines and US Airways frequent flyer programs.

THE BLUE BOOK OF EUROPEAN SKI RESORTS

FIFTH EDITION
1999 — 2000

Enzel
Heck
Muello
Schissler
Wall

Note: The Blue Book has no system for confirmation of data included herein, therefore Publishers Group International Inc. assumes no responsibility for false or misleading, or incorrect data supplied and/or published in The Blue Book of European Ski Resorts.

Publisher

Publishers Group International, Inc.
P.O. Box 3775, Georgetown Station
Washington, D.C. 20007
(202) 342-0886
FAX (202) 338-1940
E-mail: ISSBooks@aol.com

Publishers Group International, Inc., 1998

All rights reserved. No part of this publication may be reproduced, stored in a retrieval system, or transmitted in any form or by any means, electronic, mechanical, photocopying, recording, or otherwise, without the prior written permission of the publisher. Further, all base or mountain maps, and photos were supplied by various countries and other sources. However, due to considerable alteration to meet the needs of this publication, Publishers Group International, Inc. reserves the right to all maps and photos displayed in this publication.

Fifth Edition
ISBN 0-9633653-5-5

Library of Congress Catalog Number ISSN 1067-3938
Printed in the United States of America

Front Cover Photograph:

Chamonix-Mont Blanc
Photo provided by Swissair

Various photographs throughout
the book
were taken by
Fred McKinney,
Saratoga Springs, NY

Cover Design: Michael Gibbs

INTRODUCTION

Welcome to the fifth anniversary edition of *The Blue Book* of European Ski Resorts; which we believe is our best yet. As always, our goal is to give you a taste of some of the finest skiing in Europe and help you plan a memorable vacation. The editor of each section has selected attractive destination resorts for North American skiers, as well as, including a few of the up-and-coming resorts.

The editors of each section remain the same. Bob Wall edits the Austria and Germany sections; George Schissler is French resort editor; Richard Muello presents the Italian section; Ted Heck brings readers the best of Switzerland and Slovenia; and Bob Enzel edits Scandinavia, Andorra, and the Spain sections. With almost two hundred combined years in skiing, the editors of *The Blue Book* have personally visited many of the areas listed.

As a reminder to the seasoned traveler and as help to those who have not skied in Europe, we have again included our Travel Tips on page viii. The layout of *The Blue Book* remains the same and once you get the hang of it, you can compare any two areas in seconds. Though some resorts have slightly more copy than others do, the sequence is consistent. The information we have listed is all factual, not opinionated as in other directories.

Lift ticket, ski school and equipment rental rates are detailed in the back of the book. We have listed each country's rates in its own currency with the U.S. dollar exchange rate at the time of publication. With constantly fluctuating currency exchange rates readers will have a more accurate idea of pricing their trip.

Occasionally, the dollar exchange and the always-increasing cost of living do not favor travelers. We strongly suggest that spending too much money not be of too great a concern when planning your European ski vacation, because without a doubt, it will be one of your most memorable. In Europe, you will find thousand-year-old picturesque villages and sample mouth-watering homemade pastries, cheeses and wines. The après-ski scene in Europe has no resemblance to the one in the U.S.

To better illustrate the flavor of skiing in Europe, we asked Fred McKinney to again travel with us and share with readers what he sees through his camera. Fred's photos may be found throughout the book.

A major addition this year is the inclusion of Internet URL and e-mail addresses. More photos have been added and a format change that highlights and summarizes the skiing in Austria, France, Italy and Switzerland can be found at the end of each respective section.

We would like to acknowledge Swissair; Compagnie des Alps; and the Austrian National Tourist Office. Without their support, *The Blue Book* would be a more costly publication. Swissair's "The Alpine Experience" offers affordable ski vacations in Europe. CDA is the largest ski operation in France and has recently added Courmayeur, Italy to its family of areas. Their resorts are identified on the back cover and inside the book with logos. The Austrian Tourist Office represents some of the best skiing on the continent and is pleased to provide skiers with information and brochures.

The editors—George, Ted, Richard, Bob and Bob and our supporters—wish you a great ski adventure in Europe!

Bob Enzel, Senior Editor

MAPS AND MOUNTAIN PHOTOS

Austria
Mayrhoefen	3
Montafon	5
St. Anton am Arlberg—Mountain Map	**6**
St. Anton am Arlberg	**7**
Lech	8
Neustift	**12**
Stubai Glacier—Mountain Map	**13**
Innsbruck—Mountain Map	**14**
Hintertux/Mayrhoefen	15
Kitzbühel	17

France
Les Menuires	**29**
Les Portes du Soleil—Mountain Map	31
Megeve	33
Mount Blanc	**34**
Flaine	**35**
Chamonix	**36**
Chamonix—Mountain Map	**37**
L'espace Kilby—Mountain Map	**38**
Tignes	**39**
Les Arcs	**40**
Peisey Vallandry	**41**
La Plagne	**42**
Les Menuires	**43**
Méribel	**44**
Trois Vallées—Mountain Map	**45**
Val Thorens	46
Courchevel	47
Val d'Isère	48
Fondue	51

Germany
Garmisch	61
Zugspitze	62
Obertsdorf	**63**

Italy
Courmayeur	**67**
Valle d'Aosta	68
Courmayeur	**69**
Sestriere	72
Cortina	78
Marmolada	79
Madonna di Campiglio	81
San Martino di Castrozza	82
Val Senales	84
Val Gerdena	85
Dolomites	86

Switzerland
Grindelwald	93
Verbier—Mountain Map	97
Zermatt	100
Grindelwald	102
Wengen	103
Jungfrau—Mountain Map	104
Mürren	105
Davos	108
Klosters	109
Chur-Arosa	110
St. Moritz	**113**
Silvaplana	114
St. Moritz—Mountain Map	**115**

Scandinavia   121

Slovenia
Kranska-Gora	141
Bohinj (Kobla/Vogel)	143

CONTENTS

- **v** Introduction
- **vi** Mountain Photo Listing
- **viii** Travel Tips
- **x** Internet and e-mail Addresses
- **xii** Map of Europe
- **1** Austria
- **23** Spotlight: Austrian Gemütlichkeit
- **27** France
- **55** Spotlight: The French Connection
- **59** Germany
- **65** Italy
- **87** Spotlight: Italian Delight
- **91** Switzerland
- **116** Liechtenstein
- **117** Spotlight: Swiss Adventure
- **121** Scandinavia
  - **123** Norway
  - **126** Sweden
  - **129** Iceland
- **130** Andorra
- **134** French Pyrenees
- **136** Spain
- **139** Slovenia
- **145** Rates (Lift; Ski School; Rentals)
- **156** Index

TRAVEL TIPS

Although the countries and resorts featured in THE BLUE BOOK may vary in their local customs and procedures, there are some generalizations that will help skiers plan their trips and enjoy them more.

The following travel tips are offered by the editors, who collectively have spent many years skiing in Europe. They have learned some of these tips the hard way.

PLANNING

Consult a travel agent or tour operator. They eliminate a lot of detailed planning and may save you considerable time and money. Most tour operators use regularly scheduled airlines and can customize a trip.

Check with specialty ski shops or ski clubs about group tours. A local ski club just might be arranging a trip to your chosen destination.

The national tourist offices mentioned in the country sections have brochures that will let you savor a trip long before you board the plane. Airlines, too, have appropriate literature; Swissair's "Alpine Experience" is an excellent example. Tourist offices in each resort, whose telephone and FAX numbers are listed, will be happy to send additional information.

Information is available on the Internet. Check out a resort beforehand. *The Blue Book* has a list of Internet addresses and e-mail addresses.

DOCUMENTS

A visit to Europe requires a valid passport with photo. Carry it on your person, but have a photocopy of the main page in your luggage. Save time and trouble by making several extra wallet-size photos in color. Many resorts require a photo on lift passes of three or more days. Don't be waiting in the photo line when your friends are headed for the lifts.

Have a driver's license, better yet an International Driving Permit that can be purchased from an automobile association. Some European locations, particularly in Italy, demand it from drivers of rental cars.

Make sure you are covered for auto accidents by your domestic insurance carrier or credit card company. But you may still want to think about buying collision coverage to avoid possible red tape hassles.

Obtain a map of the country and the region. The larger the scale, the more the detail and the more fun you will have in identifying mountains and locating other ski areas to sample.

GROUND TRANSPORTATION

European countries have excellent roads—local, state and national superhighways. Autobahns in Germany and Switzerland are free, but most Autostrade in Italy have tolls. A car entering Switzerland from another country must pay about $30 for a special sticker authorizing travel on the superhighways.

Nearly all ski areas have fine bus transportation to move the local population and visiting skiers. The ski pass lets the skier ride free.

Gateway cities have bus service between the airport or main train station and major resorts.

Train systems are always eye-openers to Americans. They are clean, high speed and they run on time. Where trains do not go, efficient alpine bus service exists. Rail passes purchased from a travel agent before you leave home allow unlimited travel on trains and postal buses. They also earn discounts on certain uphill conveyances in ski areas.

ACCOMMODATIONS

Hotels are divided into "stars," up to five. Each category rises in amenities—in price. Rates are fixed in agreement with tourist boards and other agencies.

Prices vary by season: low season rates apply in early December, three weeks of January and often late in the season. They go up during the Christmas-New Year's holiday and the high season months of February and March.

Reservations can be made in the United States through travel agencies, hotel representatives or by writing directly to the hotel. For people who like to play it by ear, every town has a tourist office ready to help a skier find a room.

Every major city and many less-than-major ones with train stations provide a convenient baggage check at the station for a day or a month. Each station also has a tourist information stand to help with lodging and dining information at no charge. It's a very useful service.

TRIP INSURANCE

Consider a comprehensive plan for personal coverage of emergency assistance, medical expenses, lost luggage and trip cancellation or interruption.

Skiers should make sure the insurance covers a helicopter evacuation from a mountain top. There are no free ski patrol sled rides for injured skiers.

CURRENCY

Buying foreign money in a U.S. airport is a bad idea. Wait until you get to the European airport for enough money to get started with tips and incidentals. City banks will give the best exchange rate. *Blue Book* editors don't carry a lot of cash and prefer to use automated teller machines that are found just about everywhere. But make sure you know the PIN number of your card.

LIFT TICKETS

Inquire about multiple-day lift tickets. Two, three and six-day rates may represent substantial savings.

In major areas where several mountains and connecting ski circuses exist, make sure the ticket you buy covers all areas you want to ski. Ask whether the ticket price includes bus shuttles or other add-ons.

If you do not feel the need to maximize the number of runs in a day, check to see if individual ride tickets meet your needs. Some areas have single ride coupons, in addition to day and half-day tickets.

SKI SCHOOLS

These schools are among the best in the world. Their cadres can take toddlers in tow or lead advanced skiers into deep snow, where they learn that "expert" means being able to handle all snow conditions well.

LANGUAGE

Don't worry about language differences. Ski schools, restaurants, and shops usually have English-speaking personnel. But it would be advantageous to learn some basic phrases before leaving home. You will enjoy using the new language and the natives will be delighted when you make an effort to talk in their tongue.

MISCELLANEOUS

Although they are universally known, credit cards are sometimes not accepted. Some resorts, particularly in Austria, rebel against fees charged by credit card companies. Do not take for granted that your card is welcomed for lodging, food and ski activities.

Travelers on Swissair can check cumbersome ski equipment from their U.S. gateway direct to the train or bus station at your Swiss resort. This check-through may be even more important on the way home, if skiers want to spend time sightseeing in major cities.

Duty free shops are in all major airports.

The Alps usually do not have the extreme cold temperatures felt by skiers in American and Canadian resorts. Plan to dress in layers to be warm, yet be able to shed clothing as the sun warms things up.

Other helpful hints are incorporated in the narratives that precede each section of this book and also at the end of each resort.

PACK LIST

Alphorn Ski Tours of Lahaska, PA (Telephone (215) 794-5653, Fax (215) 794-7199) is a tour operator and travel agency that moves many thousands of skiers a year to the Alps. They recommend that skiers "travel right, travel light," with one each of suitcase, boot bag, ski bag and a small carry-on.

To their customers they suggest this pack list:

For skiing: skis, poles and boots . . . ski outfit of parka and pants or suit . . . shell or vest . . . ski hat and headband . . . gloves or mittens (ski and casual) . . . goggles and sunglasses . . . thermal underwear . . . wool socks . . . ski sweaters . . . turtlenecks . . . neck gaiter/face mask . . . fannypack . . . after-ski boots.

For apres ski: women should have blouses or sweater, skirts or slacks and dress shoes. Men need a sport jacket, slacks and tie (for casinos) and dress shoes.

Additional items are: underwear . . . swimsuit . . . cosmetics . . . sun cream . . . chapstick . . . extra drug prescriptions . . . extra eye glasses . . . camera, film and batteries . . . toilet articles, including washcloth and soap . . . laundry soap and small clothes line . . . converter for electricity . . . travelers checks.

Downtown Innsbruck.

Photo: Fred McKinney

Internet and e-mail Addresses

In this world of technology that is moving faster than we can schuss, we have learned that telephone and fax numbers are only a step along the way in communications.

Also, we believe that, after *The Blue Book* whets your appetite or points you toward exciting areas, you may want to talk directly to those areas by e-mail. And you can begin to enjoy your trip long in advance by studying resort information on the Internet.

Many of the resorts in this book have an Internet address for either the tourist office or a "middle man" service. A lot of the ski areas also had e-mail addresses as this fifth edition went to press. But they may change if resorts switch to other online services. In some cases you can find the e-mail address by first accessing the Web site. Remember that Internet access begins with *http://www/* and e-mail always includes an @.

	Internet	e-mail
ANDORRA		
Arinsal	andornet.ad/arinsal-pal	*emap@andornet.ad*
Ordino	andornet.ad/comuns/ordino	*ito@andorra.ad*
Pal	andornet.ad/arinsal-pal	*emap@andornet.ad*
Pas De La Casa-Grau Roig	andornet.ad/pasgrau	*pasgrau@andornet.ad*
Soldeu-El Tarter	soldeu.ad	*soldeu@andornet.ad*
Principality of Andorra		
Ski Andorra	skiandorra.ad	*skiand@andornet.ad*
AUSTRIA		
Alpbachtal	tiscover.com/albachtal	*alpbach@tirol-pur.at*
Altenmarkt/Zauchensee	salzburg.com/altenmarkt-zauchensee-tourismus	*altenmarkt-zauchensee@holidayinfo.com*
Bad Gastein	badgastein.at	*fvv.badgastein@aon.at*
Bad Kleinkirchheim	bkk.at	*office@bkk.at*
Brandnertal	brand.at	*brand@brand.vol.at*
Brixen im Thale		*tvb.soell@netwing.at*
Galtür-Silvretta	tiscover.com/galtuer	*galtuer@netway.at*
Gurgl	tiscover.com/gurgl	*tvbgurgl@netway.at*
High Montafon	tiscover.com/st.gallenkirch	*stgallenkirch@vol.at*
Innsbruck/Igls	tiscover.com/innsbruck	*info2@innsbruck.tvb.co.at*
Ischgl	tiscover.com/ischgl	*tvb.ischgl@netway.at*
Katschberg	tiscover.com/katschbergrennweg	*katschberg-rennweg@carinthia.com*
Kirchberg in Tyrol	tiscover.com/kirchberg	*kirchberg.tvb@netway.at*
Kitzbühel	tiscover.com/kitzbuehel	*office@tourist-kitzbuehel.co.at*
Lech/Zürs	lech.at	*lech-info@lech.at*
	zuers.at	*zuersinfo@zuers.at*
Montafon Valley	montafon-tourism.at	*tourismus.information@montafon.at*
Neustift im Stubaital	tiscover.com.neustift	*tv.neustift@neustift.netwing.at*
Obertauern	tcs.co.at/obertauern	*obertauern@magnet.at*
Saalbach	saalbach.com	*contact@saalbach.com*
St. Anton am Arlberg	stantonamarlberg.com	*st.anton@netay.at*
St. Johan im Pongau	salzburg.com/stjohann-tourismus	*info.tvb.st.johann@aon.at*
St. Johann in Tyrol	tiscover.com.st.johann	*tvb@st.johann.tirol.at*
Schladming		*tourist.schladming@ppl.co.at*
Seefeld	tiscover.com/seefeld	*info@seefeld.tirol.at*
Sölden Ötztal Arena	tiscover.com/oetztal-arena	*oetztal.werbung@netway.at*
Zell am See/Kaprun	esr.gold.at	*esr@gold.at*
Zillertal/Mayrhofen	tiscover.com/zillertal	*zillertal-werbung@netway.at*
. . .	tiscover.com/mayrhofen	*mayrhofen@zillertal.tirol.at*
State Tourist Offices		
. . . Carinthia	tiscover.com/carinthia	*info@carinthia.com*

	Internet	e-mail
. . . Salzburg	salzburg.com/salzburgerland	info@szgtour.co.at
. . . Styria	steiermark.com	tourismus@steiermark.com
. . . Tyrol	tiscover.com/tirol	tirol.info@tirolwerbung.at
. . . Vorarlberg	vorarlberg-tourism.at	info@vbgtour.at

FRANCE
Chamonix	chamonic.com	presse@chamonix.com
Chatel	skifrance.fr/~chatel	
Courchevel	courchevel.com	courchevel@icor.fr
La Plagne	skifrance.fr/~laplagne	ot.laplagne@wanadoo.fr
Les Angles	little-france.com/les-angles	les-angles@little-france.com
Les Arcs	lesarcs.com	wlesarcs@lesarcs.com
Les 2 Alpes	les2alpes.com	
Les Menuires	skifrance.fr/~menuires	lesmenuires@laposte.fr
Megève	skifrance.fr/~megeve	
Meribel	meribel.net	meribel@laposte.fr
Morzine	skifrance.fr/~morzine	
Tignes	tignes.net	tignes@laposte.fr
Val d'Isère	val-disere.com	infor@val-disere.com
Val Thorens	valthorens.com	valtho@valthorens.com

GERMANY
Berchtesgadener Land	berchtesgadener-land.com	info@berchtesgadener-land.com
Garmisch	garmisch.de	info@garmisch-partenkirchen.de
Oberammergau	oberammergau.de	tourist-info@oberammergau.de
Oberstdorf	oberstdorf.de	infor@oberstdorf.de
Reit im Winkl	reit-im-winkl.de	verkehrsamtreit@t-online.de

ITALY
Bormio	skiitaly.com	
Cervinia	skiitaly.com	
Cortina d'Ampezzo	skiitaly.com	
Courmayeur	courmayeur.com	
Gresonney	gresonney.com	
La Thuile	lathuile.com	
Livigno	livigno.com	staff@livnet.it
Pila	pila.com	info@pila.com
Val Di Fassa	val-di-fassa.com	
Val Di Fiemme	val-di-fiemme.com	turverb@suedtirol.com
Val Gardena	val-gardena.com	
. . . Ortisei		ortisei@val-gardena.com
. . . Selva		selva@val-gardena.com
. . . S. Cristina		s.cristina@val-gardena.com
Val Senales	valsenales.com	

NORWAY
Geilo	skiinfo.no/geilo	geilo@skiinfo.no
Kvitfjell	skiinfo.kvitfjell.no	kvitfjell.alpinanlegg@online.no
Norefjell	skiinfo.no/norefjell	norefjell@skiinfo.no

SLOVENIA
Bohinj	bohinj.si	tdbohinj@bohinj.si
Kranjska Gora	kranjska-gora.si	info@kranjska-gora.si
Mariborsko Pohorje	maribor.uni.mb.si	mom.matic@eunet.si
Rogla		turizem@unior.si
Slovenian National Tourist Board Web site is	tourist-board.si	

	Internet	e-mail
SWEDEN		
Åre (tourism)		Mikael.Kallstrm@asc.se
Bydalen (tourism)		Anders.Durling@Bydalen-fjall.se
Sälen	salen.nu	Turist.Salen@Malung.se
Swedish Travel & Tourism Council	gosweden.org	
SWITZERLAND		
Adelboden	adelbodentourism.ch	info@adelbodentourism.ch
Andermatt	topin.ch/ch/andermatt/"	verkehrsverein-andermatt@bluewin.ch
Anzère	anzere.ch	info@anzere.ch
Arosa	arosa.ch	arosa@arosa.ch
Champery	champery.ch	champery-ch@portesdusol
Chateau-d'Oex	chateau-doex.ch	chateau-doex@bluewin.ch
Crans-Montana	crans-montana.ch	information@crans-montana.ch
Davos	davos.ch	davos@davos.ch
Disentis	disentis.ch	admin@disentis.ch
Engelberg	engelberg.tourism.ch	tourist.center@engelberg.ch
Flims-Laax	alpenarena.ch	tourism@alpenarena.ch
Grindelwald	grindelwald.ch	touristcenter@Grindelwald.ch
Gstaad	gstaad.ch	tvsl@gstaad.ch
Interlaken	interlaken.ch	mail@interlakentourism.ch
Klosters	klosters.ch	info@klosters.ch
Lenzerheide	lenzerheide.ch	lenzerheide@spin.ch
Les Diablerets	alpes.ch/diablerets	diablerets@bluewin.ch
Leukerbad	leukerbad.ch	info@leukerbad.ch
Leysin	leysin.ch	tourism@leysin.ch
Malbun	searchlink.li/tourist/	
Meirgen	meiringenhasliberg.ch	info@meiringenhasliberg.ch
Mürren	muerren.ch	info@muerren.ch
Pontresina	pontresina.com	pontresina@compunet.ch
Riederalp	riederalp.ch	info@riederalp.ch
St. Moritz	stmoritz.ch	kvv@stmoritz.ch
Samnaun	samnaun.ch	info@samnaun.ch
Saas-Fee	saas-fee.ch	to@saas-fee.ch
Silvaplana	silvaplana.ch	silvaplana@bluewin.ch
Toggenburg	toggenburg.ch	buwag@toggenburg.ch
Verbier	verbier.ch	verbiertourism@verbier.ch
Villars	villars.ch	villars@pingnet.ch
Wengen	wengen.ch	information@wengen.com
Zermatt	zermatt.ch	zermatt@wallis.ch

EUROPE

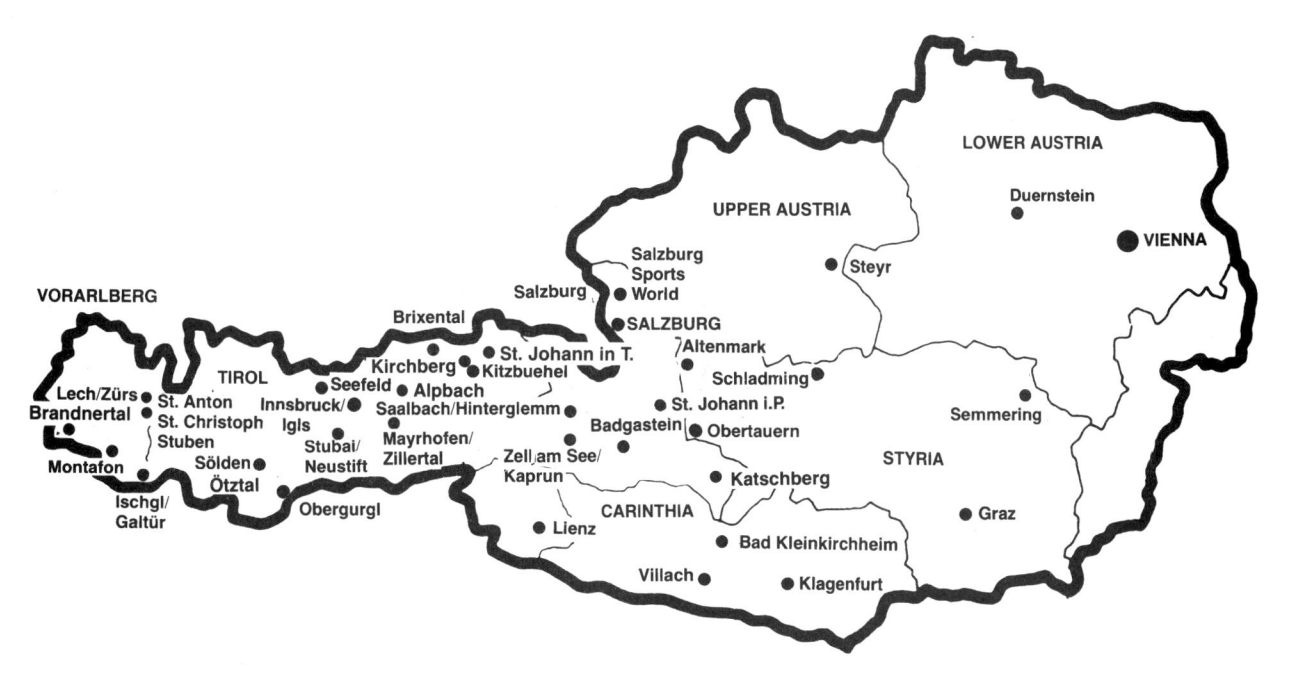

AUSTRIA

AUSTRIA

	Page No.
Alpbachtal	11
Altenmarkt/Zauchensee	20
Bad Gastein	19
Bad Kleinkirchheim	22
Brandnertal	4
Brixen im Thale/Wilder Kaiser	16
Galtür-Silvretta	9
Gurgl (Unter/Ober/Hoch)	11
High Montafon	5
Innsbruck/Igls	**14**
Ischgl	9
Katschberg*	22
Kirchberg in Tyrol	16
Kitzbühel	17
Lech/Zürs	8
Montafon Valley	4
Neustift im Stubaital	**12**
Obertauern	21
Saalbach/Hinterglemm-Leogang*	18
St. Anton am Arlberg	**7**
St. Johann im Pongau/Alpendorf	20
St. Johann in Tyrol	18
Schladming (Dachstein)	21
Seefeld	10
Sölden Ötztal-Arena	10
Zell am See/Kaprun	19
Zillertal/Hintertux/Mayrhofen	15

*Areas marked with an asterisk in the text did not update their information for this edition.

AUSTRIA

by Bob Wall

Austria is a country of Imperial cities and majestic mountains... The majesty of the Austrian Alps can be overwhelming to a first-timer on those fantastic powdery slopes. Don't be intimidated by the ever present majestic peaks, instead, enjoy the miles of untracked powder and well groomed and marked trails.

The Imperial cities of Vienna, Salzburg and Innsbruck are close to the Alps and offer an opportunity to roundout the experience of your Austrian ski holiday. Visit outstanding museums, take in the opera or attend a concert of Viennese waltzes. These are but a couple of the activities available in these glorious cities. Their unique baroque and medieval architecture houses fine restaurants, night clubs and traditional beer halls with their raucous entertainment.

Picture postcard Alpine villages with a myriad of ski slopes for skiers of every ability are another part of the Austrain experience. It is yours for the asking in the country where modern alpine skiing was born.

We hope this book will make your trip to Austria easier to plan and, consequently, more enjoyable when you arrive. There are more than 700 ski areas dotted across the Austrian landscape. Some of them are as well known as the soap products advertised nightly on television. Others are in minute farm towns with, perhaps, a single lift or tow erected so the local land owners can grab a run whenever they have a free moment.

In our attempt to catalogue and explain the highlights of Austrian skiing we have concentrated on the major resorts that have proven the most popular with skiers over the years. In the interest of clarifying the breadth of Austrian skiing we have grouped what the average American would consider a separate ski area under a single heading. For example, the statistics for Innsbruck include Igls, Hungerburg, Tulfes, Mutters and Axamer Lizum. St. Anton, St. Christoph and Stuben are also presented collectively as are Zürs and Lech. In general, areas that are tied together with a lift network or ski bus are presented as a group.

In this edition, we have included several new ski resorts. Along with these new entries are more familiar resorts dedicated to fulfilling the expectations of North American skiers. They offer special rates on package vacations that often include rooms, meals, lift tickets, and ski instruction.

Within fifteen or twenty miles of the well-known ski resort, Kitzbühel, the ski centers of the Brixental offer less expensive and uncrowded skiing. There is not the glamour and glitz that we have come to expect in "Kitz," but great skiing, intimate little inns and pensions that not only offer modestly priced accommodations, but have a menu that is guaranteed to replace every calorie you skied off.

Yes, you can find it all in Austria when it comes to skiing. Accommodations range from five star giants that offer every convenience that the royalty of the world demands and expects when on holiday, to an immaculate room in a simple farmhouse, where the bath is down the hall.

The skiing experience is as varied as the accommodations in Austria. Long groomed runs to delight any faint-of-heart novice or intermediate to some of the steepest and bumpiest runs in the world for the most advanced skier. There are thousands of miles of groomed and marked trails and nearby there are thousands of acres of ungroomed, untouched powder, soft and deep.

Off-piste skiing is recommended only with a guide. It offers the thrills and excitement of untracked slopes, virgin powder, and unexcelled mountain vistas. Every Austrian resort has a ski school that will arrange for you to hire a mountain man that knows every ridge and crevasse like the back of his hand. No need to take a chance on being in the wrong place at the wrong time.

Lift rates, ski school and guide rates and the prices for rental equipment are covered at the end of this book. Prices for the Austrian resorts are quoted in Austrian schillings and the financial page of your daily paper will tell you the exchange rate.

Cross country skiers will find their hunger for well groomed and marked trails satiated in Austria. In Seefeld, it is possible to run the same track where Bill Koch became the first American Olympic Medalist in cross country racing. More adventurous ski tourers will find a plethora of opportunities for hut to hut touring treks in the Austrian Alps.

AUSTRIA

swissair

Getting to the ski mountains of Austria is very easy. An overnight flight from several American cities to Zurich or Munich will put you within a couple of hours of Austrian skiing.

Many of the larger resorts operate a ski bus from the two gateway airports direct to your hotel. Limited access highways are well maintained and driving a rental car is quick and easy. Rail transportation in Austria and Europe is not only efficient but relatively inexpensive. Check into buying a rail pass that offers unlimited travel before leaving North America, they are not available in Europe.

Now it's time to plan your trip. Don't forget to leave time each day for the après-ski life in Austria. Little bars with a zither player are mixed with casinos, discos and some of the finest dining in the world. A ski trip to Austria is not a vacation, it is an experience. After all—skiing in Austria is a way of life.

AUSTRIAN NATIONAL TOURIST OFFICE
New York
500 Fifth Avenue, # 800
New York, NY 10110
Phone: 212-944-6880
Fax: 212-730-4568
or
New York
P.O. Box 1142
New York, NY 10108

Los Angeles
11601 Wilshire Blvd., # 2480
Los Angeles, CA 90025
Phone: 310-477-3332
              800-252-0468
Fax: 310-477-5141

SWISSAIR INFORMATION

Swissair carries skiers to the Alps from Atlanta, Boston, Chicago, Cincinnati, Los Angeles, Montreal, Newark, New York, San Francisco, and Washington, D.C., with connecting service from 21 other U.S. cities.

Swissair offers a brochure called "The Alpine Experience." It includes additional descriptions of major Swiss resorts, as well as popular resorts in Austria, France, Germany and Italy. The colorful brochure contains photos, trail maps, hotel listings and prices for package deals.

For a free copy of "The Alpine Experience" call 800-662-0021 or write to Swissair, P.O. Box 26028, Tampa, FL 33623-6028.

To book one of their exciting adventures call Swissair Vacations at 800-688-7947.

AUSTRIA

BRANDNERTAL
TVB BRANDNERTAL
A-6708 Brand
Austria
Telephone: (43) 5559 555-0 Fax: (43) 5559 555-20

Elevation: Base/Village: 1,037 m (3,401 ft); Top: 1,920 m (6,298 ft)
Vertical: 883 m (2,896 ft)
Terrain: 28 miles of wide, well-groomed runs; 8 km of snowmaking
Longest Run: 6.3 km (4 miles)
Skiing Circus: To Bürserberg 5 km & return by free post bus with lift ticket
Lifts: 12
Types: 5 double chairs; 7 surface lifts
Lift Capacity: 15,000 p/h in valley
Ski Season: Christmas - Easter
Mountain Restaurants: Several
Cross Country: 45 km of trails
Ski School: Lessons from 10 am to 1 pm. The "Surfing Academy" of Brand teaches alpine & freestyle snowboarding on the slopes & in the halfpipe
Other Winter Activities: Winter hiking trails (50 km); tennis (indoor); ski-safaris (X-C tour on the Bürserberg trails at 4,000 ft. elevation); riding hall (horseback riding indoors & outdoors); ice skating outdoors & lit for night use; bowling
Après-Ski: Winter parties with bonfire; tea dances, disco, folkore evenings
Shopping Services: 2 km long village close to the Swiss border, beauty studios, supermarkets, hairdressers, sport shops
Child Care: Nursery available; Family oriented resort - Children under 6 years old ski free
Lodging: Modern & traditional hotels - Lodging beds 4,380
Transportation: Gateway Airports: (Zurich)
Closest Provincial City:
By Auto from Airport:
By Train:
Other Information: Family resort, informal and lively

VORARLBERG
This resort lies close to the Swiss and Lichtenstein borders. The Brand Valley is oriented toward family skiing, and here children under the age of six are not required to have lift tickets. The slower pace of this resort is pointed up by the ski school hours of 10 a.m. til 1 p.m. giving everyone plenty of time to get ready and yet not miss the best time to be on the slopes.

MONTAFON VALLEY
MONTAFON TOURISMUS
Montafoner Str 21
Schruns A-6780, Austria
Telephone: (43)5556-72253 Fax: (43)5556-74856

Elevation: Base/Village: 700-1,400 m (2,297-4,593 ft); Top: 2,400 m (7,874 ft); highest point 2,394 m (7,854 ft)
Vertical: 1,700 m (5,577 ft)
Longest Run: 11.0 km (6.8 mi)
Terrain: 125 miles of maintained runs; 10% beginner, 30% intermediate, 40% advanced, 20% expert
Skiing Circus: Off-piste from Gargellen to Klosters, Switzerland
Lifts: 70
Types: 8 Gondolas; 4 cable cars; 20 Chairlifts (1 six seater, 3 quads, 2 trpls, 12 dbls, 4 sngls); 36 Surface
Lift Capacity: 78,000 p/h resort
Ski Season: Mid. Dec. through Mid-April
Cross Country: 100 km or 65 miles/12 trails with tracks, one high altitude trail (6,600 ft)
Ski School: 10 schools, 150 instructors
Other Winter Activities: Curling & ice skating/artificial; sauna; sleigh riding; natural toboggan run with lift; 26 indoor pools (partly public); 2 indoor tennis courts; hiking
Après-Ski: 25 Bars, discos
Shopping/Services: All services are available in each village
Credit Cards: MC, VISA
Child Care: Arranged by Montafon Tourismus-1 day 200-300 AS incl. lunch
6 Ski Kindergartens operate daily 10am-4pm
Lodging: 19,000 beds; 150 hotels, inns, pensions- 30 apt. houses; 2 spa hotels
Transportation: Gateway Airport: Zurich 161 km (100 mi)
Nearest Austrian Airport: Innsbruck 151 km (94 mi). Innsbruck airport is served from Frankfurt, Zurich, Paris, Amsterdam and Vienna by Tyrolean Airways
By Ski Bus from airport: 2.5 hrs from Innsbruck
By Train: 2 hrs from Innsbruck
Best Deal: Montafon Ski Pass entitles holder to the use of over 70 lifts, free bus travel and use of Montafon Railway - good at all Valley resorts

VORALBERG
The resorts of Schruns, Tschagguns, St. Gallenkirch, Gargellen, Partenen, Gaschurn, Gortipohl, Silbertal, Bartholomäberg, St. Anton/M. and Vandans combine to make up the Montafon Valley complex. Each is separate with extensive lift networks, long runs and varied terrain. 11 separate villages entertain skiers in the Valley

AUSTRIA

Many charming villages such as this one of Tschagguns are surrounded by scenic grandeur in the Montafon Valley.

Photo: Fred McKinney

HIGH MONTAFON
TOURISM
St. Gallenkirch and Gortipohl
A-6791 St. Gallenkirch, Austria
Telephone: (43) 5557-6600 Fax: (43) 5557-6659

Elevation: Base/Village: 900 m (2,953 ft)
Top: 2,380 m (7,808 ft)

Vertical: 1,480 m (4,856 ft)

Terrain: About 100 km (62 mi) of maintained runs; 10% red, 30% green, 40% blue, 20% black.

Longest run: 11.0 km (6.8 mi)

Skiing Circus: With Gaschurn and Partenen

Lifts: 29

Types: 4 Gondolas; 9 Chairlifts; 15 T-bars

Lift Capacity: 40,000 p/h resort

Ski Season: December 5-April 11

Summer Skiing: None

Cross Country: 30 km

Ski School: One school—40 instructors

Mountain Restaurants: 8

Other Winter Activities: Hiking; indoor swimming; mono-skiing; mountaineering; paragliding; snowboarding; sleigh riding; snow-trekking; sledding

VORARLBERG
St. Gallenkirch, Gartipohl, Gaschurn and Partenen are the "Five Stars of the High Montafon." Here you will find more than 100 kilometers of well groomed runs and immeasurable acres of off-piste skiing, all located on the striking Slivretta Nova mountain range.

Après-Ski: Sauna, 5 bars, 2 discos, 2 ice bars, 4 cafes, 1 with "live" music

Shopping/Services: All services

Credit Cards: EC and VISA

Child Care: Nursery, 5-days, AS 2,200; Kid's Ski School, 5-days AS 1,310-1,810

Lodging: 3,500 beds; hotels, pensions, apartments, at Gortipohl and St. Gallenkirch

Transportation: Gateway Airports: Zurich; Innsbruck

Closest Provincial City: Bludenz, 15 km

By Auto from Airport: From Zurich or Innsbruck 180 km (112 mi)

By Train: Station at Schruns

Best Deal: Special rates Jan. 7-Feb. 5, 1999; Montafon ski pass covers 70 lifts, plus free bus transportation

Other Information: All runs supplemented with snowmaking

AUSTRIA

AUSTRIA

ST. ANTON AM ARLBERG
TOURIST OFFICE St. Anton am Arlberg A-6580
Telephone: 5446-22690 Fax: 5446-2532
Stuben A-6762, Austria
Telephone: (43) 5582-761 Fax: (43) 5582-7626

ST. ANTON AM ARLBERG
In the heart of the Arlberg, St. Anton has long drawn skiers into the region. Big verticals, long runs and natural beauty make this a must for Austrian ski visitors Alpine Ski World Championships in year 2001

Elevation: Base/Village: 1,304 m (4,278 ft); Top: 2,811 m (9,222 ft). Stuben: Base: 1,407 m (4,616 ft); Top: 2,600 m (8,530 ft)

Vertical: 1,507 m (4,944 ft). Stuben 1,207 m (3,960 ft)

Longest Run: 8.0 km (5.0 mi); Valluga to St. Anton

Terrain: 20% beginner, 20% intermediate, 40% advanced, 20% expert

Skiing Circus: St. Anton am Arlberg-St. Christoph-Stuben; Lech, Zürs, Klösterle

Lifts: 82 (Arlberg Ski Area)

Types: 9 Gondolas; 1 Tram; 1 Funicular; 35 Chairlifts (12 quads, 5 triples, 16 doubles); 36 T-bars; 2 6-psngr

Lift Capacity: 111,092 p/h

Ski Season: End of Nov.-May 1

Cross Country: 41.5 km: Stanzertal 26 km, Ferwall 13 km, St. Christoph 2.5 km

Ski School: At both St. Anton and Stuben

Mountain Restaurants: Approximately 10

Other Winter Activities: Curling; hiking; ice skating; indoor swimming; indoor tennis; mono-skiing; sauna; snowboarding; hiking; tobogganing; squash; bowling; horse-drawn sleigh; paragliding

Après-Ski: Ski museum; sports center; 15 cafes, 8 ice bars, 3 discos, 8 bars; cinema

Shopping/Services: Variety of shops, library, auto repair, car rental, pharmacy, travel agencies

Credit Cards: AE,, DC, MC, VISA, Eurocard

Child Care: Babysitting on request, 5446-22690; Nursery 6-days, from 2½ years—AS 1,640; kids' ski school, from 5 years, AS 2,485 (6 days)

Lodging: 8,000 beds; hotels, gasthof, apartments, private pensions in St. Anton, St. Jakob, & St. Christoph. Stuben has 300 hotel beds and 340 private beds

Transportation: Gateway Airports: Munich/Zürich

Closest Austrian Airport: Innsbruck 103 km (64 mi) 1.5 hrs by train

Closest Provincial City: Landeck, 25 km

By Auto from airport: Munich (3.5 hrs.)/Zürich (2.5 hrs.)

By Train: Munich to Innsbruck, transfer with Arlberg Express to center of St. Anton; Zurich to St. Anton

Best Auto Route: Munich-Innsbruck-St. Anton

Best Deal: Low season Nov.-Dec., Jan. & April. Connected ticket between St. Anton, St. Christoph, Stuben, Zürs & Lech available

Other Information: 40 snowmaking machines on 20 km. Express train stops in center of resort with easy access

The Valluga peak dominates the winter wonderland above St. Anton.   Photo: Fred McKinney

AUSTRIA

LECH-ZÜRS
TOURIST OFFICE
A-6764 Lech Nr. 2
Austria
Telephone: (43) 5583/2161 Fax: (43) 5583/3155

ARLBERG
Lech caters to the lower level skier but offers challenges to the advanced adventurer in off-piste runs. Two separate villages with Lech the larger, but Zürs the more sophisticated.

Elevation: Base/Village: Lech 1,450 m (4,757 ft); Zürs 1,720 m (5,643 ft); Top: Lech 2,444 m (8,018 ft); Zürs 2,725 m (8,940 ft)

Vertical: Lech 914 m (3,000 ft); Zürs 1,006 m (3,300 ft)

Longest Run: 5 km (3 mi), Madloch

Terrain: 110 km Groomed runs; 120 km off-piste runs; 25% beginner, 40% intermediate, 35% advanced

Skiing Circus: Lech to Zürs and return via separate route; also connects to Oberlech, Zug, and Stuben

Lifts: 33 (Arlberg Region 82)

Types: 5 Gondolas; 18 Chairlifts (5 quads, 5 triples, 8 doubles); 10 Surface

Lift Capacity: 42,739 p/h resort

Ski Season: Nov. 28-April 25

Cross Country: 2 Trails—one 15 km, one 4 km

Ski School: Oberlech, Lech, & Zürs/300 instructors

Other Winter Activities: Curling; horse-drawn sleigh; helicopter skiing; ice skating/natural; indoor tennis; mono-skiing; paragliding; snowboarding; sleigh riding; winter golf; squash; hiking; tobogganing; sports center

Après-Ski: 10 Bars, 5 discos, 5 cafes, 20 ice bars, concerts

Shopping/Services: All services available, bars, cafes, restaurants, cinema, sport shops, grocery

Credit Cards: Cards accepted at shop-owners discretion: AE, DC, EC, MC VISA

Child Care: Ages 3-12 years; kids' ski school—6 days, AS 1,510; Nursery—6 days AS 1,510

Lodging: 6,732 beds; 5- and 4-star 1,899; 3-star 1,933; 2-star 2,194; private 543; apartments 163

Transportation: Gateway Airports: Zürich and Munich

Closest Provincial City: Bludenz, 40 km

By Auto from airport: Bludenz, Langen, Zürs, Lech

By Ski Bus from airport: Zürich to Zürs/Lech every Friday, Saturday & Sunday

By Train: Zürich or Munich to Langen, then bus or taxi to Lech or Zürs

Best Deal: Low season Nov. 28-Dec. 19; Jan. 9-Feb. 23, Apr. 10-25, 1999. Combined ticket with Zürs/Lech/St. Christoph/St. Anton/Klösterle

Lunch in Lech adds to the total experience in the Arlberg.

Photo: Fred McKinney

AUSTRIA

ISCHGL

TOURIST OFFICE
Post Box 24, Ischgl A-6561, Austria
Telephone: 5444/5266 Fax: 5444/5636

Elevation: Base/Village: 1,400 m (4,593 ft); Top: 2,872 m (9,423 ft).
Vertical: Ischgl 1,472 m (4,829 ft)
Longest Run: 12.0 km (7.5 mi)
Terrain: Runs, 120 km red, 40 km blue, 40 km black
Skiing Circus: You can ski from Ischgl, Austria to Samnaun, Switzerland and return via lifts from Samnaun and ski to the village center of Ischgl
Lifts: 54 including Samnaun, Switzerland
Types: 2 Trams; 3 Gondolas; 15 Chairlifts (9 quads, 4 6-seaters, 1 triple, 1 double); 21 surface lifts
Lift Capacity: 48,000 p/h resort
Ski Season: Nov. 27-May 2, 1999
Cross Country: 48 km, up to Galtür
Ski School: Each area has its own learning center
Mountain Restaurants: 12 Alpenhaus, Bodenalpe, etc.
Other Winter Activities: Curling; folklore evenings; hiking; ice skating/artificial; indoor swimming; mono-skiing; snowboarding; sleigh riding; sports center; nighttime tobogganing on 7 km run

GALTÜR—SILVRETTA

TOURIST OFFICE
A-6563 Galtür/Tirol, Austria

Telephone: (43) 5443-521 Fax: (43) 5443-521-76

Elevation: Base/Village: 1,600 m (5,249 ft); Top: 2,300 m (7,546 ft)
Vertical: 460 m (1,509 ft)
Terrain: 40 km of terrain; 4 km blue, 24 km blue-red; 12 km black
Longest Run: 1.1 km (0.7 mi) Alpkogelobfahrt
Skiing Circus: None; back-country skiing with guide; Ischgl/Samnaun short distance by car or bus
Lifts: 10
Types: 3 Chairlifts; 7 T-bars
Lift Capacity: 15,000 p/h resort
Ski Season: Mid December - Mid-April
Summer Skiing: None
Cross Country: 45 km
Ski School: One ski school
Mountain Restaurants: 3
Other Winter Activities: Hiking; ice skating/natural; indoor swimming; indoor tennis; mono-skiing; mountaineering; paragliding; snowboarding; squash; bowling alleys; telemark; hanggliding school

PAZNAUN
Ischgl is situated in the Silvretta-Samnaun Gruppe; small village with 1,280 residents; it is both a summer (mountaineering, mountain biking, swimming, tennis . . .) and a winter resort (skiing, snowboarding, cross country, ice skating . . .). A popular international resort with easy ski access to duty-free Samnaun, Switzerland.

Après-Ski: Bars, pubs, discos, cafes, coffee houses
Shopping/Services: Village has all the necessary shops-ski rentals, ski shops, souvenirs, jewelry, etc.
Child Care: Private babysitters available; rates negotiable; Nursery: 170/day, 250 w/lunch; Telephone: 5444/5452; Kids' ski school AS 1,550/6 days
Lodging: 8,600 beds; variety of hotels, pensions, private houses and apartments in Ischgl
Transportation: Gateway Airport: Munich
Closest Provincial City: Landeck, 25 km
By Air: Munich to Innsbruck, train to Landeck, bus to area
By Auto from airport: Taxi (2½ hrs.)/Bus (4 hrs.)
By Train: Munich to Innsbruck to Landeck with taxi or bus to Ischgl
By Bus: Landeck to Ischgl (55 min.); Local bus free with ski pass, connects all valley areas
Best Deal: Silvretta ski pass includes Galtür, Kappl, Ischgl/Samnaun, & See; 6-day lodging/ski package

TYROL
A high mountain resort, at the head of the Paznaun Valley, that features a variety of runs for skiers of every ability. Galtür's most famous American guest, Ernest Hemingway visited in 1925 and wrote the story "An Alpine Idyll" while visiting and skiing in the village.

Après-Ski: sauna, bars, discos, cafes
Shopping/Services: Bakery, supermarket, sports shops, electric appliances, hair salon, souvenir shop, ski rentals
Credit Cards: None
Child Care: Kindergarten from 3 years-up, 6-days w/lunch; Kid's ski school, 6-days - 4 hours p/d, age 4 and up
Lodging: Total beds 3,711
Transportation: Gateway Airport: Munich
Local Airport: Innsbruck
Closest Provincial City: Landeck, 39 km
By Auto from Airport: Innsbruck to Landeck to Galtür, 120 km (75 mi)
By Train: Innsbruck to Landeck, then take bus to Galtür
Ski Bus: From Galtür to See free with Silvretta Ski Pass
Best Deal: Silvretta Ski Pass covers Galtür, Ischgl-Samnaun, Kappl and See

AUSTRIA

SEEFELD
TOURIST OFFICE
Rathaus 43
Seefeld A-6100, Austria
Telephone: (43) 5212/2313 Fax: (43) 5212/3355

Elevation: Base/Village: 1,180 m (3,937 ft); Top: 2,100 m (6,775 ft)

Vertical: 865 m (2,838 ft)

Longest Run: 6.5 km (3.1 mi) Seefelder Joch

Terrain: Plateau surrounded by mountains-terrain for all levels. 35% beginner, 40% intermediate, 25% advanced

Skiing Circus: Happy Skicard includes ski areas around the Zugspitz-283 km of ski runs

Lifts: 23

Types: 1 Funicular; 2 Cable Cars; 3 double Chairlifts; 17 Surface lifts

Lift Capacity: 16,000 p/h resort

Ski Season: Early Dec. to early April

Cross Country: 120 km starting from Village Centre; 200 km on the Seefeld Plateau; Seefelder Joch, Härmelekopf and Gschwardtkopf areas

Ski School: 120 Alpine, Nordic & snowboard

Other Winter Activities: Curling; fitness center; indoor winter golf; hiking; ice skating/artificial; indoor swimming; ski-bobbing; indoor tennis; mono-skiing; paragliding;

SÖLDEN ÖTZTAL ARENA
(SÖLDEN/ZWIESELSTEIN/HOCHSÖLDEN/VENT)
TOURIST OFFICE ÖTZTAL ARENA,
Postfach 80 A-6450 Sölden, Austria
Telephone: (43) 5254 2212 0 Fax: (43) 5254 3131

Elevation: Base/Village: 1,377 m (4,518 ft); Top: 3,250 m (10,563 ft).

Vertical: 1,675 m (5,495 ft).

Longest Run: 10 km

Terrain: Runs: 45 red, 45 blue, 18 black—108 km of terrain including 2 glacier areas

Skiing Circus: Winter ski area of Untergurgl/Hochgurgl/Obergurgl—not connected with Sölden, 12 km

Lifts: 35 (with glacier)

Types: 2 Gondolas; 2 Funiculars; 20 Chairlifts (2 singles, 7 doubles, 5 triples, 6 quads); 11 T-bars

Lift Capacity: 55,655 p/h Ötztal-Arena

Ski Season: Mid-December-Beginning of May

Summer Skiing: On Rettenbach & Tiefenbach glaciers

Cross Country: 16 km; 8 km in Sölden, 8 km in Zwieselstein (about 3 km from Sölden)

Ski School: Sölden/Hochsölden, Vacancia, Ötztal 2000

Mountain Restaurants: 17

Other Winter Activities: Curling; fitness center; hiking; sledding; ice skating/natural; indoor tennis; mono-skiing;

INNSBRUCK LAND—TIROL
The Olympics in 1964 and 1976 have made Seefeld a prime destination area for the novice skier and the enthusiastic cross country devotee. Even if you don't ski, Seefeld is the perfect place to spend a winter vacation. All the things that make a winter day memorable and enjoyable can be found here.

sauna; snowboarding; sleigh riding; sports center; tube sliding; squash; bowling; tobogganing; aerobic

Après-Ski: Bars, discos, casino, folklore evenings

Shopping/Services: All services and shopping facilities available. Casino (jacket required.) Ski bus runs daily.

Credit Cards: AE, DC, EC, MC, VISA (hotels & shops)

Child Care: Child Care for up to 5 years, 43/5212/4459; ski kindergarten age 4-10 through Tourist Office; kid's programs for 4-13 year olds; children's theater

Lodging: 6,600 hotel beds; 1,700 apartment beds, plus private guest houses 4 (5, 4 & 3 star hotels)

Transportation: Gateway Airport: Munich (75 mi) bus or train to Seefeld (2 hrs.). Airport in Innsbruck, 22 km

Closest Provincial City: Innsbruck, 14 mi

By Auto from airport: Innsbruck to Zirl to Seefeld (25 min.); train information (43) 5212/1717

By Ski Bus from airport: 40 minutes from Innsbruck; bus service from Innsbruck on regular schedule

Best Deal: "White Weeks" Jan. 8-Feb. 4 and from March 15 to Easter

ÖTZTAL ARENA
Ski lifts spring from the Ötz Valley to serve three major skiing regions including Hochsölden with runs that start above 9000 feet. Sölden boasts summer skiing Rettenbach and Tiefenbach Glaciers and their summer skiing slopes.

mountaineering (depends on conditions); paragliding; sauna; indoor swimming; snowboarding

Après-Ski: 4 discos, 18 bars, pubs, 6 ice bars, cafes, 3 sledding parties

Shopping/Services: 6 supermarkets, 6 gift shops, 10 sport shops, plus 2 at the glacier

Credit Cards: DC, EC, MC, Euro-cheque (+ card)

Child Care: Ski school, ages 3-8 years; children's ski garden; one to six day rates

Lodging: 9,894 beds in 32 hotels, 42 pensions/guest houses, 225 apartments, 230 bed & breakfast

Transportation: Gateway Airports: Munich or Zürich Local Airport: Innsbruck

Closest Provincial City: Imst 54 km, Innsbruck 80 km

By Auto: Inntal Motorway (A12), exit Ötztal to Sölden

By Train: Innsbruck to Ötztal Bahnhof, bus from railway station to Sölden (Train and bus stop at the station)

Other Information: "Snow-Guarantee" in Ötztal-Arena. Snow machines from village to 2,090 m; average sunshine hours in Dec. (3), Jan. (4), Feb. (6), Mar. (7)

©Publishers Group International, 1998

AUSTRIA

GURGL (UNTER-HOCH-OBERGURGL)
TOURIST OFFICE: GURGL
A-6456 Obergurgl 108, Austria
Telephone: (43) 5256/6466 Fax: (43) 5256-6353

Elevation: Base/Village: 1,800 m (5,906 ft); Top: 3,080 m (10,102 ft)
Vertical: 1,276 m (4,186 ft)
Longest Run: 8.5 km (5.3 mi)
Terrain: Variety of terrain from easy groomed slopes to some very advanced, steep
Lifts: 23
Types: 2 Gondolas; 10 Chairlifts (3 h-s quads, 6 doubles, 1 single); 11 Surface (10 T-bars, 1 rope)
Lift Capacity: 33,000 p/h resort
Ski Season: Mid-Nov. to Early May
Summer Skiing: In Sölden (28 km) on Rettenbach & Tiefenbachferner glaciers
Cross Country: 12 km
Mountain Restaurants: 9 in Hochgurgl & Obergurgl
Ski School: In Obergurgl and Hochgurgl
Other Winter Activities: Curling; hiking; ice skating/natural; mono-skiing; snowboarding; squash; indoor swimming; telemarking; mountaineering; bowling

ÖTZTAL/TIROL
Obergurgl sits at 1,930 m up at the end of the Ötz Valley close to the Italian frontier. Hochgurgl, 210 m higher than Obergurgl, is accessible as is Hochgurgl, which provides more challenging skiing, with a new "Top Express" gondola connecting the two villages.

Après-Ski: 5 bars-restaurants, cafes, 4 discos, 4 ice bars, folklore evenings, concerts
Shopping/Services: 1 supermarket, 2 souvenir shops, 8 sports shops with rentals; 28 restaurants;
Credit Cards: DC, MC, VISA, Eurocard; Cards accepted in banks and some hotels
Child Care: Kindergarten Obergurgl, one to six day rates; Telephone: 05256/6305; no nursery
Lodging: 3,900 beds; 29 hotels, 5 inns, 33 pensions, 29 apartments
Transportation: Gateway Airport: Munich & Innsbruck
Closest Provincial City: Innsbruck (100 km from Obergurgl)
Train: Innsbruck to Ötztal
Ski Bus between Unter and Obergurgl
Best Deal: Ski-Fit Weeks until Dec. 21; Powdersnow Weeks Jan. 5-Feb. 1
Other Information: Hochgurgl, Obergurgl, and Untergurgl can be skied with the same lift pass

ALPBACHTAL
ALBACH TOURIST OFFICE
A-6236 Alpbach
Austria
Telephone: (43) 5336 5211 Fax: (43) 5336 5012

Elevation: Base/Village: 1,000 m (3,280 ft); Top: 2,025 m (6,642 ft); Reith, Brixlegg & Rattenberg are at 500 m
Vertical: 1,100 m (3,608 ft)
Terrain: 28 miles of runs
Longest Run: 8 km (5 mi.)
20 km of snowmaking on main runs - mostly intermediate terrain, but with 2 black runs
Skiing Circus: Reitherkogel, Wiedersbergerhorn and the main ski area of Alpbach
Lifts: 21
Types: 1 Gondola; 5 Chairs (1 single, 3 double, 1 triple); 15 Surface lifts (T-bars)
Lift Capacity: 20,000 p/h resort
Ski Season: December - April
Cross Country: 32 km of trails
Ski School: 4 Ski Schools - Alpbach & Inneralpbach, alpine & cross country instruction
Other Winter Activities: Winter hiking (40 km of cleared paths); cross country trails; indoor swimming;

TYROL
The Alpbach Valley runs south from the Inn Valley between Innsbruck and Kufstein. Its 4 villages of Brixlegg, Reith, Rattenberg and Alpbach offer a variety of accommodations and a wide range of runs. Alpbach was honored as Austria's most beautiful village and Rattenberg is famous for its blown and cut crystal.

snowboarding w/2 halfpipes; snowshoe hiking; 2 sled runs; ice skating; horse-drawn sleigh rides
Après-Ski: Sleigh rides to the inn; cafes, discothèque; ice bars
Shopping Services: Towns of Rattenburg & Brixlegg are known for their shopping (crystal blowing & cutting); supermarkets, hair stylist, sport shops, Austrian costumes
Child Care: Ski Kindergarten for skiers & for non-skiers; babysitting arranged through tourist office
Lodging: 6,504 total beds in the Inn Valley
Transportation: Gateway Airport: Munich 137 mi
Closest Provincial City: Innsbruck/Kufstein
By Auto from Airport: One hour drive
Best Deal: Guest card available at hotel offers visitor benefits
Other Information: Free ski bus

AUSTRIA

NEUSTIFT IM STUBAITAL
Tourist Office:
A-6167 Neustift im Stubaital, Austria
Telephone: (43) 5226/22 28 Fax: (43) 5226/25 29

STUBAITAL
Skiing region with total distance of approximately 30 km with Neustift Village being the centerpoint. Fulpmes, Telfes, & Neustift in the Stubai Valley retain the old Tirolean village atmosphere. Neustift with access to year-round skiing on Stubai Glacier attracts skiers from beginners to powder freaks.

Elevation: Base/Village: Neustift 1,000 m; Fulpmes 937 m; Stubai Glacier 1,750 m
Top: Fulpmes 2,260 m (7,415 ft); Stubai Glacier 3,200 m (10,502 ft) (Community of Neustift is 20 km long)

Vertical: 1,450 m (4,756 ft)

Longest Run: 10 km

Terrain: Runs in Neustift: 8 red, 17 blue, 24 black; Stubai Glacier offers variety of terrain—good lift system

Lifts: 29

Types: 4 Gondolas; 6 Chairlifts; 19 T-bars

Lift Capacity: 27,630 p/h

Ski Season: Stubai Glacier offers year-round skiing

Cross Country: 40 km connecting track in the Stubai Valley; 40 km high altitude, 5 km on Glacier

Ski School: Olympia and Neustift-Stubaier Gletscher

Mountain Restaurants: 10 huts on Elfer and Stubai Glacier; also sport/rental shops; 20 on mountain paths

Other Winter Activities: Curling; hiking; ice skating/natural; indoor swimming & tennis; sleigh riding; squash; snowboarding; bowling; tobogganing; horse riding; cross country skiing; folklore evenings; ski touring; paragliding; ice climbing, carving

Après-Ski: 12 Bars, 6 discos, 2 ice bars, 23 cafes, 14 pubs, 32 restaurants, 2 nightly toboggan runs

Shopping/Services: Farmer's market every fortnight with ecologically varied products to souvenir shops

Child Care: Kindergarten in Tourist Office Monday-Friday, 3-10 yrs. AS 100 p/d w/lunch

Lodging: 7,800 beds in Neustift im Stubaital

Transportation: Gateway Airport: Munich

Closest Provincial City: Innsbruck (19 mi) bus and train from Munich to Innsbruck-regular daily schedule

By Auto from airport: Innsbruck (25 km), take Brenner Autobahn to Schönberg/Stubaital turnoff

Ski Bus: From October until May free to all open ski areas of the Stubai Valley

By Train: Munich to Innsbruck on regular schedule (2 hrs.) then bus to Neustift (45 min.); Fulpmes and Telfes have rail connections from Innsbruck

Bus: Regular service, Innsbruck-Neustift

Best Deal: Special packages in winter, spring & autumn, incl. 6-day Glacier Ski Pass, acommodation & swimming pool entrance—rates AS 2,530-AS 7,790

These skiers seem to be waiting for a straggler on the way home to Neustift.

Photo: Galtur Tourismsverband

AUSTRIA

AUSTRIA

INNSBRUCK—IGLS
Tourist Office:
Burggraben 3, Innsbruck A-6021, Austria
Telephone: (43) 512/59 850
Fax: (43) 512/598507

TIROL
Innsbruck, internationally well known as the "heart of the Alps" and quite probably the greatest ski city in the world hosted the 1964 & 1976 Winter Olympics. Free bus service to local areas and to Stubai Glacier. A wide variety of skiing and sightseeing possibilities.

Elevation: Base/Village: 575 m (1,886 ft); Top: 3,210 m (10,528 ft)

Vertical: 1,457 m (4,780 ft)

Longest Run: 10 km (6.2 mi)

Terrain: Igls-Patscherkofel: good intermediate terrain, some tree skiing/Glungezer: gentle beginner area; Mutterer Alm: easy novice runs. Axamer Lizum & Seegrube: some high intermediate and off-piste adventure; Schlick 2000; all degrees of difficulty; 57 km red, 57 km blue, 12 km black—total 126 km of runs

Lifts: 63

Types: 10 Cable Cars; 1 Funicular; 17 Chairlifts (1 h-s quad, 4 singles, 6 doubles); 33 T-bars

Lift Capacity: 62,000 p/h resorts

Ski Season: Dec. 19-April 5

Summer Skiing: On Stubai Glacier 18 miles

Cross Country: 500 km—12 areas; free ski bus svc.

Ski School: Ski & snowboard school Innsbruck; ITS Ski School Igls 2000; Ski school "Schigls"

Mountain Restaurants: Yes

Other Winter Activities: Curling; hiking; ice skating/natural and artificial; indoor swimming; indoor tennis; mono-skiing; snowboarding; bobsleighing; fitness center; dogsled rides; tobogganing

Après-Ski: Bars, discos, cafes, coffee houses, casino, folklore evenings, concerts, cinemas, sleigh riding

Shopping/Services: Innsbruck is a city of over 120,000 and has every imaginable shop and service

Credit Cards: AE, DC, MC, VISA, Discover, EC

Child Care: Ski kindergarten for children 3 yrs. & up AS50/hr; Telephone: 43/5123/77377; Nursery on request

Lodging: 8,316 beds; from 5-star hotels to hostels

Transportation: Gateway Airports: Munich/Innsbruck

By Auto from airport: Innsbruck is a major city accessible by highway in all directions

Train and bus from Munich & Zürich: Tele-43/512/1717

Ski Bus: Free, 5 stops in city center to all 7 ski areas including Stubai Glacier, Dec.-Apr. 5, 1999

Best Deal: Super Ski Pass covers Innsbruck, the Stubai Glacier, Kitzbühel & Arlberg w/520 kms. of runs, 210 lifts—all transfers. Gletscher Ski Pass covers Innsbruck & Stubai Glacier, 126 kms. of runs, 63 lifts—all transfers

AUSTRIA

Hinterux collects so much snow that it offers glacier skiing in summer. Photo: Fred McKinney

ZILLERTAL (MAYRHOFEN)
TOURIST OFFICE
Dursterstrasse 225, Postfach 21
Mayrhofen A-6290
Telephone: (43) 5285/6760 Fax: (43) 5285/676033

Elevation: Village: 630 m (2,066 ft); Top: 2,250 m (7,380 ft)
Vertical: 1,620 m (5,314 ft)
Longest Run: 5.5 km (3.5 mi)
Regional Terrain: In the 11 areas there are 452 km (280 miles) of prepared slopes. Ziller Valley also offers many off-piste opportunities. Runs: 53 red, 27 blue, and 21 black (ski area Mayrhofen)
Skiing Circus: Lifts above Mayrhofen, on Penken or Ahorn and Horberg - Gerent slopes
Lifts: 30 local: 3 Gondolas, 11 Chairlifts, 16 Surface lifts; 146 lifts in region
Lift Capacity: 34,830 resort; 160,000 p/h in Ziller Valley
Ski Season: December to April
Summer Skiing: On Hintertux glacier
Cross Country: 20 km (13 miles), flat area
Ski School: 4 ski schools, 4 snowboarding schools
Mountain Restaurants: 15
Other Winter Activities: Fitness center; hiking; horse drawn sleigh; ice skating/natural; indoor swimming; indoor tennis; mono-skiing; paragliding; snowboarding; sleigh riding; curling; snowrafting

TIROL
This charming Tirolean village is the largest resort in the Ziller Valley, where 11 ski areas offer many possibilities. Among the others are Fügen, Hippach, Zell am Ziller, Lanersbach, Finkenberg, Gerlos, Kramsach, Kaltenbach, Hochfügen, Vanderlanersbach and Hintertux.

Après-Ski: 11 Bars/pubs, 2 discos, 29 cafes, 34 restaurants, cinema, folklore evenings, concerts, musicals
Shopping/Services: Beauty farm; woodcarving shops; supermarkets; crystal shop; wide shopping variety
Credit Cards: AE, MC, VISA - travellers checks sometimes necessary
Child Care: 3 mos-7 yrs AS 320 per day; Babysitting; Kid's ski school
Lodging: Approx. 8,000 beds in hotels, pensions & apartments
Transportation: Gateway Airport: Munich (105 mi) Local Airport: Innsbruck 65 km (41 mi)
By Auto from airport: Leave Munich-Innsbruck Autobahn at Strass; Salzburg 170 km
By Train: Innsbruck or Munich, with changes in Jenbach
Best Deal: Zillertal Superskipass includes 148 lifts serving 452 km of terrain

AUSTRIA

BRIXEN IM THALE
TOURIST OFFICE
Brixen A-6364, Postfach 17
Austria
Telephone: (43) 5334/8433 Fax: (43) 5334/8332

Elevation: Base/Village: 800 m (2,624 ft);
Top: 1,800 m (5,905 ft)

Vertical: 1,100 m (3,608 ft)

Longest Run: 8 km (5 mi) Ski-Welt; 4.5 km Brixen

Terrain: 250 km (155 mi) of prepared slopes; 122 km red, 108 km blue, 20 km black

Skiing Circus: Brixen is connected with 8 other villages—Westendorf, Hopfgarten, Itter, Söll, Going, Scheffau, Ellmau and Kelchsau

Lifts: 91 in Ski-Welt

Types: 1 Tram; 8 Gondolas; 18 Chairlifts (7 quads, 3 triples, 8 doubles); 60 Surface

Lift Capacity: 107,000 p/h in Ski-Welt, 15,000 in resort

Ski Season: Mid-December through Mid-March

Cross Country: 32 km tracks in valley connect with Westendorf, Kirchberg & Schwarzsee-Kitzbühel

Ski School: Many schools with more than 500 instructors; Brixen has 2 ski schools

SKI-WELT WILDER KAISER BRIXENTAL
Brixen im Thale is one of the 9 villages in the northeastern part of the state of Tirol. The skiing world of Wilder Kaiser-Brixen Valley is linked by an extensive lift system and is the largest connected skiing area in Austria.

Mountain Restaurants: 8 Brixen; 63 Ski-Welt

Other Winter Activities: Curling; fitness center; horse drawn sleigh; ice skating/natural; indoor tennis; snowboarding; sleigh riding; indoor swimming; hiking

Après-Ski: 4 Bars, 2 discos, 4 cafes, 1 ice bar, 7 coffee houses, folklore evenings, concerts, casino, sauna

Shopping/Services: Boutiques, clothing, drug, grocery

Credit Cards: AE, DC, Discover, EC, MC, VISA

Child Care: 9 am - 5 pm

Lodging: 23,500 beds in region, 2,700 in Brixen

Transportation: Gateway Airport: Salzburg 102 km (63 mi), Munich 130 km (81 mi), Innsbruck 80 km

Closest Provincial City: Kitzbühel, 16 km

By Auto from airport: Leave Inn Valley autobahn at Kufstein

By Train: From Munich (change in Wörgl)—station in Brixen

Ski Bus: Brixen free ski bus

KIRCHBERG IN TYROL
TOURIST OFFICE KIRCHBERG
Haupstrasse 8
A-6365 Kirchberg i.T. Austria
Telephone: (43) 5357 2309 Fax: (43) 5357 3732

Elevation: Base/Village: 860 m (2,821 ft);
Top: 2,000 m (6,560 ft)

Vertical: 1,140 m (3,739 ft)

Terrain: 75 km beginner, 66 km intermediate & 19 km expert terrain

Longest run: 8 km (5.1 mi)

Skiing Circus: Aschau-Kirchberg-Kitzbühel-Aurach-Jochberg-Pass Thurn

Lifts: 59

Types: 5 Gondolas; 22 Chairlifts (3 quads, 4 triples, 15 doubles); 32 Surface lifts

Lift Capacity: 80,000 p/h resort

Ski Season: Mid-December - Mid-April

Cross Country: 40 km

Ski School: 2 Schools: Schischule Kirchberg & Total

Other Winter Activities: Curling; hiking; horse drawn sleigh; ice skating natural; indoor swimming; indoor tennis; mono-skiing; mountaineering; paragliding; snowboarding; sleigh riding; sports center; squash

TYROL
Only four miles from the city of Kitzbühel, Kirchberg is a picturesque village in the shadow of the Kitzbüeheler Alps. The resort offers more than 120 miles of groomed runs plus another 120 miles of marked and tracked cross country trails. A free shuttle bus connects Kirchberg with Kitzbühel and the ski runs at Pass Thurn.

Après-Ski: 40 mountain restaurants; sauna; bars; discos; ice bars, cafes, coffee houses

Shopping Services: Variety of shops and restaurants

Credit Cards: Euro-Card; MC; VISA

Child Care: Krabbelstube nursery; Kid's ski school

Lodging: 8,200 beds

Transportation: Gateway Airports: Salzburg or Innsbruck

Closest Provincial City: Kitzbühel 6 km

By Auto from Airport: 80 km from Salzburg - no ski bus

By Train: From Munich (120 km) or Salzburg (80 km)

Best Deal: Private rooms; 300 apartments with shower/wc and breakfast or "Schneehasenpauschale" (children are free). Contact tourist office

Other Information: Average Snowfall: 283 cm plus 63 snowmaking guns

©Publishers Group International, 1998

AUSTRIA

KITZBÜHEL
TOURIST OFFICE
Hinterstadt 18
Kitzbühel A-6370, Austria
Telephone: (43) 5356/62155-0 Fax: (43) 5356/62307

TIROL
Romantic Kitzbühel has been a favorite with English-speaking skiers for decades, partly for its skiing, partly for its lively après-ski scene. Because it is lower, Kitzbühel is warmer than many other ski resorts in the Alps.

Elevation: Village: 800 m (2,624 ft); Top: 2,000 m (6,562 ft)

Vertical: 1,200 m (3,936 ft)

Longest Run: 6.8 km (4.2 mi), Pengelstein Süd

Terrain: 158 km (97 mi) of skiing area; Kitzbühel-Kirchberg, Jochberg-Pass-Thurn

Skiing Circus: Above Hahnenkamm, it is possible to ski back and forth to Kirchberg in another valley

Lifts: 60

Types: 5 Gondolas, 27 Chairlifts (3 quads, 4 triples, 15 doubles, 5 singles); 28 T-bars

Lift Capacity: 75,977 p/h area, 29,430 p/h resort

Ski Season: Low season: Late-Nov./early-Dec.-Dec. 22; Jan 7-31; March 11-end; High season: Dec. 23-Jan. 6; Feb. 1-Mar. 10

Summer Skiing: On Kaprun glacier 31 miles away

Cross Country: 120 km/region, 36 km/Kitzbühel

Ski School: 6 ski schools, 250 instructors

Mountain Restaurants: 24 in resort; 53 in area

Other Winter Activities: Curling; balloon trips; folklore evenings; hiking; horse drawn sleigh; ice skating/artificial; indoor swimming; indoor tennis; squash; paragliding; sauna; snowboarding; sleigh riding; downhill parties

Après-Ski: 25 Bars, 4 discos, 10 cafes, concerts, cinema, casino, fitness center, museum, wildlife park

Shopping/Services: Many shops from souvenirs to high fashion boutiques. Gourmet restaurants

Credit Cards: DC, MC; VISA AE, EC

Child Care: Nursery: 1 "Nanny" available for 400 AS Tele. 5356/75063; Kid's ski school AS 500 (+80 for lunch)

Lodging: 6,621 beds; 8,000 beds in Kirchberg plus camping on other side of mountain; hotels, pensions, inns, apts, chalets

Transportation: Gateway Airport: Salzburg 80 km; Munich 170 km, Innsbruck 100 km

By Auto from airport: Autobahn from Munich or Innsbruck via Wörgl. From Salzburg via Lofer

By Train: From Munich or Innsbruck via Wörgl

Best Deal: Kitzbühel Alpenski 6-day pass (1,100 AS child, 2,200 AS adult) covers 260 lifts, 680 kms. of trails (196 kms. with snowmaking)

Kitzbühel maintains its medieval charm around the clock.

Photo: Albin Niederstrasser

AUSTRIA

ST. JOHANN IN TYROL
TOURISMUSVERBAND
A-6380 St. Johann in Tyrol, Poststrasse 2, Austria
Telephone: (43) 5352 62235 Fax: (43) 5352 65200

Elevation: Base/Village: 663 m (2,175 ft); Top: 1,700 m (5,576 ft)
Vertical: 995 m (3,264 ft)
Terrain: 60 km (37 mi) of ski runs; 25 km blue; 28 km red; 7 km black
Longest run 5,000 m (3 mi)
Skiing Circus: St. Johann in Tyrol, Oberndorf, Fieberbrunn, St. Ulrich, Kirchdorf, Erpfendorf, Kössen
Lifts: 18 resort (66 in ski circus)
Types: 2 Funiculars; 6 Chairlifts (2 single, 2 double, 1 triple, 1 quad); 10 Surface lifts
Lift Capacity: 20,100 p/h resort
Ski Season: Mid-December - End of March
Cross-Country: 75 kms. (21 km easy, 26 km medium, 28 km difficult); 225 kms connect with other resorts
Ski School: Two schools with 130 instructors
Other Winter Activities: Tobogganing; ice skating; indoor swimming; indoor tennis; curling; sleigh rides; sports center; mono-ski; snowboarding; ballooning; winter walking paths (40 km)

SAALBACH HINTERGLEMM-LEOGANG*
TOURIST OFFICE
Saalbach-Hinterglemm A-5753, Austria
Telephone: (43) 6541/72720 Fax: (43) 6541/7900

Elevation: Village: 1,095 m (3,592 ft); Top: 2,098 m (6,884 ft)
Vertical: 1,003 m (3,290 ft)
Longest Run: 7 km (4.3 mi)
Terrain: Parallel ridges of open snowfields. 124 miles of prepared runs. Expert runs off-piste, also; 46% beginner, 49% intermediate, 5% advanced
Skiing Circus: Lifts above Saalbach connect with slopes/lifts at Leogang
Lifts: 58
Types: 1 Cablecar; 4 Gondolas; 14 Chairlifts; 39 T-bars
Lift Capacity: 62,000 p/h resort
Ski Season: Low Season until Dec. 23 & Jan. 7-27 & Mar. 11-Apr. 14; High season Dec. 24-Jan. 6 & Jan. 28-Mar. 10
Summer Skiing: Kitzsteinhorn 3,200 m, 30 km away
Cross Country: 10 km (6.2 mi) of trails from Hinterglemm to Talschluss
Ski School: 9 schools, over 200 instructors

TYROL
Situated between two of Austria's most famous mountains. The Wilder Kaiser and the Kitzbüheler Horn, St. Johann i.T. is an ideal winter holiday venue. In addition to endless miles of groomed runs, there are miles of untracked off-piste skiing.

Après-Ski: Folklore evenings; dancing, bars, pubs
Shopping Services: Wide variety of shops; full medical facilities & many other services
Credit Cards: VISA; MC; American Express; Diners; Euro-Card
Child Care: Babysitting on request; ski school kindergarten
Lodging: 5,000 guest beds in 3 or 4-star hotels; guest houses; bed & breakfast; and self catering apartments
Transportation: Gateway Airport: Innsbruck
Closest Major City: Salzburg (80 km)
By Auto: From Salzburg: Bad Reichenhall (D)/Steinpass/Lofer/B312
By Train: From Munich (150 km), Salzburg (80 km) or Innsbruck (100 km) to Bahnhof St. Johann in Tyrol. Tele. 5352/62305-385; Fax 62305-543
Best Deal: Kitzbuheler Alps area pass includes 260 lifts
Other Information: Winter preferences - Until Dec 21; Jan 2-6; Mar 8-15 room, halfboard, ski pass AS 4,220; Spring-weeks from AS 2,850 (other combinations)

SALZBURG
These two neighboring villages share their facilities to provide long runs for skiing and breathtaking views. The blend of the traditional alpine spirit and modern conveniences have made this valley an attractive resort for the young at heart. In 1991 it hosted the World Cup Championships.

Mountain Restaurants: 40
Other Winter Activities: Snowboarding, Curling; horse drawn sleigh; ice skating/natural; indoor swimming & tennis/squash; paragliding; cross country skiing
Après-Ski: 29 Bars, 14 discos, 20 ice bars, 23 coffee houses, sports center, sauna
Shopping/Services: Sports, markets and other shops
Credit Cards: AE, DC, MC, VISA
Child Care: Ages 2-7, AS 520 day, AS 1,550 4-6 days
Lodging: 17,329 beds; hotels in every category
Transportation: Gateway Airport: Munich (112 mi); Local Airport: Salzburg
Closest Provincial City: Salzburg, 100 km
By Auto from airport: Autobahn to Bischofshofen, Schwarzach, Zell am See
By Train: Via Bischofshofen to Zell am See, hourly bus to Saalbach. Skibus runs between the villages
Other Information: Austria's largest cable car.

©Publishers Group International, 1998

AUSTRIA

> **BAD GASTEIN**
> TOURIST OFFICE
> K. F. Josefstr. 24
> Badgastein, A5640
> Telephone: (43) 6434/2531-0 Fax: (43) 6434-253137

Elevation: Base/Village: 1,038 m (3,553 ft); Top: 2,700 m (8,856 ft)

Vertical: 1,700 m (5,578 ft); Sportgastein 800-1,600 m

Longest Run: 11 km (7 mi)

Terrain: 250 km (155 mi) of prepared runs on both sides of the valley and at Sportgastein 10 km away; 30% beginner, 30% intermediate, 40% advanced

Skiing Circus: Possible to ski from Bad Gastein to Bad Hofgastein and return. A ski circus also connects Dorfgastein with the Grossarl Valley

Lifts: 16, 4 cable cars; 4 chairlifts; 8 T-bars

Lift Capacity: 23,454 p/h resort

Ski Season: Early December - May

Cross Country: 35 km of tracks; high alpine-track at Sportgastein-600 m; biathlon track facilities

Other Winter Activities: Hiking; horse drawn sleigh; ice skating/natural; indoor swimming; sauna; tennis; paragliding; hang-gliding; sleigh riding; sports center; winter golf; horseback riding; ski races; local curling

SALZBURG
Bad Gastein is the main town in the Gastein Valley, a year-round spa that attracts visitors from around the world. (Only Vienna has more overnight guests.) Region has been famous for its hot mineral springs since medieval times.

Après-Ski: Casino, bars, cafes, dancing, cinema, folklore evenings, thermal indoor & outdoor pools

Shopping/Services: Array of shops and restaurants

Credit Cards: AE, DC, MC, VISA

Child Care: Kindergarten, Hotel Grüner Baum Telephone: 6434/25160; Ski kindergarten; babysitting

Lodging: 19,700 beds in Gastein Valley from pension to luxury hotels; 7 nights p/p/breakfast AS2,360-6,440; half pension 3,200-8,940

Transportation: Gateway Airport: Munich (147 mi), Salzburg (62 mi)

Closest Provincial City: St. Johann im Pongau

By Auto from airport: Tauern Autobahn to Bischofshofen, then national road to Badgastein—on major route between Germany and Italy

By Train: Trains every hour from Salzburg and Munich

Other Information: People come here to take "the cure" in thermal waters and heated "healing caves." Bad weather day trips include Salzburg and Venice

---

> **ZELL AM SEE/KAPRUN**
> TOURIST OFFICE
> Brucker Bundesstrasse
> Zell am See A-5700, Austria
> Telephone: (43) 6542/2600-0 Fax: (43) 6542/2032

Elevation: Top: 3,029 m (9,935 ft)

Vertical: 2,271 m (7,448 ft)

Longest Run: 6 km (3.6 mi)

Terrain: 130 km (80 mi) of prepared runs in total area, 30 km in glacier area; 38% beginner, 50% intermediate, 12% advanced

Lifts: 56

Types: 5 Gondolas; 6 Funiculars; 13 Chairlifts; 32 Surface lifts (T-bars)

Lift Capacity: 62,130 resort

Ski Season: November 28, 1997 - April 18, 1998

Summer Skiing: Year-round skiing on Kitzsteinhorn glacier above Kaprun

Cross Country: 200 km (124 m), including a loop at the glacier

Ski School: 10 ski schools, nearly 300 instructors

Other Winter Activities: Curling; fitness center; hiking; ice skating; indoor swimming; indoor tennis; sleigh riding; alpine flights; snowboarding; tobogganning

SALZBURG
These two resorts, 10 minutes apart by bus, promote the "Europa Sport Region." Slopes at Zell am See overlook a picturesque lake. At Kaprun vast snowfields are at a high altitude and are partly on a glacier. Served by the only subway-type mountain railway in Austria, the Kitzsteinhorn offers skiing both winter and summer.

Après-Ski: Bars, discos, cafes, coffee houses

Shopping/Services: Good shopping facilities in both communities. Excellent selection of restaurants

Credit Cards: AE, DC, MC, VISA

Child Care: Kindergarten, AS 350 p/d, Tele. 56343

Lodging: 14,000 guest beds, from pensions to 5-star hotels

Transportation: Gateway Airport: Munich (120 mi)

Closest Provincial City: Salzburg (56 miles)

By Auto from airport: Salzburg-Bischofshofen-Zell am See

By Train: Trains arrive in Zell am See from Salzburg, Innsbruck, Vienna and other directions

Best Deal: Early & late season ski packages at discount rates, Nov. 30 - Dec. 31; Jan. 4 - Feb. 8; Mar. 8-23 & Apr. 5-13, 1997

Other Information: Kaprun glacier is accessed by cable car or by unique underground train

AUSTRIA

ALTENMARKT/ZAUCHENSEE
TOURIST OFFICE
Postfach 29
Altenmarkt/Zauchensee A-5541
Telephone: (43) 6452/5511 Fax: (43) 6452/6066

Elevation: Village: 856 m (2,808 ft);
Top: 2,188 m (7,178 ft)
Vertical: 1,332 m (4,370 ft)
Longest Run: 4.5 km (2.8 mi), Kälberloch
Terrain: 350 km of prepared slopes in region and many off-piste opportunities as well; 33% beginner, 54% intermediate, 13% advanced
Skiing Circus: Possible to ski from valley to valley—Radstadt to Altenmarkt, Zauchensee to Flachauwinkel, Flachau to Wagrain, for examples
Lifts: 121
Types: 1 Tram; 6 Gondolas; 28 Chairlifts (1 triple, 27 doubles); 85 T-bars; 1 platter
Lift Capacity: 105,000 p/h in whole Sport World region
Ski Season: Early December to late April
Cross Country: 220 km (135 miles) in the resort
Ski School: 3 different ski schools in Altenmarkt/Zauchensee: Happy; Hanselmann; Top Alpin
Mountain Restaurants: 10; 2 ice bars

ST-JOHANN im PONGAU ALPENDORF
TOURIST OFFICE
St. Johann/Alpendorf Postfach 46,
A-5600 St. Johann, Austria
Telephone: (43) 6412-6036 Fax: (43) 6412-6036-74

Elevation: Base/Village: 650 m (2,080 ft)
Top: 1,900 m (6,233 ft)
Vertical: 650 m center/850 m Alpendorf (2,133/2,789 ft)
Terrain: 2 base areas—Alpendorf and Center; 128 km red, 180 km blue, & 42 km black runs
Longest Run: 5.0 km (3.1 mi)
Skiing Circus: None
Lifts: 126
Types: 5 Gondolas; 32 Chairlifts (6 triples, 26 doubles); 87 T-bars; 2 Platters
Lift Capacity: 105,000 p/h resort; 19,000 p/h St. Johann
Ski Season: December-April
Summer Skiing: Kitzsteinhorn Glacier, 30 km
Cross Country: 14 km; 220 km in region
Ski School: 3 schools; lessons for kids with 3 racing courses; snowboarding
Mountain Restaurants: 10; 40-50 in Sports World
Other Winter Activities: Curling; fitness center; hiking; horse drawn sleigh; ice skating/natural; mono-skiing;

SALZBURG
Altenmarkt/Zauchensee is one of eight resorts in the "Salzburger Sport World Amadé." Others are Kleinarl, Radstadt, St. Johann im Pongau, Wagrain, Eben, Filzmoos and Flachau. Several are interconnected with slopes and lifts. Impressive number of ski facilities within a relatively small geographic area.

Other Winter Activities: Curling; indoor tennis; snowboarding; sleigh riding; sports center; mono-ski; horse drawn sleigh; indoor swimming; sauna; squash
Après-Ski: 3 Bars, 3 discos, 5 cafes, folk museum
Shopping/Services: Two sport shops in Altenmarkt, many other shops, restaurants, four supermarkets
Credit Cards: EC, VISA; not accepted everywhere
Child Care: Ski school, 5 days AS1,450; 43/6452/4315
Lodging: 30,000 beds in region; 4,000 at resort

Transportation: Gateway Airports: Munich 250 km
Closest Provincial City: Salzburg 70 km (44 mi)
By Auto from airport: Tauern-Autobahn via Graz, 70 km
By Train: Munich to Altenmarkt or Radstadt (3 km away)
Ski Bus: Altenmarkt to Zauchensee (10 km)

Best Deal: Salzburger Sportwelt pass includes Altenmarkt, Radstadt, Flachau, Wagrain, St. Johann, Filzmoos, Neuberg & Eben. Low season special about AS 5,800 for 7 nights, halfboard, & 6-day ski pass

SALZBURG SPORTS WORLD
In the famous "Salzburg Sport Region," St. Johann is less than 40 miles from the Salzburg Airport on the Autobahn. The valley location of the village makes it an ideal starting point to ski trips to the surrounding peaks. With runs up to 5 km long, St. Johann has become a favorite destination for many skiers.

indoor swimming & tennis; paragliding; snowboarding; sleigh riding; squash; tobagganing; mountaineering
Après-Ski: Sauna, 12 bars, 4 discos, 4 ice bars, 6 cafes, 2 coffee houses; concerts, folklore evenings
Shopping/Services: Approximately 80 shops; St. Johann is a "wonderful" shopping town
Credit Cards: For shopping, hotels, restaurants—AE, EC, VISA, DC; not for ski pass
Child Care: 1-4 years, half day, AS 240; all day AS 480; Kid's Ski School
Lodging: 3,450 beds in area; 28,000 beds in Salzburg Sports World region. 5 star hotels to private pensions or farm house

Transportation: Gateway Airport: Salzburg
Closest Provincial City: Salzburg, 55 km
By Train: To St. Johann

Best Deal: Packages to Dec. 19 & from Mar. 13; 7 nights, bed & breakfast, 6 day, ski pass—AS 3,180
Other Information: Temperature average on mountain— -10C—base -½C (30F)—weather is moderate for winter conditions

©Publishers Group International, 1998

AUSTRIA

SCHLADMING (DACHSTEIN)
TOURIST OFFICE
Kuschargasse 202
Schladming A-8970, Austria
Telephone: (43) 3687/23310 Fax: (43) 3687/23232

Elevation: Schladming Village: 749 m (2,457 ft); Top: 1,894 m (6,214 ft)

Vertical: 1,243 m (4,078 ft)

Longest Run: 7.7 km (4.8 mi.)

Regional Terrain: 155 km (87 miles) of 7 prepared slopes in distinct ski areas. Good off-piste possibilities; 28% beginner, 61% intermediate, 11% advanced

Lifts: 84

Types: 7 Gondolas; 16 Chairlifts (4 quads, 1 triple, 11 doubles); 61 T-bars

Lift Capacity: 85,000 p/h in entire region

Ski Season: November-April

Summer Skiing: Dachstein glacier (June - Nov.)

Cross Country: 350 km (218 mi) of Nordic trails, Centre-Ramsau

Ski School: 12 with more than 200 instructors

Other Winter Activities: Curling; hiking; horse drawn sleigh; indoor swimming; indoor tennis; mono-skiing; paragliding; snowboarding; sleigh riding; sports center; ice skating/natural; mountaineering; sauna

OBERTAUERN
TOURIST OFFICE
Obertauern A-5562, Austria
Telephone: (43) 64 56 7252 or (43) 64 56 7320
Fax: (43) 64 56 7515

Elevation: Base/Village: 1,740 m (5,709 ft); Top: 2,350 m (7,710 ft)

Vertical: 610 m (2,001 ft)

Terrain: Terrain for all levels; access from most lodging; over 120 km of runs within resort; ski the north side and return via the south side or vice versa; 20% beginner, 30% interm., 30% advanced, 20% expert

Lifts: 37

Types: 1 Gondola; 11 Chairlifts (8 quads, 1 triple, 6 doubles); 10 T-bars

Lift Capacity: 34,760 p/h resort

Ski Season: December 1-May 1

Cross Country: 18 km (11 mi)

Ski School: 6 ski schools with 70 instructors; alpine, cross country and snowboarding instruction available

Mountain Restaurants: Yes

Other Winter Activities: Curling; winter hiking; tennis hall; mono-skiing; horse-drawn sleigh riding; cross country; squash; message; fitness center snowboarding; bobsled school

Après-Ski: Bars, discos (5), cafes

STYRIA
Although relatively unknown to Americans, Schladming in the center of Austria hosts thousands of European tourists and is one of the leading vacation centers for Austrians. Ski runs on both sides of the Enns River. Villages include Schladming, Rohrmoos, Haus/Ennstal, Pichl/Mandling, Groebming, Pruggern and Ramsau.

Après-Ski: Bars, discos, cafes, folklore evenings

Shopping/Services: Several shopping malls, sports shops, grocery stores, gift shops

Credit Cards: AE, DC, MC, VISA

Lodging: 22,000 beds in hotels, 185 pensions, 150 apartments

Transportation: Gateway Airport: Munich (131 mi), Local Airport: Salzburg 90 km (56 mi)

Closest Provincial City: Salzburg, 90 km

By Auto from airport: Tauern Autobahn, exit at Knoten/Ennstal

By Train: From Munich, change trains in Bischofshofen; From Salzburg, 1½ hours

By Ski Bus: From Schladming

Best Deal: Special bargain rates in January, plus March/April
(Nordic Ski World Championships 1999 in Centre-Ramsau)

SALZBURG
If you are looking for skiing from early December until May, the place for you is Obertauern. This unique area located at more than 5,700 feet above sea level, offers an interesting group of ski runs and the ability to ski around the bowl that completely wraps this Austrian mountaintop village.

Shopping/Services: Sport-boutiques; variety

Credit Cards: AE, DC, EC, VISA

Child Care: Kindergarten: AS1,350 p/week without lunch; AS1,850 with lunch; Nursery: Child care in Hotel Alpina-approximate cost AS300; Telephone: 06456 7336

Lodging: 6,500 beds; 118 hotels or guest houses, 2 to 4 stars; pensions, apartments and hostels

Transportation: Gateway Airport: Munich (220 km)

Closest Provincial City & Airport: Salzburg (98 km)

By Bus from Salzburg to Obertauern (Tele: 06456 7411)

By Bus from Salzburg Airport: Taxi Habersatter (Telephone: 06456 7411)

By Train from Munich, then change to bus in Radstadt to Obertauern (train station telephone: 06452 4350)

By Auto: Salzburg to Radstadt to Obertauern

Best Deal: Low season: 7 days lodging, breakfast, 6-day ski pass from AS3,380; 5 of 7 day lift pass (1,505 low season/1,735 high season); children 825/1,030; or any 10 days during season

Other Information: Low season: opening until before Xmas; Mid-Jan. to 1st week of Feb.; Last week of April

AUSTRIA

KATSCHBERG*
TOURIST OFFICE KATSCHBERG
9863 Rennweg/Katschberg, Austria
Telephone: (43) 47 34 630 Fax: (43) 4734 753
　　　　　(43) 47 34 3300　　　(43) 4734 3305

Elevation: Base/Village: 1,143 m (3,749 ft); Top: 1,640 m (2,220 ft)
Vertical: 500 m (1,640 ft)
Terrain: Longest run: 8,000 m (4.9 mi) Rennweg (1,143 m); Katschberg (1,641 m); Aineck (1,220 m)
Skiing Circus: Katschberg to Aineck to St. Margarethen (Village)
Lifts: 15
Types: 2 Chairs (1 triple, 1 quad); 13 Surface lifts
Lift Capacity: 19,000 p/h resort
Ski Season: Mid-December - Week after Easter
Cross Country: 220 kms. in Village of St. Michael and Rennweg
Ski School: 4 Ski Schools with 140 instructors
Other Winter Activities: Tobogganing; ice skating; indoor swimming; indoor tennis; curling; sleigh rides; sports center; snowboarding; Big foot; hiking

KATSCHBERG-RENNWEG
This unique resort offers mostly 4 star hotels and vacation apartments with ski in and ski out convenience; not a usual feature of European resorts. Catering to families is its specialty, with free child care offered during the ski day. A broad range of accommodations, shopping and services can be found in Rennweg.

Après-Ski: Folklore evenings
Shopping Services: Free ski bus; Ski Depot on Katschberg; 2 sport shops with rentals
Credit Cards: VISA
Child Care: In hotels
Lodging: Lodging up to 4-star hotels
Transportation: Gateway Airports:
Closest Provincial City: Spi Hal
By Auto: A10-Tauern Highway
By Train or Bus: OBB train in Spi Hal (4762/3996390); Post office for bus in Rennweg (4734/201)
Best Deal: Ski Opening - Dec. 21 and Luck of the Snowlady March 13-16

BAD KLEINKIRCHHEIM
TOURIST OFFICE
Bad Kleinkirchheim A-9546,
Carinthia-Austria
Telephone: (43) 42 40/82 12 Fax: (43) 42 40/85 37

Elevation: Base/Village: 1,100 m (3,608 ft); Top: 2,055 m (6,742 ft)
Vertical: 1,364 m (4,475 ft)
Terrain: 56 mi (85 km) of runs; 35% beginner, 60% intermediate, 5% expert. Open slope off-piste skiing on the Nockalm, above the picturesque village of St. Oswald/Bad Kleinkirchheim
Lifts: 32
Types: 3 Gondolas; 6 Chairlifts; 16 T-bars, 7 children's lifts
Ski Season: Beginning December-Early April
Cross Country: 16 km (10 mi) and 42 km (25 mi) in surrounding area
Ski School: 3 schools, 120 instructors
Other Winter Activities: Curling; bowling; hiking; horse drawn sleigh; horseback riding; ice skating/natural; indoor swimming; indoor tennis; solarium; sauna; tobogganing; spa; squash; indoor shooting range; billiards; snowboarding; ski-hockey

CARINTHIA
Bad Kleinkirchheim is a lively ski and spa resort. Radon baths and ski slopes share the time of the skier and the non-skier at this wonderful little town. The skiing on runs that are used by World Cup racers will offer challenges for the most advanced; other runs are interesting for the beginner and the intermediate skier.

Après-Ski: Bars, discos, folklore evenings
Child Care: Kindergarten: Half day without meals AS100 p/d; AS450 p/week; Kid's Ski School: Ski Kindergarten, 6 days with meals AS1,650
Lodging: 7,200 beds; hotels, inns, pensions; 199 apartment houses
Transportation: Gateway Airport: Frankfurt; to Klagenfurt via Austrian Air Lines
Closest Provincial City: Klagenfurt (31 mi)
By Train or Bus from airport: Munich and return—3 times daily to Spittal to Bad Kleinkirchheim
By Train: From Klagenfurt to Spittal—4 times daily, then change to bus to Bad Kleinkirchheim
Best Deal: Bad Kleinkirchheim Supercard—Variety of options including lifts, swimming, tennis, sports facilities

©Publishers Group International, 1998

Austrian Gemütlichkeit

by Bob Wall and Fellow Editors

Austria's role in the history of skiing has been chronicled throughout the 20th century. Museums in many resort villages have exhibits about pioneers and heroes of the sport and the development of equipment and techniques. And the friendliness of the apres-ski scene has been saluted in literature.

Ernest Hemingway wrote, "I remember the snow on the road to the village squeaking at night when we walked home in the cold with our skis and ski poles over our shoulders, watching the lights and finally seeing the buildings, and how everyone on the road said, 'Grüss Gott.'

"There were always country men in the Weinstube with nailed boots and mountain clothes and the air was smoky and the wooden floors scarred by nails. We drank together and we all sang mountain songs."

Hemingway found the Montafon Valley a good place to work more than 70 years ago. Modern day skiers can still pick up some of that flavor, particularly in the Hotel Taube in Schruns, where he hung out. They can build their own memories.

THE MONTAFON VALLEY

Skiers in the United States identify their resorts by the names of mountains or towns they hover over. European skiers often think in terms of valleys, which can contain nearly a dozen ski areas along a relatively short drive.

One valley well-known to continental skiers is the Montafon in western Austria's state of Vorarlberg, a diversion to the right shortly after entering the country from Switzerland and before rising to the Arlberg pass. In the summertime this is the popular scenic Silvretta high alpine road; in winter meters of snow form a barrier at the far end of the valley. Between the autobahn and Partenen are small villages and large ski areas, some of them dwarfing anything in New England. In addition to Hemingway's Schruns there are Tschagguns, Gaschurn, Gargellen, St. Gallenkirch, Gortipohl, Sibertal and Vandans.

More than 70 lifts serve 125 miles of maintained runs, mostly intermediate and advanced, with some vertical drops almost a mile high. And there are many opportunities for off-piste adventure, including a back-country trip around the Madrisa Horn mountain from Gargellen to Klosters in Switzerland.

The editors of *The Blue Book* visited the Montafon and stayed in the village of Gaschurn. Frau Sohler, owner of the Hotel Pension Nova, checked them in, told the group where the best conditions were on the mountain, had a cup of coffee with them after skiing and retreated to the kitchen to chop the fillets for the Fondue Bourguignone dinner she personally served. The editors felt they were part of the family.

Such friendliness is one of the reasons the Madrisa Hotel in Gargellen is full most of the season with guests who return year after year to the Montafon's highest resort. Hans Karl Rohmberg is the owner, who cruises the dining room and lounge, but he is also the porter who schlepps luggage to a guest's room.

SHAMED OUT OF THE SAUNA

The editors also remember Rohmberg as a helluva skier. Ted Heck's chief memory of the Madrisa Hotel, however, was indoors—in the nude and mixed sauna. During an earlier visit to Gargellen and with American decorum, he went into the sauna in sneakers and wearing a bathing suit. The stares of other males, sitting nude on the hot wooden seats, made Ted feel less than macho. He withdrew.

Ted remembers, "The next day I quit skiing early, figuring I would have the sauna all to myself and could avoid any condescending glances. I was five minutes into sweat when the door opened and a vision of loveliness entered. She stepped by me and took a seat in the row up and behind me. And she engaged me in conversation. How was the skiing? Where was I from? Did I like Austria?

"It was more challenging than skiing the toughest slope in the Montafon—trying to talk to a naked lady without looking back up over your shoulder. For the second time I had to flee. When I entered the dining room that night, the lady from the sauna smiled as I passed her table. But I am not sure she recognized me with my clothes on."

The Montafon Valley drapped by the Silvretta Mountains.   Photo: Helmut Häusle

AUSTRIA

THE ZILLERTAL

Another valley visited by *The Blue Book* editors was the Zillertal, less than an hour east of Innsbruck in the colorful state of Tyrol. It is a ski region popular with Germans, whose country abuts Austria on the north.

The Zillertal has impressive statistics. Between the Innsbruck-Munich autobahn and the Hintertux glacier at the end of the Zillertal are 11 ski areas offering a total of 282 miles of ski runs, 197 Nordic miles, 14 cable cars, 47 chair lifts and 88 drag lifts. Major ski areas include the nearly two-mile-high Hintertux glacier, where you can ski all year long. Most Americans are not familiar with names of other areas, such as Krenzjoch, Hochfügen, Spieljoch, Penkenjoch and Rastkogel.

Mayrhofen, one of the best known villages in Zillertal, is popular with ski groups, who seek a combination of excellent skiing and a lively après-ski scene. However, throughout the valley a skier can detour to almost any other kind of winter sport, plus indoor games like squash and tennis.

AN EDITOR'S VIEW OF THE SKIING

Richard Muello's responsibility in this book is the section on Italy. But he remembers the Zillertal well: "The Alps reach heights of over 10,000 feet, while snow cover and terrain often vary from groomed to powder to forgiving moguls—all on the same

Blue Book photographer Fred McKinney, having just arrived from the U.S., changes clothes in the parking lot for a day of skiing at Hochfüggen. George Schissler looks on in amusement.

wide slope. Advanced skiers have the opportunity to experience the thrill of glacier skiing at Hintertux, where national ski teams train during the summer.

"Brendt, our genial Austrian guide/instructor from the Mount Everest Ski School in Mayrhofen, many years ago was a race coach in Stowe, Vermont. He escorted us on a memorable day of skiing on the glacier. The 50 miles of ski runs covered steep, wide slopes from the summit, mogul lessons for the hardy, and a number of fast, challenging runs on the far side. And everywhere the view was fantastic."

ANOTHER EIDTOR'S VIEW OF THE APRÈS-SKI SCENE

The streets of Mayrhofen seemed deserted at night, but in the several fine hotels, such as the Alpenhotel Kramerwirt, guests danced in the bar area before and after dinner. Behind many a pub door was lots of action—disco music in some, oldies and soft piano in others. And in the Tirolerstube country music was on tap for anyone wanting to try a Texas two-step.

Editor George Schissler is big on France, but wrote about his Austrian experience this way: "Americans are discovering these valleys with their vast and varied ski terrain, excellent accommodations and friendly atmosphere. There is a laid back attitude and a sense of appreciation for the natural surroundings and Austria's glorious past."

INNSBRUCK, CAPITAL OF THE TYROL

You can do so some serious skiing in the eight ski areas around Innsbruck in a region that boasts of 200 lifts, 300 miles of well-maintained pistes and 300 miles of cross country tracks. Among the downhill slopes is the twisting, wooded trail on the Patscherkofel Mountain at Igls, above the town. It was the venue in two Olympics that Innsbruck hosted in 1964 and 1976. Television viewers in the past two decades have

Austrian super-guide, Brendt leads The Blue Book editors around the Hintertux Glacier.

Photo: Fred McKinney

©Publishers Group International, 1998

AUSTRIA

seen many replays of Franz Klammer's careening run for the gold in '76.

Farther from town are many choices at Axamer Lizum, including the mostly treeless, wide track of the women's downhill. It passes along spectacular cliffs and is a comfortable intermediate run—unless you go into and maintain a tuck.

On the Stubai glacier in another part of the region, it is possible to ski year round. Even low intermediates feel like Olympic racers on many wide and gently pitched slopes.

Innsbruck is certainly not a ski in/ski out place, something a compulsive skier may insist on. Free ski buses pick skiers up near their hotels and transport them to the day's choice of areas. But compensating for this is the opportunity to live downtown with history, to tour castles and museums.

When Doctor Johann Cammerlander, owner of the Goldener Adler Hotel, points to freedom fighters pictured on the dining room wall, he says, "Just after you won your independence from the British, we lost ours to Napoleon, but only temporarily." He also directs attention to the list of nobles and celebrities who have stayed in his hotel in the last 450 years. Fifty yards up the street is the Golden Roof, where Emperor Maximilian waved to his people at a time when Columbus was talking to Indians.

The opportunity to blend art, architecture and history with exciting outdoor adventures is one of the reasons your editors frequently recommend Innsbruck as a ski destination. It is a cosmopolitan city of 120,000 inhabitants, a quarter of whom are university students. The culture and the shopping are especially interesting to mismatched couples, i.e. when one spouse or friend does not feel it necessary to devote every daytime moment to a search for the perfect turn.

ARLBERG AMENITIES

Bus rides do not plague snow chasers in St. Anton, the mega resort in the Arlberg region, where the states of Tyrol and Vorarlberg meet. Boundless snow and lifts to carry skiers up over it are only a few

Snowboarder cuts across the ultra-steep Seegrube/Hafelekar above Innsbruck.
Photo: Innsbruck-Igls Tourist Office

minutes walk from many hotels and pensions.

There are some aficionados who feel there is nothing in Austria to compare with St. Anton. From the top of the Valluga peak, which dominates the ski area, one sees endless snowfields, some still untouched, others engraved by powder skiers. Many smooth trails, scooped out of the deep, are stitched together by chair lifts, T-bars and cable cars. A common ski pass lets skiers ride 85 lifts in the Arlberg.

St. Anton will host the World Championships in alpine skiing in 2,001, the same year that the Arlberg Ski Club celebrates its 100th anniversary. Town fathers will need to make room for more exhibits in the Heimat Museum, which traces the colorful history of the village and its place in skiing. It was here that Hannes Schneider went into a crouch and introduced a new technique for turning awkward planks of wood in the snow.

The après-ski scene in St. Anton is action packed. The pedestrian zone at the end of the day is like Grand Central Station during rush hour, but with people carrying skis instead of briefcases.

An Austrian gem; St. Anton am Arlberg sparkles day or night.
Photo: St. Anton Tourist Office

AUSTRIA

UP THE PASS A PIECE IS LECH

Across the state line in Vorarlberg is Lech, a charming village with its own group of dedicated fans. Some of them stay in hotels along the main street and stream; others opt for Oberlech. The hillside is studded with many hotels, several of which have sunny terraces where nearly everybody on the mountain seems to stop for lunch. The menu gets less attention than the elegantly dressed men and women, bronzed faces turned toward the sun.

Many Oberlech hotels are connected underground by a tunnel in which electric carts move tourists' luggage and hotels' foods and sundries up from Lech.

Lech is a sometime day trip for expert skiers who drop from the top of the Valluga in St. Anton into ungroomed snow. But it is a one-way trip, requiring a bus or taxi for the return. More popular with skiers lodging in Lech is the opportunity to stay in the sun all day in a big circuit between Lech and the village of Zürs. They work the mountains on the west side of the main road in the morning and the east in the afternoon.

One unusual bit of après-ski action is an aerial tram ride up one of the Lech mountains. The cable car is temporarily redone as a bar and guests watch the sun set and drink champagne, while the car moves at quarter speed. The operator wears a tuxedo and becomes a croupier on the terrace above.

The gambling at roulette and blackjack is with funny money, given to passengers as part of their $35 ticket. There is legalized gambling in some Austrian resorts, but this is not one of them. What you lose goes to charity. Anyone who wins gets a voucher for a modest gift at a local shop or restaurant.

Lech and St. Anton are two of 11 resorts in four countries that promote themselves as "Best of the Alps."

The cradle of alpine skiing, Lech am Arlberg . . . a winter paradise.
Photo: Tourist Office, Lech am Arlberg

MIXING SKIING WITH MUSIC

Another happy compromise, like Innsbruck, for couples whose thirsts for skiing are not a perfect match is the romantic city of Salzburg.

In the state of Salzburg are 24 ski areas, some of them unknown to Americans, even though they are impressive in size. For example, the Sportworld Amade region, just one of those 24 areas, actually consists of 10 separate villages with name such as Altenmarket, Zauchensee, and Filzmoos. Another is Flachau, home of Herman Maier, skiing hero of the last Olympics.

A Panorama Tour's program known as Salzburg Ski Safari picks skiers up at their hotels each morning for an hour's ride to one of the resorts. One route goes through the narrow enclave of Germany that juts down into Austria. Nearby is Berchtesgaden, where 60 years ago Adolf Hitler in his mountain aerie covetously stared out toward Salzburg.

Another trip passes Hohenwerfen Castle, where segments of "Where Eagles Dare" was filmed. Remember that movie in which Richard Burton and Clint Eastwood wiped out the whole German army?

There are few après-ski scenes to match the color of Salzburg, Mozart's hometown. He got there before Julie Andrews. And although "The Sound of Music" is still heavily promoted, Amadeus's melodies get more attention. An evening concert of his music is a far cry from a disco and a different way to end a great day of skiing.

Altenmark balloon festival.

©Publishers Group International, 1998

FRANCE

FRANCE

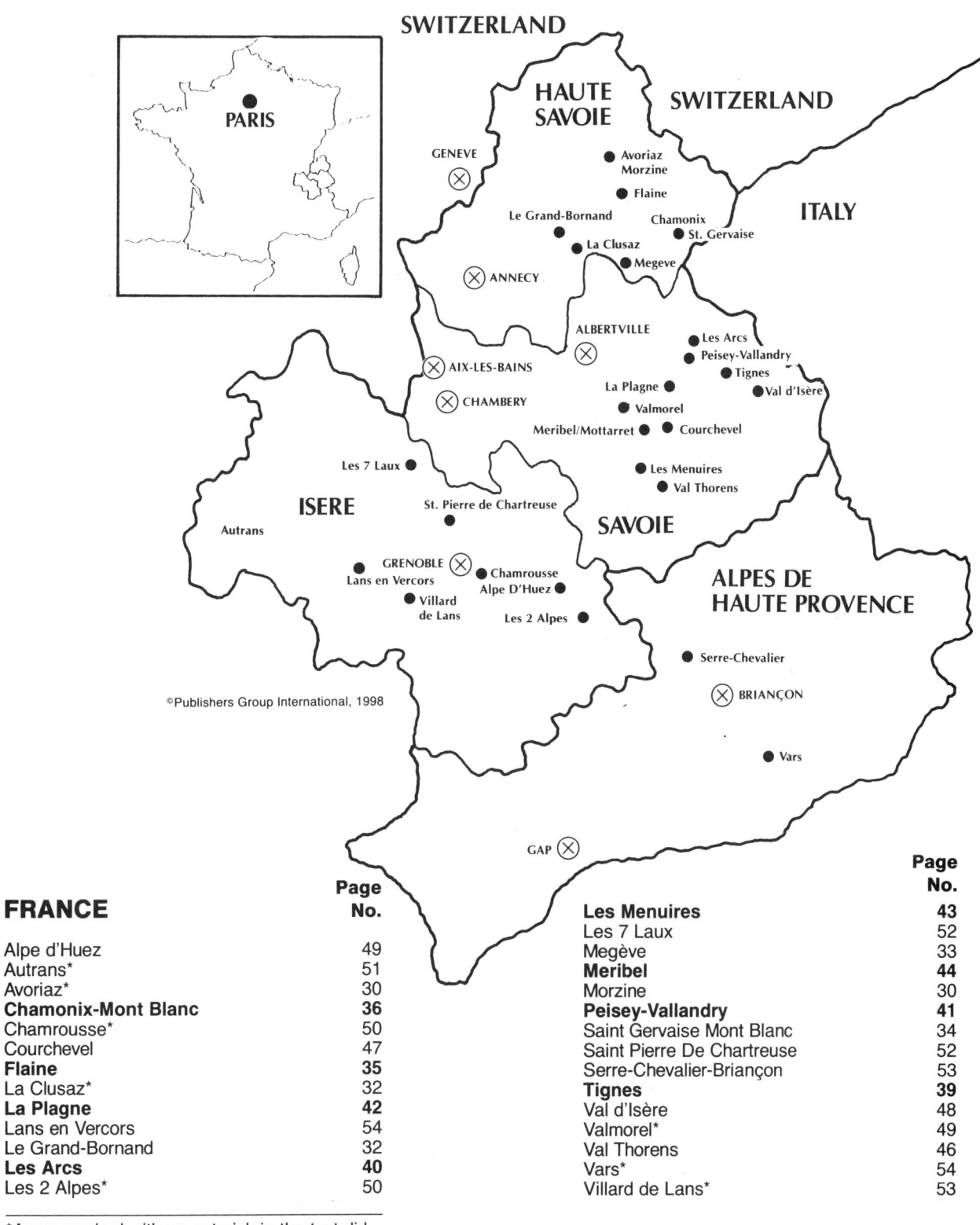

	Page No.
Alpe d'Huez	49
Autrans*	51
Avoriaz*	30
Chamonix-Mont Blanc	**36**
Chamrousse*	50
Courchevel	47
Flaine	**35**
La Clusaz*	32
La Plagne	**42**
Lans en Vercors	54
Le Grand-Bornand	32
Les Arcs	**40**
Les 2 Alpes*	50

	Page No.
Les Menuires	**43**
Les 7 Laux	52
Megève	33
Meribel	**44**
Morzine	30
Peisey-Vallandry	**41**
Saint Gervaise Mont Blanc	34
Saint Pierre De Chartreuse	52
Serre-Chevalier-Briançon	53
Tignes	**39**
Val d'Isère	48
Valmorel*	49
Val Thorens	46
Vars*	54
Villard de Lans*	53

*Areas marked with an asterisk in the text did not update their information for this edition.

FRANCE

by George Schissler

The French have a long and glorious past when it comes to winter sports. The country has hosted the Olympic Games on three occasions and the French Alps boast many of the world's premier ski resorts.

Visitors taking a ski vacation in France will be pleasantly surprised at what the resorts have to offer both on and off the snow. First, the Alps themselves overwhelm anyone with an eye toward scenic beauty. Majestic vistas appear everywhere, each one more captivating than the one before, and for the skier boundless snowfields hold challenge and pleasure.

Skiing in the French Alps is rated among the best in the world and resorts such as Chamonix, Les Arcs, Tignes and Flain, among many others, have been attracting skiers to their slopes for years. They have the reputation for making vacationers welcome and satisfied. Of course it is easier to satisfy skiers if snow conditions are good. This is usually the case in the French Alps, but in the event that Mother Nature is not cooperative, many resorts now have extended snowmaking systems. At some of the resorts glacier skiing can take place year round.

Skiing is a family activity and here amidst some of the world's loftiest peaks every family member can enjoy ski vacations in the majestic Alps. At many resorts marked trails enable skiers of varying abilities to ski safely and confidently top to bottom without detracting from the fun.

Most of the country's larger resorts are located in the Savoie and Haute Savoie regions. This section of *The Blue Book of European Ski Resorts* has listed destination resorts which are renowned for providing a totally enjoyable ski experience. Good snow, efficient lift systems, fine dining facilities, active night life, child care, shopping, accommodations and affordability. Not all French resorts are listed, but those that are represent a factual and honest taste of skiing in France.

If you are entertaining thoughts of taking a ski vacation in France, *The Blue Book* will get you off to a good start. Also look into Swissair's travel packages. The airline will transport travelers to Zurich with connections to many gateway cities. Most ski resorts can be accessed from Geneva or Zurich, Switzerland and Lyon, France. Although these three cities are the most convenient, there are several

The French are avant garde *in lifts, such as this in Les Menuires.*   Photo: Hemon

FRANCE

other European international airports which provide bus, rail or automobile transportation.

A vacation in the French Alps is a skier's dream. Make yours come true this season. You'll still be talking about it next summer.

THE FRENCH ALPS COMMISSION
610 Fifth Avenue
New York, N.Y. 10020-2452
Telephone (212) 582-3439.

THE FRENCH GOVERNMENT TOURIST OFFICE
New York
610 Fifth Avenue
New York, NY 10020-2452

Chicago
645 North Michigan Avenue
Chicago, IL 60611-2836

Dallas
2305 Cedar Spring Road
Dallas, TX 75201

Los Angeles
9454 Wilshire Boulevard
Beverly Hills, CA 90212

AIR FRANCE
888 Seventh Avenue
New York, NY 10106
(212) 830-4482

SWISSAIR INFORMATION

Swissair carries skiers to the Alps from **Atlanta**, Boston, Chicago, Cincinnati, Los Angeles, **Montreal, Newark, New York, San Francisco, and Wash**ington, D.C., with connecting service from 21 other U.S. cities.

Swissair offers a brochure called "The Alpine Experience." It includes additional descriptions of major Swiss resorts, as well as popular resorts in Austria, France, Germany and Italy. The colorful brochure contains photos, trail maps, hotel listings and prices for package deals.

For a free copy of "The Alpine Experience" call (800) 662-0021 or write Swissair, P.O. Box 26028, Tampa, FL 33623-6028.

To book one of their exciting adventures call Swissair Vacations at 800-688-7947.

The well-established resort of Peisey Vallandry is connected to Les Arcs 1800 level.   Photo: Fred McKinney

FRANCE

AVORIAZ*
OFFICE DU TOURISME D'AVORIAZ
Place Central
74110 Avoriaz/Morzine, France
Telephone: (33) 4 5074 0211 Fax: (33) 4 5074 1825

Elevation: Base/Village: 1,805 m (5,790 ft); Top: 2,466 m (7,988 ft)

Vertical: 550 m (1,806 ft)

Longest Run: 11 km (6.8 mi)

Terrain: 672 km (420 mi) in Portes du Soleil; 150 km in Avoriaz; 26% beginner, 58% intermediate, 15% advanced

Skiing Circus: See Morzine listing

Lifts: 42 in Avoriaz; 218 in Portes du Soleil

Types: 126 Chairlifts; 79 Surface

Lift Capacity: 47,000 p/h resort; 230,000 p/h in region; 224 total lifts

Ski Season: December 17-April 30

Cross Country: 150 km (93 mi) of tracks in the region; 47 km in Avoriaz

Ski School: 150 instructors; over 600 in region

HAUTE-SAVOIE (PORTES DU SOLEIL)
Major area in the Portes du Soleil resort complex and only 14 km from Morzine. You can also make a Swiss skiing connection from Avoriaz to Les Crosets, Champery and Morgins. Cars and buses not allowed— a pollution-free atmosphere. Horse & sleigh transfer from parking area.

Mountain Restaurants: 8

Other Winter Activities: Paragliding; sauna; sports center; squash; ice skating; dog sleigh, horse sleigh, snowboard park

Après-Ski: Bars, 3 discos

Child Care: Nursery from 3 months, ½ day 115FF; 1 day 205; 6 days 1,025FF; Children's Village; Nursery: 3 years & up; Tele: (33) 4 5074 0446; ½ day 105FF; full day 190FF; 6-½ days 510; 6 days with lunch 1,095FF

Lodging: 15,000 beds; 1 hotel (100 beds); 493 chalets and apartments

Transportation: Gateway Airport: Geneva, 80 km (50 mi). Auto parking for 1,500 vehicles 300 m from resort—cost 40FF p/d, 240FF p/w—transfer is by sleds

Other Information: Active atmosphere, but decidedly French speaking. Purpose built resort but with pleasing wood exteriors situated in a winter wilderness

---

MORZINE
TOURIST OFFICE:
Place La Crusaz
74110 Morzine, France
Telephone: (33) 4 5074 7292 Fax: (33) 4 5079 0348

Elevation: Base/Village: 1,000 m (3,281 ft); Top: 2,240 m (7,347 ft)

Vertical: 1,020 m (3,346 ft)

Longest Run: 11 km (6.8 mi)

Terrain: 19% beginner, 35% intermediate, 33% advanced, 13% expert

Skiing Circus: Portes du Soleil-650 km (410 mi) to 12 different villages, connecting with Swiss slopes.

Lifts: 24; 219 in Portes du Soleil

Types: 4 Cablecars; 10 Gondolas; 79 Chairlifts; 120 Surface lifts in Portes du Soleil

Lift Capacity: 230,000 p/h in Portes du Soleil on 219 total lifts

Ski Season: December - April

Cross Country: 97 km; 5 different areas

Ski School: E-S-F; 650 instructors in Portes du Soleil

Other Winter Activities: Folklore evenings; ice skating/artificial; mono-skiing; mountaineering; snowboarding; sleigh riding; sports center; curling; snowshoe walking; paragliding; bowling; ice climbing

PORTES DU SOLEIL
Traditional French resort with lifts from the town center. Morzine, coupled with Avoriaz, offers 65 lifts servicing 75 marked runs and 83 miles of skiing. The region offers 290 runs and 420 miles of ski terrain.

Shopping/Services: Supermarkets, sport shops, optician, pharmacies, doctors/dentists, bakeries, butcher, etc.

Child Care: L'outa; Nursery: 6 × ½ day: 525 F 6 × Full day: 940 F; English speaking Tele: (33) 4 50 79 26 00

Lodging: 16,000 beds; 67 hotels with 3,300 beds; Reservations: (33) 4 50 79 11 57

Transportation: Gateway Airport: Geneva (70 km)

By Ski Bus from airport: Direct to resort from Geneva

Other Information: Largest internationally linked ski area in the world. Other French ski villages in the Portes du Soleil are: Avoriaz, Les Gets, Chatel, Abondance, La Chapelle d'Abondance, St. Jean d'Aulps.

©Publishers Group International, 1998

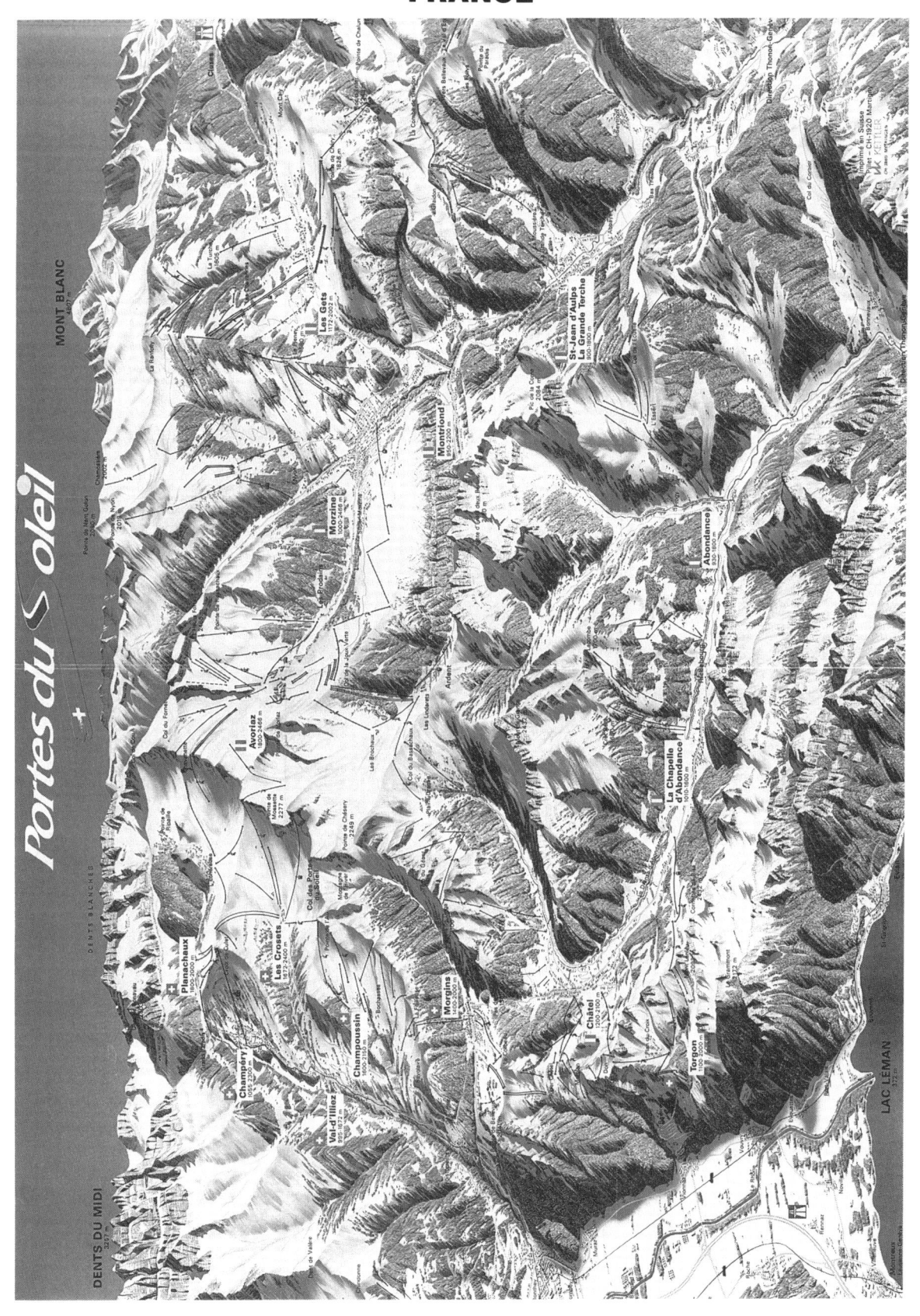

FRANCE

FRANCE

LA CLUSAZ*
TOURIST OFFICE:
Place de l'Eglise
74220 La Clusaz
Telephone: (33) 4 5031 6500 Fax: (33) 4 5032 6501

Elevation: Base/Village: 1,100 m (3,609 ft); Top: 2,600 m (8,528 ft)
Vertical: 1,500 m (4,920 ft)
Longest Run: 4.0 km (2.5 mi)
Terrain: 76 marked runs for 81 miles; 33% beginner, 37% intermediate, 25% advanced, 5% expert
Skiing Circus: The surrounding areas (Espace Aravis) combine to offer skiers 96 lifts and 117 runs for 121 miles of ski terrain
Lifts: 56
Types: 3 Cable cars; 2 Gondolas; 13 Chairlifts (3 triples, 10 doubles); 38 Surface
Lift Capacity: 49,500 p/h resort
Ski Season: Mid-December–May
Cross Country: 70 km cross country at two separate areas
Ski School: 170 instructors
Other Winter Activities: Ice skating/artificial; mono-skiing; snowboarding; sleigh riding; sports center; telemark; outdoor swimming

LE GRAND-BORNAND
OFFICE DU TOURISME
Le Grand-Bornand
F-77450
Telephone: (33) 4 50 02 78 00 Fax: (33) 4 50 02 78 01

Elevation: Base/Village: 1,299 m (4265 ft) (Chinaillon); Top: 2,099 m (6,890 ft)
Vertical: 1,099 m (3,609 ft)
Longest Run: 4 km (2.5 mi)
Terrain: 43 runs covering 40 miles. Also many off-piste opportunities (Espace Aravis: 115 runs for 121 miles); 31% beginner, 38% intermediate, 26% advanced, 5% expert
Skiing Circus: Between both communities, Le Grand-Bornand and Chinaillon
Lifts: 38 (Espace Aravis: 96)
Lift Capacity: 35,500 p/h resort
Ski Season: December 19-April 25
Mountain Restaurants: Seven
Cross Country: 56 km of doubletrack loops
Ski School: 100 Instructors (25 English-speaking)

MASSIF DES ARAVIS
One of the oldest ski resorts in France. Has retained its picturesque buildings and village atmosphere. Good lift system provides easy access to all terrain on 3 mountains. Lift access from town center.

Après-Ski: Bars, discos, coffee houses
Shopping/Services: Restaurants, cinemas, gift shops
Credit Cards: AE, DC, MC, VISA; Credit cards widely accepted but not by all shops and services
Child Care: Club des Mouflets (8 mos-4½ yrs) Club des Champion (3½-6 yrs); Tele: 450 32 65 00
Lodging: 1,500 beds; 1,990 hotel beds; 6,132 apartment beds; 9,000 beds in second homes; 400 camping beds
Transportation: Gateway Airport: Geneva (50 km)
Closest Provincial City: Annecy
By Auto from airport: Annecy-Thones-La Clasaz via RN509; Annemasse - Bouneville
By Train: Nearest RR station is Annecy; bus runs to La Clusaz 4 times each day
By Bus: See Le Grand-Bornand for bus information

HAUTE-SAVOIE (Massif des Aravis)
A traditional type resort with some lift access from the town center. Le Grand-Bornand has two communities— the village at 1,000 m and Chinaillon at 1,300 m, with connecting terrain.

Other Winter Activities: Fitness center; ice skating/natural; hang-gliding; sauna; sleigh riding; mono-ski; snowboarding
Après-Ski: Bars, discos, cinema, restaurant variety
Shopping/services: Variety available; bakeries, restaurants, sport shops, service stations, tobacco shops, etc.
Child Care: Kindergarten from age 3, 9:30 am-1 pm & 2:30 pm-5:30 pm
Lodging: Hotel Rates: 3-Star $78/2-Star $42 pp/pday/½ board
Transportation: Gateway Airport: Geneva
By Bus: Day bus service from airport. Several bus companies service airport; Tele: (011-41) 22 798 20 00 or Fax: (011-41) 22 788 00 82 for centralized information
Best Deal: Rates are lowest in January & April

FRANCE

> **MEGEVE**
> OFFICE DE TOURISME
> B.P. 24-74120,
> Megeve, France
> Telephone: (33) 4 5021 2728 Fax: (33) 4 5093 0309

Elevation: Base/Village: 1,113 m (3,658 ft); Top: 2,350 m (7,710 ft)

Vertical: 1,237 m (4,059 ft)

Longest Run: 3.6 km (2.25 mi)

Terrain: 17% beginner, 29% intermediate, 40% adv., 14% expert. Runs: 50 red, 21 green, 37 blue, 17 black

Lifts: 81

Types: 7 Gondolas; 2 Cable Cars; 25 Triples; 47 T-bars

Lift Capacity: 87,036 p/h resort

Ski Season: Mid-December - Mid-April

Cross Country: 75 km

Ski School: 228 Instructors; Kid's Ski School limited to 10 students, with 36 instructors; Kindergarten Ski School ages 3-10; 12 or 24 hours of instruction

Mountain Restaurants: 34

Other Winter Activities: Flying; hiking; ice skating/artificial; indoor swimming; indoor tennis; mono-skiing; paragliding; snowboarding; sleigh riding; sports center; curling; climbing wall; tobogganing; beauty farm

Après-Ski: 20 Bars, 9 discos, casino, cinema, bowling, museum, French linguistic courses, folklore evenings

HAUTE-SAVOIE (Pays du Mont-Blanc)

Megeve is well suited to the leisure skier with alternating alpine pastures and conifer forest at altitudes of between 1,100 and 1,850 m. Above this open skiing up to an altitude of 2,350 m awaits the more adventurous skier. Part of the huge skiing area covering the 13 resorts of the Mont-Blanc region.

Shopping/Services: Over 200 shops, 85 restaurants and brasseries, typical bistros, tea rooms; medical care

Credit Cards: AE, MC, VISA

Child Care: Meg 'Loisirs, Tele: 04 5058 7784; Alpage, Tele: 04 5021 1097; Caboche, Tele: 04 5058 9765; Princesse, Tele: 04 5093 0086; Child care rates, 100 ½ day; from 1,200-1,800 FF for 6 days (with meal)

Lodging: 43,185 beds; hotel rates p/p p/d ½ board; 4-Star 675-1,565, 3-Star 450-1,950, 2-Star 290-450

Transportation: Gateway Airport: Geneva (70 km)

Closest Provincial City: Annecy (60 km)

By Auto from airport: Geneva/Sallanches A40-Sallanches/Megeve RN212 (13 km)

By Ski Bus from airport: Bus Tele: 04 5021 2518

By Train: Train to Sallanches then bus or taxi to resort; Tele: 8 3635 3235

Best Deal: Low season all inclusive packages (6 day Evasion ski pass covering 300 km/200 miles of ski slopes plus 7 days lodging) from 1,315 FF in apartment (4 person basis) from Jan. 9–30 Mar. 13 to Apr. 17, 1999. Book through Megeve Res. 04 5021 2952 Fax 04 5091 8567

Megeve has night scenes to match the daytime beauty of sunny slopes.

Photo: Megeve Tourist Office

FRANCE

SAINT GERVAIS MONT BLANC
OFFICE DE TOURISME
115 Avenue du Mont Paccard F
74170 Saint Gervais Mont Blanc
Telephone: 4 5047 7608 Fax: 4 5047 7569

SAINT-GERVAIS
A charming village that possesses one of the most famous attractions in the world: The Mont Blanc. It offers 300 km of ski slopes between fir trees and alpine chalets.

Elevation: Base/Village: 850 m (2,185 ft); Top: 2,350 m (7,780 ft)

Vertical: 1,500 m (4,965 ft)

Terrain: 20% beginner, 40% intermediate, 25% advanced; 15% expert

Skiing Circus: Saint Gervais, Saint Nicolas, Mont Joly, Mont d'Arbois, Megève

Lifts: 82

Types: 9 Gondolas; 1 Funicular; 25 Chairlifts; 47 T-bars

Lift Capacity: 38,000 p/h resort

Ski Season Dec. 19 to April 18

Summer Skiing: No

Cross Country: 30 km

Ski School: French Ski School (2) and Ski Ecole International

Other Winter Activities: Curling, fitness center, hiking, horse drawn sleigh, ice skating, indoor swimming, monoskiing, mountaineering, paragliding, snowshoeing

Après-Ski: Bars, discos, cafes, concerts, festival

Shopping Services: Resort offers all services: shops, stores, banks etc.

Credit Cards: AE, EC, MC, USA

Child Care: French Ski School 4-6 yrs; Nursery 6 months - 6 yrs. Tel. (33) 4 5047 7621

Lodging: 1,500 beds in hotels but 25,000 beds available throughout the resort

Transportation: Gateway Airports: Geneva (70 km)

Closest Provincial City: Annecy (80 km)

By Auto from Airport: 45 min.; Ski bus available from airport

By Train: Transfers and shuttle from Geneva

Other Information: Weather phone: (33) 8 3668 0274

Abundant snow in Chamonix, France's oldest ski resort and site of the first Winter Olympics.

©Publishers Group International, 1998

Ski in good Company

COMPAGNIE DES ALPES

World leader in ski area management

**Méribel ▪ La Plagne ▪ Les Arcs ▪ Tignes ▪ Flaine-Grand Massif
Les Menuires ▪ Les Grands Montets ▪ Courmayeur ▪ Peisey-Vallandry**

Tignes

World-class skiing — 365 days a year.

Tel. 33 4 79 40 03 03
Fax 33 4 79 40 03 04
e-mail : tignes@laposte.fr

La Plagne

The world's largest single ski resort.

Tel. 33 4 79 09 79 79
Fax 33 4 79 09 70 10
e-mail : laplagne@wanadoo.fr

Les Arcs

Skiing for everyone... at every level.

Tel. 33 4 79 07 68 00
Fax 33 4 79 07 68 99
e-mail : reservation@lesarcs.com

Les Menuires

Ski the wide open spaces of the world's largest ski area — Les 3 Vallées.

Tel. 33 4 79 00 79 79
Fax 33 4 79 00 60 92
e-mail : lesmenuires@laposte.fr

Méribel

Beautiful sylvan slopes in an international atmosphere... and great après ski.

Tel. 33 4 79 00 50 00
Fax 33 4 79 00 31 19
e-mail : meribel@laposte.fr

Flaine

The only major ski resort that's also a Bauhaus work of art.

Tel. 33 4 50 90 80 01
Fax 33 4 50 90 86 26
e-mail : flaine@laposte.fr

Les Grands Montets

Exceptional mountain skiing for that all-out ski experience.

Tel. 33 4 50 53 23 23
Fax 33 4 50 53 58 90
e-mail : reservation@chamonix.com

Courmayeur

The Italian side of Mont-blanc. Skiing with an Italian accent.

Tel. 39 0165 84 23 70
Fax 39 0165 84 28 31
e-mail : courmayeur.com

Peisey-Vallandry

An alpine village resort, with access to Les Arcs and La Plagne.

Tel. 33 4 79 04 20 30
Fax 33 4 79 07 95 34
e-mail : peiseyvallandry.com

FRANCE

FLAINE

TOURIST OFFICE:
Galerie des Marchands
74300 Flaine, France
Telephone: (33) 50 90 80 01 Fax: (33) 50 90 86 26

Le Grand Massif — COMPAGNIE DES ALPES

Elevation: Base/Village: 1,600 m (5,249 ft); Top: 2,500 m (8,202 ft)

Vertical: 900 m (2,952 ft)

Longest Run: 14 km (8.7 mi) blue run

Terrain: Runs: 54 red; 15 green; 47 blue, 16 black

Skiing Circus: 160+ miles of connected trails in Le Grand Massif ski area. Flaine is linked to the resorts of Samoëns, Les Carroz d'Araches, Morillon and Sixt

Lifts: 77 in Le Grande Massif

Types: 5 Gondolas; 1 Cable Car; 24 Chairlifts; 45 Surface Lifts, 2 Yogurt pots

Lift Capacity: 28,000 p/h resort; Lift Capacity 74,000 p/h in total ski complex with 77 lifts

Ski Season: Mid-December - May 1

Cross Country: 8.8 km (8 mi) and a ring of 8 km at the top of the Grandes Platieres

Other Winter Activities: Ice skating/natural; indoor swimming; mono-skiing; hang-gliding; snowboarding; sports center; ice driving; skidoos; sauna; snowpark

HAUTE-SAVOIE

Mostly intermediate terrain but good off-piste skiing for the advanced skier. Settled in a huge snow bowl Flaine is a car-free purpose built resort ideally suited for families and children. Due to its height, it has excellent snow conditions. Ski-in, Ski out.

Après-Ski: Concerts, shows at the auditorium

Shopping/Services: Post office, banks, supermarkets, bakery, hairdresser, physiotherapist, approx. 30 bars & restaurants

Credit Cards: AE, DC, MC VISA

Child Care: Hotel Lindars: Club Aquarius Kindergarten or ski school; Tele: 50 90 81 66

Lodging: 9,500 beds; 1100 hotel rooms (packages)

Transportation: Gateway Airport: Geneva 44 mi, Lyon 131 mi

Closest Provincial City: Cluses

By Auto from airport: Geneva to Chamonix on motorway exit "Clusez Center," right onto N205-1 mile then left to D6 to Flaine

By Bus: Several bus companies operate from Geneva and information is centralized. Tele: (011-41) 22 798 20 00

Auto Parking limited to 60 minutes to enable loading & unloading—car-free resort

Skiers are probably in cafes after a busy day on the trails of Flaine.

Photo: E. Guilpart

©Publishers Group International, 1998

FRANCE

CHAMONIX-MONT-BLANC
TOURIST OFFICE:
Place de l'Eglise
74400 Chamonix, France
Telephone: (33) 4 5053 0024 Fax: (33) 4 5053 5890

HAUTE-SAVOIE

Chamonix allows access to several ski areas along the valley—all bus connected; the largest one is Les Grands Montets with 9 lifts and a 7,220-ft vertical. Excellent terrain for advanced skiers. Chamonix is France's oldest ski resort and can boast of having the world's highest lift-served vertical.

Elevation: Base/Village: 1,035 m (3,396 ft); Top: 3,842 m (12,605 ft)

Vertical: World's highest lift-served vertical, 2,807 m (9,205 ft); Les Grands Montets 3,275 m

Longest Run: 21 km (15 mi) on Vallée Blanche

Terrain: 63 runs for 136 km (Mont-Blanc: 299 runs for 425 miles)

Types: 13% beginner, 24% intermediate, 32% advanced, 31% expert

Lifts: 51; Mont-Blanc 209

Types: 6 Gondolas; 1 Funicular; 6 Cable Cars; 18 Chairlifts; 20 Surface

Lift Capacity: 64,250 p/h resort

Ski Season: Early December - May

Cross Country: 45 km

Ski School: 300 Instructors

Mountain Restaurants: 8, serving lunch only

Other Winter Activities: Ice skating/natural; ice skating/artificial; indoor swimming; indoor tennis; paragliding; sauna; sleigh riding; sports center; squash; curling; bowling; alpine museum

Après-Ski: Bars, discos, cafes, coffee houses, casino

Shopping/Services: All services available

Child Care: Tele: 4 50 54 04 76; ski nursery in Argentière 1,400 FF, 6-days with lunch. Ski Kindergarten (Ski School 4 5053 2257) from ages 4-12 yrs., 1400 FF 6 days with lunch

Lodging: 61 hotels with 6,855 beds and more than 4,000 apartments. Booking Service Tele. 4 50 53 23 33

Transportation: By Auto from airport: Geneva (88 km)—follow signs to Mont Blanc or by coach

Local bus services Argentière at eastern end of Chamonix Valley

Best Deal: Rates lowest early Dec. & in April

Other Information: Five separate ski areas along valley floor

In the Haute Savoie region picturesque chalets are often at the end of a run. Photo: Chamonix Tourist Office

©Publishers Group International, 1998

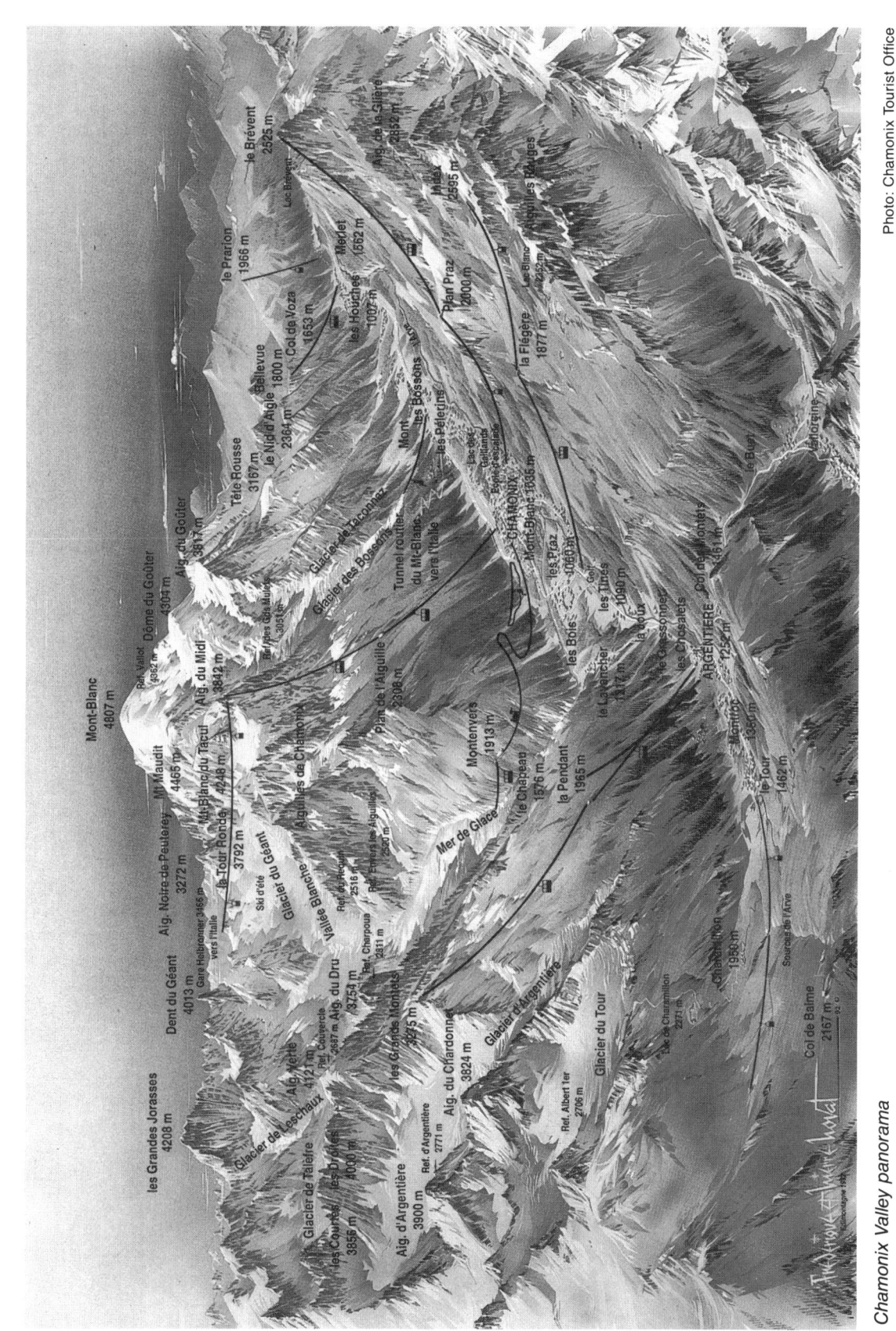

FRANCE

Chamonix Valley panorama

FRANCE

l'Espace Killy . . . Tignes and Val d'Isère

FRANCE

TIGNES
OFFICE DE TOURISME DE TIGNES
73320 Tignes, France

Telephone: (33) 479 06 55 37 Fax: (33) 479 06 37 63

Elevation: Base/Village: 1,550 m (5,085 ft); Top: 3,656 m (12,008 ft)

Vertical: 1,559 m (5,115 ft)

Longest Run: 5.5 km (3.4 mi), Genepy

Terrain: Including Val d'Isère, 300 km of alpine skiing with 129 runs; 14 black, 36 red, 59 blue, & 20 green; 20% beg., 50% intermediate, 20% adv., 10% expert. Slalom, mogul & snowboarding stadiums

Skiing Circus: Tignes-Val d'Isère-Espace Killy-Tignes/Champagny/La Plagne-Tignes/Peisey-Nancroix/Les Arcs (1 day ski pass)

Lifts: 96, including Val d'Isère

Types: 6 Gondolas; 2 Funiculars (1 in Val d'Isère, 1 in Tignes); 4 Cable cars; 40 Surface; 50 Chairlifts

Lift Capacity: 135,015 p/h both resorts (67,185 Tignes)

Ski Season: mid-December–early September

Summer Skiing: Tignes is open 365 days a year for skiing, but Espace Killy is only open Dec. - May

Cross Country: 44 km. Cross Country also possible on glacier during summer months

Ski School: 6 Ski schools E.S.F./Evolution 2/Tignes Ski School International (800 Instructors)

Mountain Restaurants: 6

Other Winter Activities: Fitness centers; husky drawn sleigh; helicopter skiing; ice skating/natural; swimming; snowshoe; indoor tennis; mono-skiing; paragliding; squash; hang-gliding; iced waterfall climbing; ice driving; UVA; rock climbing; many fitness & health activities

Après-Ski: 70 bars & restaurants, 4 discos, cafes, health activities; bowling; cinema; bridge

Shopping/Services: Complete shopping facilities

Credit Cards: AE, MC, Eurocard, Diners

Child Care: Garderie les Petits Lutins (3 mos-6 yrs) Tele: 47906 5127; Gardens Les Marmottons (2½-10 yrs) Tele: 47906 5167

Lodging: 28,000 beds

Transportation: International flights to Lyon-Satolas & Geneva-Cointrin & from Paris to Chambery. Bus transfers to resort

Closest Provincial City: Bourg-Saint Maurice, 26 km

By Auto: A6 motorway to Albertville to Moûtiers "A" road N90 to B. St.-Maurice "B" road D902 to Tignes

By Train: Daily trains including h-s APT & night trains from Paris to Bourg Saint Maurice, regular bus service & taxis available

Other Information: Dec. 4-6, 1998 "Tignes 98 Acrobatic Ski World Cup"; Jan. 6-8, 1999 "European Women's Cup"; Jan. 10-16 "British Senior Championship"

Terrain: Including Val d'Isère, 300 km of alpine skiing with 129 runs; 14 black, 36 red, 59 blue & 20 green; 20% beg., 50% intermediate, 20% adv., 10% expert. Slalom, mogul & snowboarding stadiums

SAVOIE

On its own Tignes must be rated as one of the finest ski resorts in Europe. Great weather and skiing for all levels of skiers and an extensive lift system. When coupled with Val d'Isere there are over 100 lifts and more than 200 miles of trails.

Tignes is doubly impressive in this photo of its man-made lake.

FRANCE

LES ARCS
TOURIST OFFICE: BP45
Arc 1800
73706 Arc 1800 Cedex
Telephone: (33) 4 79 07 12 57 Fax: (33) 4 79 07 45 96

Les Arcs

COMPAGNIE DES ALPES

SAVOIE
Purpose built resort is comprised of 3 village-sections on 3 separate levels. Arc 1600 the lowest section is followed by Arc 1800 which now makes up the main village, and then Arc 2000 higher up the mountain. Access is from the center of the village of Bourg St. Maurice on a funicular or by auto via a winding mountain road.

Elevation: Base/Villages: Arc 1600 (5,250 ft); Arc 1800 (5,900 ft); Arc 2000 (6,450 ft)

Vertical: 2,125 m (6,976 ft); has longest vertical in Europe on black run

Longest Run: 7 km (4 mi)

Terrain: 200 km (125 mi) of groomed slopes; also many un-groomed off-piste possibilities; 10% beginner, 30% intermediate, 38% advanced, 22% expert. Ski Runs: 38 red, 13 green, 50 blue, 16 black

Skiing Circus: Three levels offer many interconnected lifts and trails. Linked to E'space Killy, La Rosiere and La Plagne (see Peisey Vallandry)

Lifts: 78 including Peisey Vallandry

Types: 2 Gondolas; 1 Cable car; 1 Funicular; 31 Chairlifts (4 detachable quads, 27 doubles); 31 Surface tows; 11 Baby tows

Lift Capacity: 85,400 p/h resort

Ski Season: December 12-May 2

Cross Country: 15 km in Les Arcs and 30 in Bourg St. Maurice

Ski School: 250 Instructors at 3 locations

Mountain Restaurants: 4 restaurants, 4 bars

Other Winter Activities: Ice skating/natural; hang-gliding; sleigh riding; squash; luge; halfpipe (Arc 1800); ski jump (Arc 1800); speed skiing (Arc 2000)

Après-Ski: 20 Bars, 7 discos, cafes, coffee houses, concerts, 4 piano bars

Shopping/Services: Shops at all levels; Arc 1800 houses the most varied services including banks and post office, 50 restaurants

Credit Cards: AE, MC, VISA; Most credit cards accepted

Child Care: Garderie d'enfants (3 mos.-6 yrs.) from 690 FF/week; Tele: 4 79 41 55 55

Lodging: 30,000 beds; 32 residences from 1,840 FF/Studio 3/4 persons per wk)

Transportation: Gateway Airport: Geneva 170 km (106 mi); Lyons 210 km (131 mi)

Closest Provincial City: Lyon

By Auto: 15 km from Bourg-St.-Maurice (uphill) to Arc 1800; 27 km to Arc 2000. Gondola connects Arc 1800 to the valley of Arc 2000

By Ski Bus from airport: 4 times daily

By Train: From Chambery, resort is 8 miles from RR station at Bourg-St.-Maurice; funicular to Arc 1600

Best Deal: With a military pass, free one day access to Tignes/Val d'Isere, La Plagne and the Trois Vallées. 30% discount on lifts at Les Arcs before Dec. 18 and after April 18

An inviting scene from one of the three levels of purpose-built Les Arcs. Photo: E. Guilpart

FRANCE

PEISEY VALLANDRY
TOURIST OFFICE
73210 Peisey Nancroix
Telephone: (33) 4 7907 9428
Fax: (33) 4 7907 9534

COMPAGNIE DES ALPES
Peisey.Vallandry

SAVOIE
One of the oldest ski resorts in France. Peisey and Les Arcs share the same Massif, an area where intermediate and beginner skiers can feel comfortable, but also some high level ski trails through forests nearby the Vanoise National Park.

Elevation: Base: 1,650 m (5,413 ft); Village: 1,350 m (4,429 ft); Top: 3,200 m (10,496 ft)

Vertical: 2,000 m (6,560 ft)

Terrain: 52 km (32 mi) of downhill runs at Peisey-Vallandry; 192 (93 mi) of downhill runs at Peisey-Vallandry-Les Arcs; 25% beginner, 40% intermediate, 35% expert. Eleven snowmaking guns

Skiing Circus: Peisey Nancroix-Vallandry to Les Arcs via lifts and ski trails. Nearby to La Plagne

Lifts: 14; with Les Arcs, 78

Types: 7 Chairlifts: (1 h-s quad, 4 quads, 2 doubles); 5 T-bars

Lift Capacity: 15,000 p/h resort; over 80,000 when combined with Les Arcs

Ski Season: Dec. 19, 1998 - April 25, 1999

Cross Country: 40 km

Ski School: 45 instructors

Mountain Restaurants: 3

Shopping/Services: 25 restaurants, grocery stores, cinemas, banks, variety of gift, sport & souvenir shops

Credit Cards: AE, MC, VISA, EC

Lodging: 9,000 beds; 8 hotels-150 beds-additional 9,000 beds in condominiums

Transportation: Gateway Airport: Geneva (2 hrs.)

Closest Provincial Cities: Chambery (1½ hrs./100 km); Albertville (1 hr/60 km)

By Auto from airport: Highway from Geneva (80 km), Lyon (180 km)/also from Paris to Bourg St.-Maurice

Airport Bus: Geneva-Les Arcs runs 4 times daily

By Train: TGV (highspeed train) from Paris to Landry, then bus shuttle, 4½ hrs.

Best Deal: Olympic ski pass allows access to Les 3 Vallées & Espace Killy terrain and a total of 77 lifts. Good also at several other resorts. Inquire when making lift ticket purchase as to which resorts are included

Other Information: New in 1998, slope "les Rhodes"

Going to ski school is a welcome assignment in the beautiful surroundings at Peisey Vallandry. Photo: E. Lemaire

FRANCE

LA PLAGNE
OFFICE DU TOURISME
B.P. 62
73211 Aime Cedex, France
Telephone: (33) 4 7909 7979 FAX (33) 4 7909 7010

SAVOIE
Comprised of 10 villages, both modern purpose-built and traditional; mostly ski-in, ski-out. 120 runs for 130 miles. A family-oriented resort with some challenging terrain. Well-suited for beginner and intermediate level skiing; also excellent off-piste skiing with guide.

Elevation: Base/Village: 1,250-2,100 m (4,100-6,737 ft); Top: 3,250 m (10,663 ft)

Vertical: 2,000 m (6,565 ft)

Terrain: Runs: 6 black, 33 red, 67 blue, 14 green; 12% beginner, 48% intermediate, 33% advanced, 7% expert

Longest Run: 15 km (9 mi)

Lifts: 110

Types: 1 Cable Car; 8 Gondolas; 33 Chairlifts; 68 Surface

Lift Capacity: 120,600 p/h resort

Ski Season: December 19-April 18, everything open

Summer Skiing: July to August on glaciers

Cross Country: 96 km

Ski School: 550 Instructors located in 11 separate areas of the resort

Mountain Restaurants: Approximately 20-serving lunch only (mostly cafeteria style)

Other Winter Activities: Snowshoes; pedestrian walks; night skiing; trekking; motor biking; ice skating natural (3); indoor swimming; mono-skiing; paragliding; sauna; snowboarding; sports center; tobogganing; squash; hang-gliding; rock & wall climbing; fitness, gym, sauna, Jacuzzi, Turkish bath

Après-Ski: Bars, discos, cafes, coffee houses, snow motor bikes, cinema, bowling, game rooms, folklore evenings, Olympic bobsleigh run open to the public

Shopping/Services: All services are available throughout the villages

Credit Cards: AE, MC, VISA

Child Care: Several with rates from 80/185 to 105/230 FF with meals; Kid's Ski School: Snow Garden 2½ hr lesson from 75/115 FF; Nursery: Full day with meals 85/230 FF; Nurseries are spread throughout the village with ½ day-7 day rates w/wo meals

Lodging: 45,000 Beds; Hotels: 3-Star $90; 2-Star $75 p/p p/d ½ board

Transportation: Gateway Airport: Geneva or Lyon

By Auto from airport: Motorway to Albertville (A43 and A430) 4 lane road from Albertville to Moutiers to Aime

Train Info: 4 79 85 50 50

Bus Info: 4 79 09 72 27

Best Deal: Super discount before holidays; children under 7 ski free all times. Jr. tariff from 7-15 years

La Plagne in Savoie has 10 villages in its amazing complex.

Photo: J. Favre

FRANCE

High rise apartments like these in picture postcard Les Menuires are often seen in villages specially designed for skiing.

LES MENUIRES
TOURIST OFFICE: BP22
73440 Les Menuires, France

Telephone: (33) 4 7900 7300 Fax: (33) 4 7900 7506

Elevation: Base/Village: 1,850 m (6,070 ft); Top: 3,200 m (10,499 ft)

Vertical: 1,468 m (4,818 ft)

Longest Run: 3.5 km (2.2 mi) La Masse

Terrain: 61 marked trails for 62 miles (3 Vallées: 600 kms of runs/375 miles) (6 green-12 blue-32 red-11 black); 10% beg., 20% interm., 50% adv., 20% expert

Skiing Circus: Trois Vallée: Les Menuires, Val Thorens, Méribel, Courchevel, Saint Martin de Belleville, La Tania

Lifts: 45 (les Menuires)

Types: 6 Cable cars; 3 Bucket lifts; 18 Chairlifts; 18 Surface; 200 lifts in les Trois Vallées

Lift Capacity: 49,204 p/h resort; 230,000 in Trois Vallées

Ski Season: Mid-December–end of April

Summer Skiing: Val Thorens (9 km)—Peclet Glacier

Cross Country: 28 km; 3 trails (1 blue, 1 red, 1 green); 132 km/Trois Vallées

Ski School: 2 Schools, 210 instructors

Mountain Restaurants: 14

Other Winter Activities: 2 Fitness centers; 1 ice skating (artificial); 2 outdoor heated swimming pools; mono-skiing; paragliding; sauna; snowboarding; hang gliding; snowmobiles; snowshoe outings

Après-Ski: Discos. Unlimited access for the week to either swimming pool or ice skating rink: 40 FF p/p

SAVOIE
Ski area of the Trois Vallées which comprise the largest ski area in the world (Courchevel-Meribel-La Tania-Les Menuires & Val Thorens). Modern, purpose-built resort, ski-in-ski-out. Snowmaking from 5,640 to 6,630 ft.-315 snowguns, foremost in Europe. Easily accessible off-piste skiing.

Shopping/Services: 32 bars and restaurants, about 100 shops, 2 cinemas

Credit Cards: MC, VISA, AE, EC

Child Care: 3 mos to 12 yrs old-169 FF per day-116 FF ½ day; Nursery: Smurf's Village—Tele: 4 7900 6379; In Saint Martin 4 7908 9309. Kid's Ski School (ages 4-6) from 890 FF for 6 days

Lodging: 23,600 beds; Hotels, apts., chalets, tourism residences

Transportation: Gateway Airport: Geneva 145 km or Lyon 180 km

Closest Provincial City: Albertville; 57 km Chambery 100 km/Lyon 185 km); Bi-pass from RR station or airport to resort

By Auto from airport: Motorway A43 to Albertville-N90 to Moutiers RD 915A to Les Menuires. The last town before climbing to Les Menuires is Moutiers (27 km) where there is a train station and bus connection

By Train: RR Station at Moutiers-27 km to Les Menuires-Info: 363 535 35; RR Office in Les Menuires 479 00 63 90/"Belleville buses": 479 00 61 38

Best Deal: Lowest before Dec. 19 & after April 20

Other Information: When connected with 3 Vallées resorts the area has 600 km of pistes, 132 km cross country tracks, 1,306 snowguns, 200 ski lifts with a passenger flow of 230,000 skiers per hour

43

©Publishers Group International, 1998

FRANCE

MÉRIBEL
OFFICE DU TOURISME DE MÉRIBEL B.P. 1, 73551 MÉRIBEL, FRANCE Telephone: (33) 4 7908 6001 Fax: (33) 4 7900 5961

SAVOIE
One of the sites of the 1992 Winter Olympic Games, and a major resort of the Trois Vallées ski complex. Vast expanse of terrain suited to all abilities.

Elevation: Base/Village: 1,450 m (4,760 ft); Top: 2,952 m (9,685 ft)

Vertical: 2,349 m (7,712 ft) down to Brides

Longest Run: 5 km (3 mi)

Terrain: 74 runs for 150 km: 9 black, 21 red, 33 blue, 11 green; 15% beg., 43% interm., 28% adv., 14% expert

Lifts: 60 (3 Valleys over 200)

Types: 16 Gondolas; 18 Chairlifts; 18 Surface, 8 telebabies

Lift Capacity: 64,609 p/h resort; Lift Capacity: 200,000+ p/h in Three Valleys 200 total lifts

Ski Season: December 5 to May 2

Summer Skiing: Val Thorens-Peclet Glacier

Cross Country: 23 km in Méribel plus 8 km towards Courchevel

Ski School: 300 Instructors; Tele 4 7908 6031

Other Winter Activities: Ice skating/artificial; indoor swimming; mono-skiing; snowshoeing; ski-touring; hang-gliding and parasailing; flying school; fitness centers; discos; library; bowling; snowboarding; squash; ski-doo

Shopping/Services: More than 110 stores and shops offering all services, cinemas, concerts

Credit Cards: AE, MC, VISA

Child Care: Kindergartens in Méribel & 1 in Méribel-Mottaret (3-5 yrs), Tele: 4 7908 6690 & 4 7908 6060; 6 days, w/o meals 1,063 FF; w/meals 1573 FF; Child Ski School: 3 to 12 yrs old

Lodging: 30,000 beds; 29 hotels: 4-4-Star, 16-3-Star, 10-2-Star, & 2 unclassified; 19 rental agencies; Rates: 4-Star 700-1,470 FF p/p, 3-Star 340/1190 FF, 2-Star 280-800 FF; Rates p/p-p/d ½ board

Transportation: Gateway Airport: Lyon Satolas (180 km), Geneva (130 km)

Closest Provincial City: Moûtiers. Chambery/Aix 90 km with an international airport

By auto from airport: Motorway to Albertville, 4 lane road to Moûtiers, then 18 km of mountainous road up to area

By Ski Bus from airport: Direct connections from 3 airports; by helicopter or plane on request

By Train: Station at Moûtiers (18 km) 11 miles

Other Information: 20 km snowmaking coverage (210 acres), 366 snowguns in Meribel (1,100 in 3 Valleys)

All the buildings in Meribel have the style of this chalet.

Photo: J. M. Gouedard

FRANCE

The Three Valleys (Trois Vallées) that make this one of the world's largest skiing arenas combines (from left to right) Courchevel, Méribel, Les Menuires, Val Thorens and several smaller resorts.

FRANCE

Val Thorens is the highest ski resort in all the Alps of Europe.
Photo: F. Gros

VAL THORENS
TOURIST OFFICE:
73440 Val Thorens, France

Telephone: (33) 4 7900 0808 Fax: (33) 4 7900 0004

Elevation: Base/Village: 2,300 m (7,546 ft); Top: 3,200 m (10,496 ft)

Vertical: 1,468 m (4,820 ft) down to Les Menuires

Longest Run: 3.0 km (2.25 mi)

Terrain: Highest lift elevation is 10,890 ft. Resort has 54 slopes for 87 miles, 126 snowmaking guns; Trois Vallées area: 286 slopes for 600 km of runs; 1,303 snowmaking guns. Ski Runs: 107 red, 49 green, 93 blue, 37 black

Lifts: 30 Val Thorens; 3 Valleys 200

Types: 150 Passenger Cable Car; 4 Gondolas: including 1 30-passenger gondola; 16 Chairlifts (9 quads, 3 triples, 5 doubles); 9 surface lifts

Lift Capacity: 52,000 p/h; 200,000+ p/h in Trois Vallées

Ski Season: End of October - Early May

Summer Skiing: Months of July & August—Peclet Glacier

Cross Country: 132 km (82 mi) in Trois Vallées

Ski School: 200 instructors; Trois Vallées 1,220

Mountain Restaurants: 11

Other Winter Activities: Indoor swimming; 3 indoor tennis courts; mono-skiing; sauna; sports center; gymnasium; whirlpool; golf simulator; snow scooters; roller blades; squash; Turkish baths; badminton; wall climbing, paragliding, ULM; snowshoe trekking; free jazz and classical music concerts weekly

Après-Ski: Bars, discos, cafes, coffee houses, cinema

Shopping/Services: Parking garages, gas station, radio station, banks, medical center, post office, change office, booking center

Credit Cards: AE, MC, VISA

Child Care: Winter: French Ski School: Tel. 04 79 00 02 86, 6 days w/meals 1,350 FF Summer: Les Ouistitis: Tel. 04 79 00 09 20, 6 days w/meals 550 FF (1998 rates)

Lodging: Accommodations range from luxury hotels to private residences; Hotels: 4-Star $127, 3-Star $55, 2-Star $47-93 p/p-p/d, ½ board; 21,000 beds

Transportation: Gateway Airport: Geneva or Lyon

Closest Provincial City: Chambery 112 km; 36 km from Moutiers RR station, 189 km from Lyon airport, 154 km (96 mi) from Geneva

Best Deal: Rates are lowest before Dec. 19 and after April 17 and between Jan. 7-Jan. 27; children under 5 ski free. Reduced rates for families of 5 or more and seniors 60+.

SAVOIE
Modern, purpose-built area; ski-in, ski-out. When linked with Méribel and Courchevel the 3 Vallées total 200 ski lifts (including the world's 2 biggest cable cars, 160 persons in Courchevel and the 150 passenger lift in Val Thorens). They total 286 slopes and 375 miles of marked runs.

©Publishers Group International, 1998

FRANCE

COURCHEVEL
OFFICE DU TOURISME
B.P. 37 - La Crousette
Courchevel, France 73122
Telephone: (33) 4 79 08 00 29 Fax: (33) 4 79 08 15 63

SAVOIE
Part of Les Trois Vallées (Three Valleys) complex and perhaps offering the most challenging terrain. Resort is built on five levels or separate villages the largest and highest of which is Courchevel 1850 named so to reflect its height. Easy lift access. Most extensive ski area in the world.

Elevation: Base/Village: 1,100 m
Top: 2,738 m (8,985 ft)

Vertical: 1,638 m (5,371 ft)

Longest Run: 3.8 km (2.3 mi)

Terrain: 100 runs for 150 km (3 Vallees: 291 runs for 600 km); Runs in Courchevel: 36 red, 26 green, 27 blue, 11 black

Skiing Circus: Trails connect to slopes of Val Thorens, Les Menuires, Meribel and Mottaret and *La Tania*.

Lifts: 67

Types: 10 Gondolas; 16 Chairlifts; 40 Surface; 1 cable car

Lift Capacity: 64,533 p/h resort; Lift Capacity: 229,340 p/h in Three Valleys on 195 total lifts

Ski Season: November 29 - May 2, 1999

Summer Skiing: Val Thorens

Cross Country: 66.5 km of prepared tracks

Ski School: 450 instructors, largest in Europe

Mountain Restaurants: 11

Other Winter Activities: Fitness center; ice skating/artificial; indoor swimming (in hotels); hang-gliding; sauna; sleigh riding; ski jumping; paragliding; tobogganing; snowboarding; ice climbing cascade, climbing wall

Après-Ski: Bars, 6 discos, cafes, coffee houses, folklore evenings, concerts, bowling ski shows; ice skating show; cinema, casino in Brides les Bains

Shopping/Services: Grocery stores, dish satellite, jewelry shops, butcher & bakery shops, dress and gift shops, art gallery, optician, furniture & hardware stores

Credit Cards: AE, MC, VISA

Child Care: Children 2 yrs+; Tele: 79 08 07 72 Le Village des Enfants

Lodging: 32,000 beds; Hotel rates: 4-Star 1360-5500/3-Star 500-3700/2-Star 320-950 p/p-p/day

Transportation: Gateway Airport: Geneva 140 km; Lyon 180 km; Chambery Aix Las-Bouns 100 km; Courchevel (private) Airport

By Auto from airport: Service runs several times daily directly to resort

By Train: to Moutiers then bus or taxi 25 km. From Paris take TGV (4 hours)

New this Winter: New Snowboard Park

The tiered terrain of Courchevel has skiing above and below the treeline.

Office of Tourism Val D'isere, M. Junak

©Publishers Group International, 1998

FRANCE

VAL D'ISÈRE
TOURIST OFFICE:
B.P. 228, 73155 VAL D'ISERE CEDEX, FRANCE
Telephone: (33) 4 79 06 06 60   Fax: (33) 4 79 41 12 06

Elevation: Base/Village: 1,850 m (6,070 ft); Top: 3,550 m (11,647 ft)

Vertical: 1,307 m (4,290 ft)

Longest Run: 4,824 km (3.0 mi) "La Verte"

Terrain: 17% beginner, 47% interm, 26% advanced, 10% expert. Runs: 36 red, 19 green, 58 blue, 11 black

Skiing Circus: Ski the Espace Killy (Val d'Isere & Tignes); off-piste runs to Bonneval 5/Arc and to Les Arcs, La Plagne

Lifts: 102

Types: 4 Trams; 6 Gondolas; 2 Funiculars; Underground funicular; 49 Chairlifts; 41 Surface

Lift Capacity: 64,480 p/h resort (131,665 l'Espace Killy)

Ski Season: November 28 - May 2

Summer Skiing: End of June through mid-August on Pissaillas glacier

Cross Country: 44 km La Daille, Manchet; Lac de L'ouillette

Ski School: 10 Ski schools w/ 350 French Nat. Instructors

Mountain Restaurants: 12

SAVOIE
Linked with Tignes to offer some of the best ski terrain in Europe (the Espace Killy). Year-round skiing. A premier ski resort. Connected to Tignes and regarded by skiers as the place to ski while in France. Home of Olympic champions, it offers some of the finest ski terrain in Europe, especially off-piste.

Other Winter Activities: 3 fitness centers; folklore evenings; helicopter skiing; hiking; ice skating/natural; indoor swimming; mono-skiing; paragliding; tobogganing; snowboarding; sleigh riding; snow scooters

Après-Ski: Bars, restaurants, dancing

Shopping/Services: Local radio station, 7 doctors/physiotherapists, 2 pharmacies, optician, 4 banks, TV & car rental, sports & camera shops, florist, beauty shops

Credit Cards: Eurocard, Mastercharge, VISA

Child Care: 2 Facilities; Nurseries 210 FF p/d; 160 p/½ day with lunch - either morning or afternoon with lunch (Tele: 79 06 13 97; 79 41 12 82)

Lodging: 14,004 beds; 2,521 in hotels; 4-Star $150, 3-Star $100-137, 2-Star $82, p/p/day

Transportation: Gateway Airports: Lyon; Geneva
Closest Provincial City: Bourg St. Maurice (30 km)
By auto from airport: A41(N90) D902—Geneva 180 km
Train from Bourg St. Maurice then regular bus service
Regular bus service from train stations and airports

Best Deal: Springski: mid April - closing. Free skiing: child under 5, seniors over 75

Photo: Office of Tourism Val D'Isere, M. Junak

FRANCE

VALMOREL*
MAISON DE VALMOREL
Bourg-Morel
Valmorel, France
Telephone: (33) 79 09 8003

Elevation: Base/Village: 1,103 m (3,619 ft); Top: 2,403 m (7,884 ft)

Vertical: 1300 m (4,265 ft)

Terrain: 560 hectares (1,384 acres); each hamlet in Valmorel has a connecting ski lift to the main ski slopes; 81 slopes, 3,600 hectares (acres combined)

Skiing Circus: Tarentaise-Maurienne link creates the "Grand Domaine" with Saint François Longchamp

Lifts: 30 (47 with St. François Longchamp)

Types: One cable car; 9 chairlifts; 19 surface lifts; and a Telebourg (free cable car) that connects the hamlets

Ski Season: Early December through May

Cross Country: In nearby village Les Avanchers and the District of Aigueblanche. Shuttle service provided

Ski School: 90 instructors, private; off-slope powder courses; beginner area w/slow-speed chairlift

Mountain Restaurants: 6 (walk to 3)

Other Winter Activities: Paragliding; tobogganing; marked winter pathways around the resort; mountaineering (guides available); snow-shoe outtings

---

ALPE D'HUEZ
TOURIST OFFICE:
38750 Alpe d'Huez, France

Telephone: (33) 4 76 11 44 44 Fax: (33) 4 76 80 69 54

Elevation: Base/Village: 1,860 m (6,100 ft); Top: 3,328 m (10,926 ft)

Vertical: 2,230 m (7,317 ft)

Longest Run: 16 km (10 mi)

Terrain: Marked runs for 140 miles; 36% beginner, 29% intermediate, 25% advanced, 10% expert

Skiing Circus: Interconnected snowfields on several mountain ridges

Lifts: 82

Types: 6 Trams; 9 Gondolas; 23 Chairlifts; 44 T-bars

Lift Capacity: 90,000 p/h resort

Ski Season: December - May 1

Summer Skiing: Available on the Sarenne Glacier-lift serviced

Cross Country: 50 km (31 mi)

Mountain Restaurants: 13

Other Winter Activities: Curling; ice skating/artificial; indoor and outdoor swimming; indoor tennis; paragliding; hang-gliding; sauna; sports center; ice hockey; cinema

---

SAVOIE
Valmorel opened in the mid-70's, but unlike purpose-built resorts of the same era has maintained its original architecture. It's divided into 6 connecting hamlets, compact and without the need of an automobile, plus a dedication to children's activities makes Valmorel an ideal family resort.

Après Ski: Movie house; discos, casino evenings, bars, restaurants, concerts and shows; sauna; health club

Shopping Services: Several grocery stores, drugstore, banks, auto repair, post office, clothing and sport shops

Child Care: Qualified nursery personnel for ages 6 mos-18 mos; ages 18 mos-3 years—full program; Kid's Ski School with many activities, ages 3-8 years

Lodging: 6 hotels, apartments to rent or reserve; Holiday home for children, ages 5-10

Transportation: Gateway Airports: Lyon and Geneva

Local Airport: Chambéry

Closest Provincial City: Moûtiers

By Train: Nearest railway station is in Moûtiers

By Bus: Ski bus links and Valmorel-Moûtiers coach service information, contact tourist office

Other Information: Over 40 snowmaking guns. Small airport at Arenouvillaz allows quick access to the Trois Vallées and Mont Blanc. Cable car between main street and hamlets makes a car unnecessary

---

ISERE
Known for great snow, especially sunny weather and panoramic mountain views. A modern, purpose-built resort with ski-in, ski-out accessibility. Nicknamed "The Island in the Sun".

Après-Ski: Bars, discos, cafes, coffee houses

Lodging: 4,276 beds; 27 hotels/3,400; total number of beds 32,000; 4-Star $158-164/3-Star $62-128/2-Star $50-78

Transportation: Gateway Airport: Lyon (164 km) and Geneva (220 km)

By Auto from airport: RN 91: Grenoble, Bourg d'Olsans Huez

By Train: From Lyon or Paris take the TGV ("super-fast") train to Grenoble, then bus from train station. For info (800) 345-1990

By Air: Air Inter connects Paris to Grenoble; bus meets all incoming flights

Other Information: If you opt to take the TGV train be ready to board immediately & quickly

FRANCE

LES 2 ALPES*
OFFICE DU TOURISME
BP7
38860 Les 2 Alpes, France
Tel. (33) 476 79 22 00 Fax: (33) 476 79 01 38

Elevation: Base/Village: 1,650 m (5,414 ft); Top: 3,568 m (11,810 ft)
Vertical: 2,300 m (7,546 ft)
Terrain: 30% beginner, 34% intermediate, 26% advanced, 10% expert; 200 kms (122 mi)
Lifts: 63
Types: 3 Cable; 4 Gondolas; 1 Funicular; 23 Chairlifts; 32 Surface
Lift Capacity: 61,280 p/h resort
Ski Season: Early December to early May, also end of October and early November
Summer Skiing: On Mont De Lans glacier
Cross Country: 27 km of tracks
Ski School: Two schools with 300 instructors
Other Winter Activities: Ice skating/artificial; indoor swimming; squash; paragliding; sauna; cinema

ISERE
Two Alps connected by an extensive ski circus. Similar to its neighbor, L'Alpe d'Huez, Les 2 Alpes usually has moderate weather and sunny skies. There is a good variety for all levels, but the east-facing slopes are great for beginning skiers and children. Built in 1945.

Après-Ski: Bars, discos, cafes, coffee houses, 2 fitness centers
Lodging: 30,000 beds; 40 hotels/3,700 beds
Transportation: Gateway Airport: Lyon or Geneva
Closest Provincial City: Grenoble (1 hr)
By Air: Air Inter flies between Grenoble and Paris
By Bus: Tennet operates bus transfers from Grenoble after each flight—transfer time is 2 hours
By Train: TGV service to Grenoble, transfer to bus at train station. Train schedule info, call Rail Europe (800) 345-1990
Other Information: TGV train waits for no one—be ready to board quickly

CHAMROUSSE*
TOURIST OFFICE:
38410 CHAMROUSSE, FRANCE

Telephone: (33) 476 89 92 65 Fax: (33) 476 89 98 06

Elevation: Base/Village: 1,650 m (5,413 ft); Top: 2,250 m (7,382 ft)
Vertical: 600 m (1,968 ft)
Terrain: 9 red, 6 green, 13 blue and 9 black runs
Lifts: 26
Types: 1 tram; 9 chairlifts (3 high-speed quads); 16 T-bars
Lift Capacity: 26,668 p/h resort
Ski Season: December - End of April
Cross Country: None
Mountain Restaurants: 2
Ski School: French Ski School, 120 instructors
Other Winter Activities: Ice skating/artificial; indoor swimming; mono-skiing; snowboarding; paragliding; fitness center, sauna

ALPES DU NORD/MASSIF DE BELLEDONNE
"The first ski resort in France." Ideal for children and families. Easy to reach all winter - near to Grenoble. Abundant snowfalls from December to May.

Après-Ski: 20 restaurants, cinemas; 16 bars, 2 discos
Shopping Services: Banks, gift and souvenir shops; ice driving school
Credit Cards: VISA, MC, EC
Child Care: Kid's Ski School, 90 FF ½ day; nursery, 125 FF per day
Lodging: 13,000 beds in the resort
Transportation: Gateway Airports: Lyon, 130 km
Closest Provincial City: Grenoble, 30 km
By Train: To Grenoble, then ski bus with "train correspondence"

©Publishers Group International, 1998

FRANCE

Fun with fondue is de rigeur *in the French après-ski scene.*   Photo: Arnal

AUTRANS*
TOURIST OFFICE: 38880 Autrans
France

Telephone: (33) 476 95 3070 Fax: (33) 476 95 3863

Elevation: Base/Village: 1,050 m (3,475 ft); Top 1,710 m (5,657 ft)
Vertical: 660 m (1,160 ft)
Terrain: 16 slopes: 1 Black, 4 Red, 2 Blue, 9 Green, 18 km groomed
Skiing Circus: No
Lifts: 16
Types: 1 Chair, 15 Surface lifts
Lift Capacity: 8,000 p/h resort
Ski Season: Opens Mid-December
Cross Country: 11 tracks (160 km)
Ski School: 20 instructors - English spoken
Other Winter Activities: Horseback riding; mini-golf; tennis; sports center

ISERE
In addition to its alpine tradition, Autrans is considered to be the number one cross country ski area in France. Its long history of international participation in winter sports has made it into a popular family activities center. For alpine skiers there is a large boulevard in the midst of the woods without avalanche or crevasse concerns.

Après-Ski: Cinema, game room
Shopping Services: Butcher shop, bakery, tobacco-news, beauty shop, restaurants, library, sports shop
Lodging: 8,000 beds. 10 Hotels. Also apartments and private homes
Transportation: Gateway Airports: Geneva & Lyon
Closest Provincial City: Lyon (184 km)
By Auto from Airport: A48 - Grenoble/St. Etienne de St. Geoirs
By Train: Lyon 1 hr; Geneva 2 hrs. Shuttle service from RR station
Other Information: Night skiing on 3 slopes (8.5 km). mountain restaurant

FRANCE

LES 7 LAUX
TOURIST OFFICE: Q. T. Les 7 Laux
38190 Prapoutel les 7 Laux, France

Telephone: (33) 4 76 08 1786 Fax: (33) 4 76 08 7192

Elevation: Base/Village: 1,350 m (4,470 ft); Top: 2,400 m (7,945 ft)
Vertical: 1,050 ft
Terrain: 42 slopes: 3 black, 19 red, 11 blue, 9 green
Skiing Circus: No
Lifts: 31
Types: 9 Chairlifts, 22 ski tows
Lift Capacity: 33,000 p/h resort
Ski Season: Opens Mid-December
Summer Skiing: No
Cross Country: 12 km on Prapoutel, 12 km on Pleynet
Ski School: French Ski School, 89 instructors. English, Spanish, German spoken
Other Winter Activities: Disco, sports club. Tele. 76 08 1786
Après-Ski: Cinema

LES 7 LAUX
Les 7 Laux is considered the third ski area of the Dauphine region. Skiers can ski in solitude to the southeast or experience 100 km of terrain on 42 designated alpine slopes from green to black runs. A high altitude inhabited village.

Shopping Services: Butcher shop, bakery, tobacco and news stands, hairdresser, barbershop, restaurants, library, sports shop, hardware store, service station, parking garage, doctor, dentist, laudromat
Credit Cards:
Child Care: Ages 3-8
Lodging: 8,720 beds; 6 hotels (in the village, 10 km from the slopes)
Transportation: Gateway Airports: Grenoble, Lyon (134 km), Geneva
Closest Provincial City: Lyon
By Auto from Airport: Rt. A41 from Grenoble/Chambéry. Transfers: Tel. 76 65 4848
By Train: Closest Grenoble. Transfers: Tel. 36 35 3535
Best Deal:
Other Information: Snowmaking (26 guns)

SAINT PIERRE DE CHARTREUSE
TOURIST OFFICE: LeBourg
38380 St. Pierre de Chartreuse, France

Telephone: (33) 476 88 6208 Fax: (33) 476 97 3088

Elevation: Base/Village: 900 m (2,979 ft); Top: 1,800 m (5,958 ft)
Vertical: 900 m (2,979 ft)
Terrain: 19 runs—3 black; 7 red; 4 blue, 5 green. 30 km of ski terrain
Skiing Circus: None
Lifts: 13
Types: 2 Chairlifts; 1 cable car; 10 tows
Lift Capacity: 9,600 p/h resort
Ski Season: Opens 15 December
Summer Skiing: No
Cross Country: 7 tracks (80 km)
Ski School: 30 instructors. English, Spanish & German spoken

SAINT PIERRED DE CHARTREUSE
A resort that is different from the expected. A village that is "magical" throughout the entire year. It offers the visitor a "big surprise" and a place to relax. Monastery at Chartreuse open for tours.

Other Winter Activities: Horseback riding; sports club
Shopping Services: Butcher shop, bakery, tobacco and sports stores, hairdresser, library, doctor, dentist
Child Care: Age 4-12; 2 hrs 70FF
Lodging: 3,800 beds; 6 hotels; 64 apartments; 4 private houses
Transportation: Gateway Airports: Grenoble-St. Ceoirs, Lyon (100 km), Geneva (140 km)
Closest Provincial City: Lyon
By Auto from Airport: Shuttle from airport. Tele. 76 87 4848
By Train: Paris 3 hrs; Lyon 1½ hrs; Geneva 2½ hrs
Other Information: 5 slopes (30 km) lighted for night skiing

©Publishers Group International, 1998

FRANCE

VILLARD DE LANS*
BP 54
38250 Villard de Lans, France

Telephone: (33) 4 76 95 1038 Fax: (33) 4 76 95 9839

Elevation: Base/Village: 1,060 m (3,478 ft); Top: 2,170 m (7,120 ft)
Vertical: 1,110 m (3,642 ft)
Terrain: 130 km of runs; 9 red, 4 green, 12 blue and 10 black runs
Lifts: 31
Types: 2 gondolas; 6 chairlifts; 23 T-bars
Lift Capacity: 30,000 p/h resort
Ski Season: Mid-December - April 20
Cross Country: 160 kms; Villard de Lans/Correncon/ St. Julien en Vercors/St. Martin en Vercors
Ski School: Ecole du Ski Francais; Tele. 4 76 95 10 94
Mountain Restaurants: 3 alpine and 4 cross country
Other Winter Activities: Tobogganing; ice skating/ artificial; indoor swimming; indoor tennis (2); sports center; mono-ski; snowboarding; hiking
Après-Ski: Folklore evenings; bridge, library; cinema; discos; restaurants

---

SERRE-CHEVALIER
OFFICE DU TOURISME
SERRE-CHEVALIER, BP20
05 240 Serre-Chevalier, France
Telephone: (33) 4 92 26 98 98 Fax: (33) 4 92 26 98 84

Elevation: Base/Village: 1,350 m (4,429 ft); Top: 2,800 m (9,186 ft)
Vertical: 1,450 m (4,757 ft)
Longest Run: 6.4 km (4.0 mi)
Terrain: Along with nearby (2 km) Monetier there is every type of ski terrain imaginable. Groomed and off-piste through high forest and above tree line. Gentle and demanding terrain. 109 prepared runs and over 250 km (155 mi) of trails; 70 km (31 mi) beginner, 80 km (46 mi) intermediate, 50 km (31 mi) expert; 13 black, 55 red, 21 green, 20 blue trails
Skiing Circus: The Serre-Chevalier ski slopes are linked with the Briancon (3 miles) Slopes.
Lifts: 72
Types: 6 Gondolas; 3 Trams; 16 Chairlifts; 47 Surface
Lift Capacity: 70,500 p/h resort
Cross Country: 45 km; 5 prepared tracks
Ski School: 250 instructors/5 ski schools
Mountain Restaurants: 11
Other Winter Activities: Snowshoe walking; ice skating/natural; indoor swimming; paragliding; hang-

VERCORS-DAUPHINE
Villard De Lans offers skiing for both downhill (130 km) and cross country (160 km) with 31 lifts.

Shopping Services: More than 100 shops offering all services, including restaurants, bakeries, bank, doctors, dentists
Credit Cards: VISA, MC
Child Care: Kid's Ski School, 80 FF/2 hours; 6 days, 2 hours p/d 390; 12 days 610
Lodging: Hotels, rental apartments, hotel residences, camping, pensions
Transportation: Gateway Airports: Lyon Satolas Airport
Closest Provincial City: Grenoble
By Auto from Airport: Lyon - Grenoble/Grenoble - Villard de Lans
By Train: Rail Europe (914) 682-2999; (800) 345-1990
Other Information: 100 snowmaking guns at 1,150 m & 1,800 m. Ski school area for beginners and children

SOUTHERN ALPS
Resort is made up of 3 villages (Saint Chaffrey & Villeneuve et Monetier) and offers an extensive variety of ski terrain and usually sunny skies. Off-piste skiers will like its tree-lined powder fields. Serre Chevalier has been in operation for more than 50 years and is the largest destination resort of the southern Alps.

gliding; sauna; sledding; horseback riding; ice driving car school, on snow pose
Après-Ski: Bars, discos, cafes, coffee houses
Shopping/Services: All services & shopping available
Credit Cards: AE, MC, VISA
Child Care: Each village has its own child care facilities
Lodging: 30,000 beds; 31 hotels & pensions, but condominium units house most visitors
Transportation: Gateway Airport: Geneva/Lyon; Turin, Italy; Paris/Grenoble
Closest Provincial City: Grenoble, 108 km
By Auto from airport: N91 from the east and N94 from the west to Briançon
By Train: Geneva to Grenoble to Briançon then ski bus to Serre-Chevalier
Other Information: Some snowmaking capability usually ensures lower level skiing.
Snow telephone 9224 2929 or 9224 9898

FRANCE

VARS*
OFFICE OF TOURISM
05560 Vars les Claux, France

Telephone: (33) 492 46 51 31 Fax: (33) 492 46 56 54

Elevation: Base/Village: 1,650 m (5,413 ft); Top: 2,750 m (9,022 ft)

Vertical: 1,100 m (3,608 ft)

Terrain: 23 red, 10 green, 20 blue and 8 black runs

Skiing Circus: To Risoul (resort)

Lifts: 31 (54 for Vars/Risoul)

Types: 1 Telécabine; 6 Chairlifts; 24 Surface

Ski Season: December 8 - April 21

Cross Country: 25 km; 5 itineraries for cross country and a winter pedestrian path

Ski School: France Ski School; Int'l Ski School

Other Winter Activities: Helicopter flying; fitness center; ice skating natural; mountaineering; paragliding (2); sauna (3); snowboarding; speed skiing

Après-Ski: 38 restaurants & bars, discos, cinema, conferences

Shopping Services: Grocery, bakeries, pharmacy, souvenirs, hair dresser, sport shop, complete variety

HAUTES ALPES
Bathed in 2 hours of sunshine per day - 300 days of sunshine per year. Vars is in the domain of la Forêt Blanche and has 170 km of runs and 58 lifts making the resort one of the largest in the southern Alps. Mild temperatures.

Credit Cards: Visa, MC

Child Care: Kid's Ski School, 2 years and up

Lodging: 17,000 beds (1 - 3 star, 11 - 2 star hotels, 5 guest houses, 20 holiday centers, 2 club-hotels); average lodging cost is between 2,100 FF - 3,500 FF for a 2 star hotel week, high season

Transportation: Gateway Airports:

Closest Major City: Grenoble, 160 km

By Auto from Airport: From Grenoble N91 to Briancón to Guillestre to Vars. From Marseille (250 km) via A51

By Train: From Paris to Briancón (TGV) Reservations Tele. 43635 3535

Bus service from Dec. 8 - April 21 - Montdauphin/Guillestre to Vars; Reservation Tele. 492 45 18 11

Other Information: Temperature between −15°C (night) to +15°C (noon)

LANS EN VERCORS
TOURIST OFFICE: Place de l'Eglise
38250 Lans en Vercors
France
Telephone: (33) 76 95 4262 Fax: (33) 76 95 4970

Elevation: Base/Village: 1,020 m (3,310 ft); Top: 1,983 m (6,600 ft)

Vertical: 963 m (3,145 ft)

Terrain: 24 km of groomed slopes. Runs: 19, 5 Red, 8 Blue, 6 Green

Skiing Circus: No

Lifts: 16

Types: 16 Surface lifts

Lift Capacity: 12,700 p/h resort

Ski Season: Opens Mid-December

Summer Skiing: No

Cross Country: 22 tracks (70 km)

Ski School: French Ski School - 25 instructors English spoken; 2 hour group lessens or 1 hour private

Other Winter Activities: Swimming, sports center, tennis, ice skating, mini golf, horseback riding

LANS EN VERCORS
Lans en Vercors is located in the Regional National Park of Vercors. A family village with a climate suitable for both summer and winter activities. Cultural events continual year round, but particularly in the wintertime when skiing competitions take place.

Après-Ski: Cinema, disco, game room

Shopping Services: Butcher, bakery, tobacco & news, hairdresser-barber, restaurants (some on Mt.), library, sport shop, garage, parking, souvenirs, dentist, doctor

Credit Cards:

Lodging: 7,000 beds; 5 hotels, 2 inns, 40 private homes, 180 apartments

Transportation: Gateway Airports: Geneva & Lyon

Closest Provincial City: Lyon, 100 km (62 miles)

By Auto from Airport: Shuttle (33) 7647 7777

By Train: Lyon 1 hour, Geneva 3 hrs.
Shuttle - Tel (33) 7647 7777

Other Information: 15 km (4 slopes) lighted for night skiing

The French Connection

by George W. Schissler

France has a distinguished ski history dating back to 1924 with the first Winter Olympic Games in Chamonix. This site was chosen for its abundance of snow and terrain to test the world's best skiers.

Forty-four years later France was again chosen as the host nation for this winter competition. Grenoble was selected as the site of the 1968 Olympics. It was at Grenoble that Jean-Claude Killy, anchor of the dominant French ski team, swept three alpine events to become a national hero. France was awarded the Winter Games for a third time, with Killy heading the organizing committee, when Albertville was selected as the site for the 1992 Winter Olympic Games. (The U.S. is the only other country to host three Winter Olympics—1932, 1960 and 1980).

Back in February, 1992 when the eyes of the world focused on France and the XVI Olympic Winter Games, the center of activity was Albertville, but Les Menuires, Les Arcs, and Meribel became internationally known ski resorts thanks to exposure from the Games.

These resorts, among Europe's best, have long enjoyed success drawing skiers from all countries on the continent. The added exposure brought about by the Olympics resulted in an increased number of Americans taking ski vacations in the French Alps. They came away with glowing reports of fantastic skiing on large expanses of snow.

Because of the enormous area, skiers with the use of a trail map have the ability to ski from village to village. Begin a ski day at home base after breakfast, take a few runs, enjoy a leisurely lunch in a neighboring village, take an afternoon break in yet another, and with an eye on the clock (make very sure of lift closing time) catch the appropriate lift(s) back to the original departure site. You will most likely have covered many miles on the snow and never once used the same lift or descended the same terrain. The trail map is essential. Don't leave home without it!

The 1994 edition of *The Blue Book* highlighted the 1992 Olympic venues after an in-depth visit by the editors. Although not as publicized as some of its neighbors, the French resorts are every bit as appealing and exciting as anything Europe has to offer. There usually is an abundance of snow to cover some of the most demanding and scenic terrain in the world. There are slopes and trails which allow skiers of all abilities to cruise with style. Snowmaking has been added to insure that good conditions prevail at lower levels.

GETTING AROUND IS EASY

Any skier making an initial visit to the French Alps will be amazed at what surely must be the most prolific and efficient lift service anywhere. This efficiency is due in large part to, Compagnie des Alps (CDA), the premier ski lift company in Europe. Regarded as the leader in lift management, its development and research have resulted in advanced technology which allows huge numbers of skiers to be transported uphill in state-of-the-art lifts with minimum waiting or inconvenience. CDA resorts are identified on the back cover and are identified in the French and Italian sections of *The Blue Book*. Their company logo will be in the resort box at the top left handside of the page. When you visit one of the resorts with Compagnie des Alps managed lifts, you will spend a full day on the snow. Swissair will get you to a destination city quickly and efficiently and CDA will transport you over the slopes with ease.

During our visit to Les Grande Montets in Chamonix, Meribel, Les Arcs, Les Menuires, Tignes and La Plagne not once did we waste time. Tram, chair and gondola—all are state-of-the-art and even dreaded surface lifts are well maintained and organized, devouring even the longest lift lines. The lifts move quickly and skiers spend little or no time in line before being whisked to the top for another run.

Equally efficient and convenient is the land transportation system. Getting from one ski resort to another by auto is accomplished on highways which are up to date and the speed limit allows travelers to reach their destinations in reasonable time.

From the Geneva airport the ride to the Haute Savoie, where many of the best known resorts are located is roughly 2½–3 hours on Route 90N. This is a super highway equal to major routes in the U.S. Car rental companies are conveniently located at the airport and all arrangements are efficiently handled in advance when you book a Swissair tour package.

The lovely, quaint village of Saint Martin de Belleville in the Three Valleys.

Photo: Meribel Tourist Office

FRANCE

Although arrangements are easy and convenient, the cost is neither. Be advised that in Europe the cost of gasoline is high (at least double that of the U.S.) and rental expenses vary greatly. But these expenses are offset when you consider that you can travel freely at your own pace to visit world famous resorts throughout the country, or just roam through scenic tiny villages and into a bygone era of history. Take some time off from the ski slopes to enjoy the beauty of France at every turn of the road. Get off the highway and ride secondary paths. Getting lost can be a pleasurable experience and may result in a memorable day of sightseeing.

Should you elect *not* to rent a car but want to travel about the country—no problem. Another advantage to a French ski vacation (or any vacation in France for that matter) is the proximity to many of the country's larger cosmopolitan cities. They can be accessed by an efficient rapid railway system. The fast-moving TGV railway enables travelers to enjoy the view of the countryside, while heading for city streets. Train stations in many of the small ski villages enable travellers to ski one day and tour a large city the next, without taking to the highway. You can ski one day and sightsee in Paris, Grenoble or Lyon the next. What could be better or more convenient?

The Blue Book of European Ski Resorts will aid you in planning a ski trip to one of the countries represented in this book. Each of them will fulfill your dream of a vacation, with skiing as the primary motive for seeking pleasure in this winter wonderland. But you will miss out if you do not visit the French Alps using a convenient Swissair flight to Geneva, Switzerland with access to some of the best and most adventurous skiing in Europe.

An awesome view in Chamonix.
Photo: French Government Tourist Office

Lyon, France's third largest city is known for many things, a few of which are: cuisine, sightseeing and arrival city to ski the French Alps.

If this is to be your initial visit to ski the French Alps, please be advised that what you see (at first) is not what you get. You get much more. The larger resorts, and almost all of the smaller and lesser known areas may have only a single lift at the base or village center, but as soon as you step off the initial lift conveyance there will be a large and varied choice of lifts to carry you higher and further. The lift system in the French Alps is prolific and efficient.

THE CHAMONIX EXPERIENCE

Chamonix, France's oldest ski resort and one of the world's best known, has an aerial tramway serving the Aiguille du Midi; an experience to be remembered for a lifetime. And you will certainly recall forever the walk across the bridge, through the ice tunnel to sunlight. At the tunnel exit you hand your ski poles to your guide, who then ties you to the other members of your party for the perilous trek down on foot in clumsy ski boots. Here at the very crest of the peak (so scared you dare not peek) you follow exactly in footsteps of those who have traversed before you to reach the relative safety of a small plateau. You breathe a momentary sigh of relief, catch your breath and prepare yourself for the descent on the famed, Valleé Blanche. The guide cautions you to follow in his tracks closely, as crevasses and other dangers are ever-present. You only have to be told once. Eyeing what lies ahead, you use good judgment and follow his track exactly.

This first descent leads to what is probably the world's most famous ski run down to the Mer de Glace. Looking ahead you may be intimidated. Have no fear. The guide is aware of your ability and leads the way through vast powder fields, around crevasses which cut hundreds of feet below your skis and then cuts a path around gigantic blocks of ice which nature bowled through the valley many years ago. But for all its ruggedness the Mer de Glace can be negotiated by intermediate skiers and skied with a sense of accomplishment and pleasure. Your guide picks spots where you can free ski in

©Publishers Group International, 1997

FRANCE

absolute safety, although it is a good idea to tailgate him closely when possible. Be assured that he will not let you venture too far off his track and he will not hesitate to let you know that you must keep close to him. To have fun in the Vallée Blanche, the mountain guide is the key. No one should venture into the Vallée Blanche and through the Mer de Glace without a guide; he is the one who allows you to have a full day of exciting skiing in safety.

Before embarking on this adventure, you might inquire as to whether there is enough snow to enable you to ski all the way out. *The Blue Book* editors had to climb out on a series of super-steep ladders, almost completely vertical, in full ski dress and carrying their ski equipment to reach the train station high above, for the ride down the mountain and home. If you climb these ladders, you will forget neither the ride up to the Aiguille du Midi or the lengthy climb out.

From the top of the Aiguille du Midi there is nothing between you and God, and most people on the Midi have already had a few words with Him. Up there to be heard by God one only needs to whisper. At the bottom you can shout a loud "Thank You."

The ski season in the French Alps usually begins in late November and continues on through late May at most resorts. Of course, there is year-round skiing on glaciers (check the resort listings for these locations).

MORE TOP RESORTS

Visitors may purchase the Olympic lift pass that also includes *Val d'Isere, Tignes, La Plagne* and *Les Arcs*. This is a great way to explore several of the country's top resorts. The pass is valid for a maximum of one day at each of the major ski resorts leaving time off for sightseeing.

The *La Plagne* complex is comprised of 10 different areas and offers skiers of every ability challenging terrain suitable to their individual comfort level. *Courchevel*, one of France's premier ski resorts is situated in a vast snow bowl and is part of "The Three Valleys" complex. The area is built on five levels, each with its own compact village. Hotels are located to provide easy access to lifts, Courchevel also lays claim to the largest tram in the world, accommodating over 160 passengers.

While Chamonix may operate the highest lift in the country, it is *Tignes* in the Savoie's L'Espace Killy which certainly has undisputed claim to the lowest. Here, where skiing is available 365 days a year, skiers can ride to the top of the mountain in warmth and relative comfort on an underground funicular which connects the lower portion of Val Claret to "The Panoramic" restaurant of the Grand Motte. This lift travels beneath the glacier and can transport 3,000 persons per hour (skiers and non-skiers) and it operates in severe weather conditions in complete safety. There are no panoramic views on the way up. The reward comes at the mountain-top, whether it be for the eye or the palate. Tignes has ski terrain to make all skiers comfortable on its 110 miles of trails and 57 lifts. This resort also makes it possible to ski to Val d'Isere on the other side of the valley.

Skiers carefully track down into the Vallée Blanche at Chamonix.

Of course, from Val d'Isere you can also get back to Tignes on snow.

Once you have made the crossover in either direction you have the option of returning by skis, or catching a free shuttle bus which runs between the resorts. In Val d'Isere you are in the village several Olympic champions call home. Jean Claude Killy, Henri Oreiller and the Goitschel sisters, medalists all, are based here. A vertical drop of 4,800 feet and 56 lifts gives skiers a choice of 95 miles of ski terrain to explore. You just might get to ski with one of the Olympic heroes. This resort is considered by informed skiers as the place to be in the French Alps in the winter. It was the site of the 1992 Olympic downhill, giant slalom and combined events. The village, a combination of the old and new, has retained its charm with narrow streets and steepled church. Active nighttime activities or just a stroll through the lighted village center completes the perfect ski day.

The modern resort of La Plagne offers skiers superb skiing and aprés-ski.

FRANCE

CDA RESORTS... SOME OF THE LARGEST IN THE WORLD

France boasts the largest ski area in the world, "The Three Valleys", with 375 miles of runs and more than 200 lifts. *Les Menuires* and *Val Thorens*, only 7 km from each other by road in the south of the Savoie, offer skiers more than 300 km of terrain and 75 lifts to get them to the skiing. These resorts, along with *Meribel, Courchevel* and *LaTania* make up the Three Valleys. These resorts provide more ski terrain than most skiers will manage to test while vacationing. There is also the added treat of being able to ski during the summer months on the Peclet Glacier.

At *La Plagne*, located in the center of the Savoie and site of the 1992 Olympic bobsled and luge events, skiers will come to understand the meaning of the word "circus" as it pertains to terrain availability and accessability in Europe. The word simply implies that skiers can travel from one village or resort to another on snow. At La Plagne this could be referred to as a "traveling circus" because this "circus" allows the skier to visit the 10 levels which make up this complex and all with the purchase of one Olympic six-day lift pass. LaPlagne has more skiing than you can handle in a six-day period and still sleep in the same bed every night.

Long before the 1992 Olympics, *Les Arcs* was already well-known for its great snow and diversity of terrain. There is something for every member of the skiing family—from beginner to the adventurous extreme skier. The Olympic speed track is here and you can test your skill and daring on it. There are also gentle, well groomed slopes and deep off-piste powder. This three-tiered resort (Arc 1600, Arc 1800, and Arc 2000) is serviced by a gondola connecting the three separate areas. Each area allows skiers to travel to the top of the mountain to either ski or take in the views which overlook the Mont Blanc Valley. Les Arcs is a family-oriented resort and children's activities are well planned to keep them busy and tire them enough to make them sleep well in the evening. Or, just maybe, after a full day of skiing at Les Arcs, Mom and Dad will be the first to call it a day.

Skiers visiting Les Arcs are advised to spend some time on the neighboring slopes of *Peisey Vallandry* which are accessible from Arc 1800. Both resorts share the same Massif and each seems to be an extension of the other.

Peisey Vallandry and **Les Arcs** carry skiers on 78 lifts with 112 trails and approximately 90 miles of runs which can accommodate all ability levels. This area is more of an authentic village resort than just a ski resort. It is one of the country's oldest areas serving skiers, and is divided into two small villages affording breathtaking views of the summits of the Vanoise National park. The authentic Alpine identity has been preserved and visitors will be transported back in time by the baroque treasures of the chapels and churches. The village has stood still, but the skiing has kept up with the times.

Located in the heart of the High Savoy, Flaine in the shadow of Mont Blanc is another resort sharing the Grand Massif. It has 2,952 feet of vertical terrain, 31 lifts and when connected to the four neighboring resorts of Samoens, Les Carroz d'Arachs, Morillon and Sies, offers skier's access to 80 lifts and 265 km of snow on which to ski. Due to its elevation and abundant natural snowfall, Flaine is a favorite resort for those looking for off-piste adventure in deep, light powder.

It is difficult to describe and write about only a few of the many resorts listed in this section of *The Blue Book*. Each resort visited brought us away with a positive impression. The efficient lifts; breath-taking scenery; excellent ski conditions; genial hosts; diet-busting foods and wines, are just some of the things the resorts in the French Alps offer the vacationing visitor.

It is our hope that *The Blue Book of European Ski Resorts* will help you make an informed decision when considering a ski vacation in Europe. We have tried to gather as many facts on the resorts listed so that you will have a good idea as to where you might want to go; when the best time may be to vacation in the Alps and what is available when you get there. We have had great times in the French Alps and highly recommend it as the place to ski in Europe.

Maybe you owe it to yourself. Give it a try!

Les Grands Montets at Chamonix.

The Grand Massif and the resort of Les Arcs.   Photo: Nicole Nicolas

©Publishers Group International, 1997

GERMANY

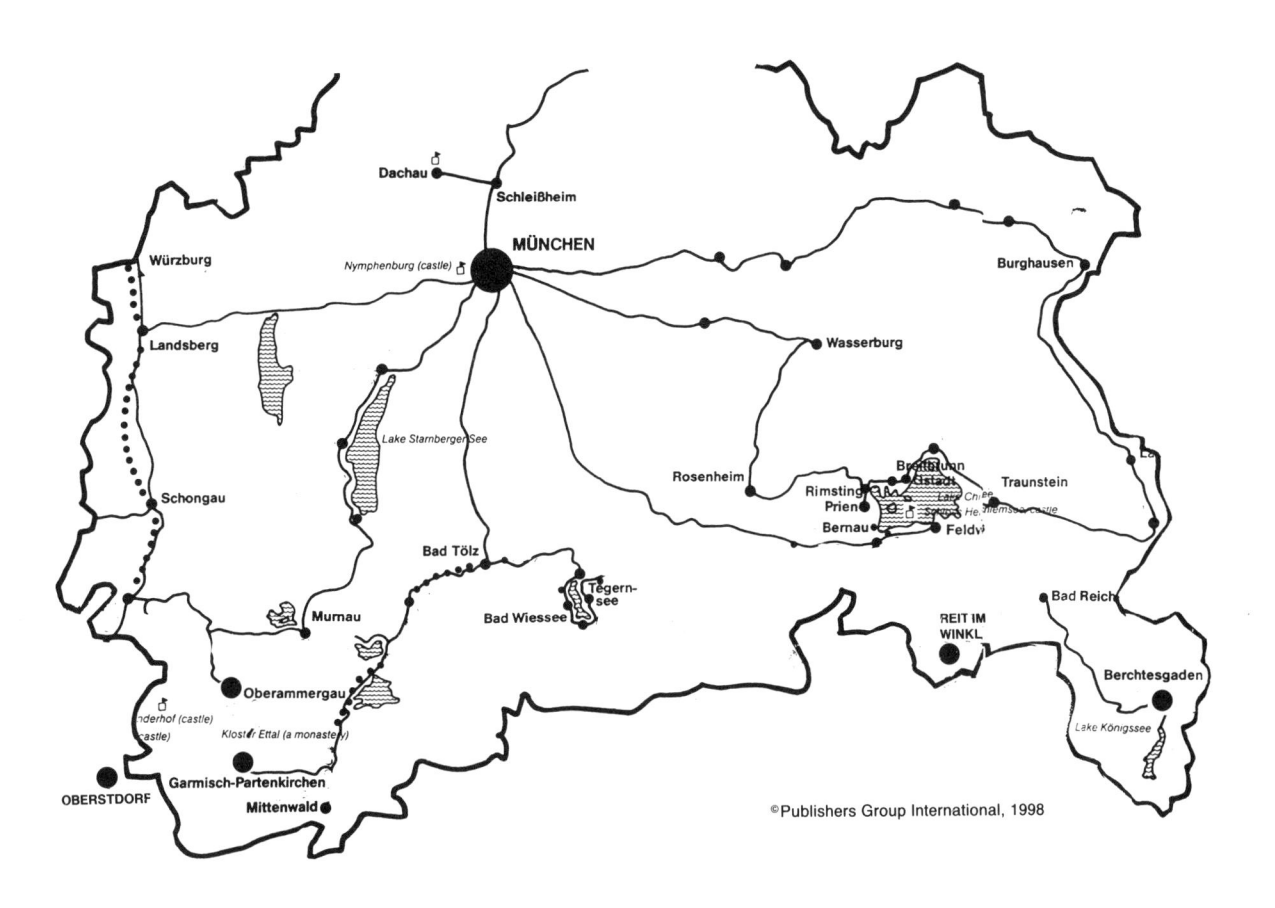

GERMANY

	Page No.
Berchtesgadener Land	64
Garmisch-Partenkirchen	**61**
Oberammergau	62
Oberstdorf	**63**
Reit im Winkl/Steinplatte/Winklmoos-Alm	64

*Areas marked with an asterisk in the text did not update their information for this edition.

GERMANY

by Bob Wall

Germany must be considered as a contender in the field of ski resorts. The Alps of Bavaria are close to Munich, which offers a convenient gateway for skiers from North America. The new Munich airport is less than two hours from the major ski centers of Germany via a well-maintained limited-access highway network and an efficient high-speed rail system. Alpine and cross-country skiers will find excellent facilities with plenty of terrain for skiers of all abilities.

Without a doubt, Garmisch-Partenkirchen is the easiest German resort to reach from the Munich Airport. Located about 35 miles south of the Bavarian capital and connected by an Autobahn, Garmisch is less than hour from the baggage claim area. This charming pair of cities, Garmisch and Partenkirchen are separate municipalities located at the foot of Germany's highest peak, the Zugspitze.

Garmisch-Partenkirchen gained international fame when it hosted the 1936 Winter Olympics. In order to accommodate the Games, ski jumps, skating rinks and a bobsled run were built making it a first class winter resort.

Many millions of Americans have visited Garmisch while serving in the Armed Forces in Europe. The military has maintained a recreation center there ever since the end of World War II. Returning veterans help make the twin towns one of the most popular resorts in the "Best of the Alps" group.

Oberstdorf in the Allgauer Alps is well known to American television fans for its ski flying hill. Jumpers regularly soar more than 150 meters from this giant ski jump. Oberstdorf is also a superb alpine ski resort with runs to satisfy skiers of every ability. It is also possible to ski from Oberstdorf into the Kleinwalsertal in Austria.

Nordic skiers will find hundreds of kilometers of groomed cross country trails at Nordic centers throughout the country and especially in the Black Forest.

The lifestyle in the Bavarian and Allgauer ski resorts reflects the joy of living that is so prevalent among southern Germans. There is always time to stop for a coffee or a beer and exchange views and ideas with visitors. Accommodations vary from five star hotels that often resemble a mountain chalet, to a simple farmhouse. The pensions of the Alps of southern Germany certainly set the standard and mode for what the English and Americans call the bed and breakfast.

A ski trip to Germany also gives you the opportunity for some great sightseeing. Near the resorts of Upper Bavaria, several of the castles erected by Ludwig II, the King of Bavaria, are open to view. The most remarkable of the group is Neuschwanstein, reputed to have been the inspiration for the castles at Disneyland and Disneyworld. Neuschwanstein is but a short drive from Garmisch-Partenkirchen, but also close by are Linderhof and the two castles on the islands of Chiemsee.

A ski trip to Germany will reward you with some fantastic skiing and an opportunity to understand that great German word *Gemütlichkeit*—hospitality, relaxed pleasure and friendly atmosphere.

For brochures and more information:

GERMAN NATIONAL TOURIST OFFICE
122 E. 42nd St.
New York, NY 10068-0072
Telephone: (212) 661-7200

LUFTHANSA GERMAN AIRLINES
680 Fifth Ave.
New York, NY 10019
(718) 895-1277

SWISSAIR INFORMATION

Swissair carries skiers to the Alps from Atlanta, Boston, Chicago, Cincinnati, Los Angeles, Montreal, Newark, New York, San Francisco, and Washington, D.C., with connecting service from 21 other U.S. cities.

Swissair offers a brochure called "The Alpine Experience." It includes additional descriptions of major Swiss resorts, as well as popular resorts in Austria, France, Germany and Italy. The colorful brochure contains photos, trail maps, hotel listings and prices for package deals.

For a free copy of "The Alpine Experience" call (800) 662-0021 or write Swissair, P.O. Box 26028, Tampa, FL 33623-6028.

To book one of their exciting adventures call Swissair Vacations at 800-688-7947.

©Publishers Group International, 1998

GERMANY

A typical Bavarian street Scene in Garmisch.

GARMISCH-PARTENKIRCHEN
TOURIST OFFICE
Richard-Strauss-Platz
82467 Garmisch-Partenkirchen
Telephone: (49) 8821-1806 Fax: (49) 8821-180755

Elevation: Base: 720 m (2,362 ft); Top: Zugspitze 2,964 m (9,732 ft)

Vertical: Alpspitze area 1,330 m (4,364 ft)

Longest Run: 8.7 km (5.4 mi); Wank area

Terrain: 118 km (73 mi) of marked runs; Zugspitze, Germany's only glacier ski area; Runs: 21 red, 8 green, 13 blue, 2 black; 10 snowmaking machines from village to 1,100 m

Skiing Circus: skiiing possible 5 glaciers

Lifts: 39

Types: 1 Tram; 8 Gondolas; 3 Chairlifts (doubles); 27 T-bars

Lift Capacity: 50,000 p/h resort

Ski Season: November - May

Cross Country: 200 km in the valley

Ski School: 5 ski schools with 200 instructors

Mountain Restaurants: 11

Other Winter Activities: Curling; horse drawn sleigh; folklore evenings; hiking; ice skating/natural & artificial; indoor swimming; indoor tennis; mono-skiing; sauna; paragliding; snowboarding; sleigh riding; sports center; mountaineering; fitness center; ice hockey

UPPER BAVARIA
Site of the 1936 Olympics, Garmisch-Partenkirchen sits at the foot of the Zugspitze, the country's highest mountain. There are 5 mountains in all, several are interconnected as well as glacier skiing on the Zugspitze.

Après-Ski: Casino; 9 discos, 12 bars, 17 cafes, concerts, theaters, cinema

Shopping/Services: Variety of shops in the center: boutiques, jewelry, antiques, souvenir, handicrafts, fashion, sports, pharmacies, etc.

Credit Cards: AE, DC, MC, VISA, EC in hotels, restaurants and shops

Child Care: Ski kindergarten, ½ day or day, 5 days with/without meals

Lodging: 9,651 beds; 3,182 beds in 37 hotels, 2,272 beds in holiday apartments, 2,400 beds in breakfast pensions, 1,204 beds in private houses

Transportation: Gateway Airport: Munich

By auto from airport: Highway A95 Munich to Garmisch-Partenkirchen, 140 km

By Train: Hourly train service from Munich station

Best Deal: "Happy Ski Card" ski pass for 3 days or more includes 113 lifts around the Zugspitze

Other Information: Free local bus service for guests; Avg. sunshine hours: Dec. 65, Jan. 78, Feb. 99, Mar. 141

GERMANY

Germany's highest mountain, the Zugspitze, is impressive from all sides. Photo: Best of the Alps

OBERAMMERGAU
TOURIST OFFICE
Eugen-Papst Str. 9A, Ammergauer Haus
82487 Oberammergau, Germany
Telephone: (49) 8822/92310 Fax: (49) 8822/7325

Elevation: Village: 850 m (2,789 ft); Top: 1,683 m (5,522 ft)

Vertical: 866 m (2,814 ft)

Terrain: Mostly beginner and intermediate-one longish run with alternate (double black) steep pitch from top of gondola to St. Gregor-Wellenberg

Lifts: 8

Types: 1 Gondola; 1 Chairlift; 6 Surface (5 T-bars)

Ski Season: Mid-December-March

Cross Country: 100+ km, prepared trails, flat to steep

Ski School: 2 schools, 35 instructors

Mountain Restaurants: Two

Other Winter Activities: Curling; fitness center; folklore evenings; hiking; horse drawn sleigh; ice skating/natural; indoor swimming; indoor tennis; paragliding; sauna; snowboarding; sleigh riding; sports center; tobogganing

UPPER BAVARIA
Famous for its Passion Play staged every 10 years since the 17th century. Mostly a Nordic rather than downhill area, but if you visit the town in winter you can ski and look down on Ettal.

Après-Ski: Bars, discos, cafes, coffee houses, folklore evenings, concerts

Shopping/Services: Year-round resort town with a full range of shopping and services

Child Care: Yes

Transportation: Gateway Airport: Munich

Closest Provincial City: Munich (60 mi)

By Auto from airport: Via Autobahn-A95

By Train: Yes

Other Information: Sightseeing is a must in the Ammer Valley—nearby the Benedictine Abbey of Ettal and within 50 km (31 mi) are 2 castles of King Ludwig II: Neuschwanstein, and nearby Linderhof

GERMANY

Television viewers of international ski jumping events have seen this lift and ski jump in Oberstdorf.

OBERSTDORF
TOURIST OFFICE:
Markplatz 7, D-87561 Oberstdorf
Germany
Telephone: (49) 8322/700-0 Fax: (49) 8322/700-236

Elevation: Base/Village: 815 m (2,673 ft); Top: 2,224 m (7,295 ft)

Vertical: 1,379 m (4,523 ft)

Longest Run: 7.5 km (4.7 mi), Nebelhorn to village

Terrain: 44 km (27 mi) of groomed slopes; 26% beginner, 64% intermediate, 10% advanced

Skiing Circus: A combination of 3 individual areas: Nebelhorn, cable car direct from town; Söllereck and Fellhorn-Kanzelwand: From the Fellhorn you can ski to the Kleinwalsertal ski complex in Austria and return by gondola

Lifts: 32

Types: 1 Gondola; 4 Cable cars; 6 Chairlifts; 20 Surface lifts (19 T-bars)

Lift Capacity: 26,300 p/h: Söllereck area 4,300 p/h; Nebelhorn areas 6,000 p/h; Fellhorn/Kanzelwand area 16,000 p/h

Ski Season: December-April

Cross Country: 85 km (52 mi) of tracks, including high altitude ones for beginners

Ski School: 8 schools with 200; 3 snowboard schools

Mountain Restaurants: 9, Nebelhorn 4; Fellhorn 4 & Söllereck 2

ALLGÄU REGION
Oberstdorf where the World Nordic Championships were held in 1987 is the leading wintersports resort of the Allgäu Region of southern Germany. Oberstdorf is popular with natives as a ski, spa and holiday resort. Proximity to Austria's Kleinwalsertal area gives it a continental ambiance.

Other Winter Activities: Curling; hiking; horse drawn sleigh; ice skating stadium; paragliding; indoor horseback riding; tobogganing; indoor swimming; indoor tennis; snowboarding, bungy jumping; ski jump

Après-Ski: Bars; discos; cafes; folklore evenings; concerts; sauna; spa; solarium, fitness center; icebars at all 3 skiing areas; casino in Kleinwalsertal, 12 km

Shopping/Services: Varied nightlife, many restaurants, variety of shops in the center, cozy wine taverns, theater performances, cinema, museum

Credit Cards: AE, DC, EC, VISA in many hotels, shops, & restaurants but not all

Child Care: 5-day Ski Kindergarten, DM 180

Lodging: 17,000 beds; over 300 hotels, lodges, pensions and apartments; also holidays on a farm

Transportation: Gateway Airport: Munich 210 km (130 mi); Zürich 220 km (132 mi); Stuttgart 245 km

Closest Provincial City: Kempten

Auto: B 12 Munich-Kempten/B 19 Kempten-Oberstdorf

Train: Available to Oberstdorf from Munich and Stuttgart

Best Deal: Ski pass Oberstdorf/Kleinwalsertal (Austria). Also, low season last 3 weeks of January

GERMANY

REIT IM WINKL/WINKLMOOS-ALM/ STEINPLATTE
TOURIST OFFICE
Rathausplatz 1; 83242 Reit im Winkl, Germany
Telephone: (49) 8640/80020 Fax: (49) 8640/80029

Elevation: Base: 700 m (2,297 ft); Top: 1,860 m (6,102 ft)
Vertical: 1,160 m (3,806 ft)
Terrain: 3 red, 4 green, 4 blue and 1 black
Longest Run: 9.6 km (5.6 mi)
Skiing Circus: Winklmoos-Alm (Germany)-Steinplatte (Austria)
Lifts: 12
Types: 6 Chairlifts (2 h-s quads, 1 triple, 3 doubles); 6 Surface
Lift Capacity: 22,000 p/h resort
Ski Season: Middle of December until after Easter
Cross Country: 80 km; Areas: Reit im Winkl, Winklmoos-Alm, Hemmersuppenalm, beg., intermediate, and advanced terrain; Langlaufschule Dorner
Ski School: Alpine: Skischule for Reit im Winkl/Winklmoos-Alm; Also snowboard and mono-ski school
Mountain Restaurants: Several

BERCHTESGADENER LAND
TOURIST OFFICE:
Königsseer Strasse 2
D-83471 Berchtesgaden, Germany
Telephone: (49) 8652/9670 Fax: (49) 8652/63300

Elevation: Base/Village: 600 m (1,968 ft); Top: 1,800 m (5,905 ft)
Vertical: 1,170 m (3,838 ft)
Terrain: Variety of terrain for all levels at Jenner; good for families and beginners at Rossfeld, beginner-intermediate terrain in Götschen, and families and beginners in Hochschwarzeck; night skiing at 3 locations
Skiing Circus: Areas not connected, however, skiing Austria is possible via Zinkenkogel and Bad Dürrnberg
Lifts: 22
Types: 2 Trams; 1 Gondola; 19 Surface lifts
Lift Capacity: 15,000 resort
Ski Season: Mid-December-Mid-April
Cross Country: 61 km cross country skiing in the 5 communities of the Berchtesgadner Land
Ski School: At Berchtesgaden, Bischofswiesen, Ramsau, Königssee, Oberau, Schönau, Unterau and Marktschellenberg, Monday-Friday 10-noon & 2-4 pm
Other Winter Activities: Luge; bobsled; curling; fitness center; ice skating/natural; indoor swimming; snowboarding; 3 indoor tennis courts; ballooning; mountaineering school;

UPPER BAVARIA
Reit im Winkl in southeast Bavaria is popular with alpine and cross-country skiers. Its terrain of open snowfields and tree-lined slopes straddles the German-Austrian border and can be accessed from either country. All mountain restaurants accept both marks and schillings.

Other Winter Activities: Ice skating/artificial; indoor swimming; indoor tennis; mono-skiing; snowboarding; curling; hiking; horse drawn sleigh; mountaineering
Après-Ski: Folklore evenings; sauna; bars; discos and cafes; concerts
Shopping/Services: Ski, sportshops; village shopping
Credit Cards: Eurocard, Visa
Child Care: Kids Ski School for age 3 and older with or without meals (without meals 160 DM p/5 days; 10 days 290 DM); Other: Private babysitting by school girls and private individuals, cost 15 DM p/h, contact tourist office
Lodging: 2 hotels; 5,000 beds in all

Transportation: Gateway Airport: Munich, 130 km
Closest Provincial City: Berchtesgaden (37 mi)
Closest Austrian City: Salzburg (35 mi); Kitzbühel, (18 mi)
By Auto from airport: 1 ½ hours Munich to Salzburg, exit Bernau-Prien, then Bernau south to Reit im Winkl
By Bus from airport: Every hour Prien am Chiemsee, then transfer to bus to Reit im Winkl. Ski bus in town

UPPER BAVARIA
Jenner, Rossfeld, Zinkenkogel, Götschen, Hochschwarzeck and Berchtesgaden are ski areas surrounding the city of Berchtesgaden which encompasses about 250 sq. km (120 sq. mi) utilizing a lift network of six separate locations. Plenty of sightseeing with a variety of winter activities.

sleigh riding; sports center; tobogganing; skibobing; med. & high ski jumps, 5 squash courts
Après-Ski: Bars, discos, cafes, concerts, horse-drawn sleigh, feeding the deer, folklore evenings, folk museum
Shopping/Services: Complete shopping and services
Credit Cards: Many restaurants, hotels, gift shops and clothing stores accept credit cards
Child Care: Full day care w/lunch 5 days at 8 locations; Kid's Ski School; Nursery: Babycare 2 hours DM20
Lodging: Full range of hotels, guest houses, bed & breakfast, pensions, private rooms & holiday apartments
Transportation: Gateway Airport: Munich; Salzburg
Closest Provincial City: Berchtesgaden, 96 miles
By Auto: Autobahn A8 to B-20 Road to Berchtesgaden
Best Deal: Weekly pass includes bus transportation
Other Information: 1st week of Dec. is "Buttnmandln" (straw-clad figures ringing cowbells chase through town); "Xmas & New Years Shooting" on 12/24 and 12/31

©Publishers Group International, 1998

ITALY

ITALY

	Page No.
Alpe Siusi-Sciliar*	79
Altopiano di Asiago 7 Comuni*	77
Arabba	77
Ayas	68
Bardonecchia*	72
Bormio	76
Cervinia/Valtourenche	70
Claviere-Cesana Torinese*	75
Cortina d'Ampezzo	78
Courmayeur	**69**
Forgárida-Marilleva*	80
Gressoney	71
La Thuile	70
Limone Piemonte*	73

	Page No.
Livigno	75
Macugnaga-Monte Rosa*	74
Madonna di Campiglio	81
Monte Bondone	80
Piancavallo*	86
Pila	71
S. Caterina Valfurva	76
Sauze d'Oulx*	74
Sestriere*	73
Solda-Tra Foi*	82
Val Di Fassa	83
Val Di Fiemme	83
Val Gardena-Selva-S. Cristina	85
Val Senales/Schnalstal	84

*Areas marked with an asterisk in the text did not update their information for this edition.

©Publishers Group International, 1998

ITALY

by Richard Muello

When considering Europe for that special ski adventure, Italy has all the winning features. World class skiing facilities coupled with a cosmopolitan atmosphere and extensive choices of artistic and cultural events has made it a mecca for skiers from around the world for more than sixty years.

Nature has bestowed upon Italy magnificent mountains, abundant snow and ideal winter temperatures. It is the only alpine country to encompass the entire 868 mile Alpine Arc. The lofty Alps, the most captivating mountains in Europe, divide Italy from France in the northwest, Switzerland and Austria in the north and the former Yugoslavia in the northeast.

The immense mountains of Mont Blanc (15,771 ft.) and the Gran Paradiso (13,324 ft.) form backdrops for many of the challenging slopes in the Aosta Valley region. These peaks, possibly the most beautiful of the alpine range, harbor such internationally renowned resorts as Cervinia, Courmayeur and La Thuile.

The Dolomites, among the most exquisite and spectacular mountains in the world, are in the eastern Alps, a mere hundred miles north of Venice, all within Italy's borders in the provinces of Belluno, Bolzano and Trento. They are a unique manifestation of nature with towering peaks of vertical rocky spires shaded in multi-colors. Cortina d'Ampezzo, site of the 1956 Winter Olympics, is one of many outstanding ski resorts in this beautiful natural setting. These mountains, with vast snowfields, offer an endless variety of terrain for all skiers. The "Dolomite Super Ski Pass" incorporates the largest circuit in the world with 464 lifts and 1,100 km. of ski runs in 12 valleys at 38 different ski centers.

A second range of mountains, the Apennines, "The backbone of Italy," traverses the entire length of the peninsula.

The main objective of *The Blue Book* is to assist readers in planning their European ski vacation by providing accurate information regarding terrain, ski facilities, rates, off-mountain activities, accommodations and travel. We also strive to provide an attractive book that is appealing and a pleasure to read.

Skiers have a most pleasant dilemma of determining which region and ski resorts they want to visit. Fear not, it is a win-win situation, because all of them are very special and unique. Twenty-eight resorts have been selected from Italy's six northern regions: Aosta Valley, Piedmont, Lombardy, Trentino Alto-Adige, Veneto, and Fruili Venezia Giulia. For easy reference, the regions and resorts are presented in a west to east sequence.

These areas represent a small fraction of Italy's overall ski resorts. However, they have a reputation for exceptional ski facilities and extensive après-ski activities. Many outstanding resorts such as Bormio and Livigno are linked by interconnected or reciprocal lift systems forming circuses, like the Alta Valtellina Ski Pass in the Lombardy region.

For special ski experiences, Italy offers the most inter-country ski opportunities in Europe: Cervinia to Zermatt in Switzerland; Courmayeur to Chamonix in France; La Thuile to La Rosiere in France; and Claviere/Casane Toriese to Montgenevre in France.

The proximity of many Italian resorts, such as Macugnaga or Val Senales, to Austria and Switzerland make day trips convenient for skiing or sightseeing.

A language difference is not a barrier to communicating. At least some English is spoken at most resorts, hotels, shops, and aboard planes, trains and buses. Although Italian is the official language, a majority of the residents of the alpine regions are multilingual—French is officially recognized in Aosta Valley and an ancient German-Swiss dialect is spoken in Gressnoy Valley.

The Trentino Alto-Adige Region is involved with two cultures; in Trentino the principal language is Italian, while in Alto-Adige language and tradition are German. Before World War I this South Tirol region was part of Austria. The Ladin minority present in both areas adds even more ethnic and linguistic variety.

Prices will differ substantially, according to the season. Although high and low seasons may vary slightly from region to region, this time frame will serve as a guideline. High season: Christmas week through the first week in January, and the month of February to the middle of March. For the Dolomite Super Ski Pass, the seasons and costs are included with the resorts in the rate section in the back of the book.

©Publishers Group International, 1998

ITALY

Much of Italy's history and art are reflected in its churches, monuments and museums, not only in the cosmopolitan cities of Milan, Venice and Turin, but in each provincial city and town as well. Although major cities are easily accessible from the resorts, works of art and cultural events are always at your doorstep.

Italy is crowned by mountains and is rich with a unique atmosphere, culture and climate. However, it is the people that distinguish a ski vacation and make the difference. Visitors immediately sense the hospitality which is expressed with delicious foods, fine wines and hearty laughter. The link for skiers with art, literature and nature is complete in Italy.

For additional information, contact:

ITALIAN GOVERNMENT TRAVEL OFFICES
Chicago
(312) 644-0996   Fax: (312) 644-3019

New York
(212) 245-4822   Fax: (212) 586-9249

Los Angeles
(310) 820-1898   Fax: (310) 820-6357

Québec
(514) 866-7667   Fax: (514) 392-1429

ALITALIA AIRLINES
666 Fifth Avenue
New York, NY 10103
(212) 903-3300
(800) 223-5730 (reservations)

SWISSAIR INFORMATION

Swissair carries skiers to the Alps from Atlanta, Boston, Chicago, Cincinnati, Los Angeles, Montreal, Newark, New York, San Francisco, and Washington, D.C., with connecting service from 21 other U.S. cities.

Swissair offers a brochure called "The Alpine Experience." It includes additional descriptions of major Swiss resorts, as well as popular resorts in Austria, France, Germany and Italy. The colorful brochure contains photos, trail maps, hotel listings and prices for package deals.

For a free copy of "The Alpine Experience" call 800-662-0021 or write to Swissair, P.O. Box 26028, Tampa, FL 33623-6028.

To book one of their exciting adventures call Swissair Vacations at 800-688-7947.

ITALY

This gondola accesses Punta Helbronner and the famed Vallee Blanche ski adventure.
Photo: Italian Government Travel Office

AYAS

AYAS/CHAMPOLUC A.P.T.
Localita Varase, 16-CAP 11020, Aosta, Italy
Telephone: (39) (125) 307113 Fax: (39) (125) 307785

Elevation: Base/Village: 1,570 m (5,151 ft); Top: 2,727 m (8,947 ft)

Vertical: 1,157 m (3,796 ft)

Terrain: 180 km (112 mi) of downhill slopes, well protected with good snow cover. Recommended for beginners-intermediate skiers; 33% beginner, 55% intermediate, 12% advanced

Skiing Circus: The three ski resorts in the Ayas Valley have an interconnected lift system, and can also cross-over to Gressoney-La Trinite (Monterosa ski)

Lifts: 18

Types: 1 Cableway; 9 Chairlifts

Ski Season: December-April

Summer Skiing: Plateau Rosa (May-November)

Cross Country: 35 km of excursion and cross-country ski tracks (1 ring, 5 km and 1 cross country track)

Ski School: Two schools/40 instructors at Champoluc and at Antagnod

Other Winter Activities: Helicopter skiing; ice skating; mono-skiing; mountaineering; snowboarding

Après-Ski: Discos, nightclubs, casino at St. Vincent

AOSTA VALLEY

Ayas Valley lies in the heart of the Western Alps and is composed of many quaint little villages, including the three ski resorts of Antagnod, Champoluc and Frachey. The glaciers of the Mont Rosa range provide a fine background for one of the most beautiful and popular valleys in the province.

Shopping Services: Restaurants, shops, first-aid, cinema

Credit Cards: AE, VISA, Mastercard

Child Care: Kindergarten

Lodging: 21 Hotels/pensions-743 beds, plus chalets/apartments, private homes

Transportation: Gateway Airports: Milan; Turin; Geneva

Closest Provincial City: Aosta 63 km (39 mi)

By Auto from Airport: Motorway from gateway airport to Ayas Valley

By Bus from Airport: Bus services from Milan, Turin, Verres

By Train: Nearest railway station: Verres, 27 km (17 mi) to Ayas

Bus service from Verres, Turin, Milan to Ayas

Best Deal: Network of lifts from three resorts in Ayas Valley, and with adjoining Valley of Gressoney

Other Information: Reliable snow conditions plus good ski facilities provide skiers with a wide slope variety

ITALY

COURMAYEUR
Tourist Office: COURMAYEUR APT
P. le Monte Bianco 13-CAP 11013
Courmayeur (AO) Italy
Telephone: (39) (165) 842060 Fax: (39) (165) 842072

COMPAGNIE DES ALPES

AOSTA-VALLEY (Languages Italian and French) Courmayeur lies at the foot of Mont Blanc in the Aosta Valley, on the Swiss and French borders of Italy. As many as 14 peaks in the Mont Blanc range exceed 4,000 m (13,000 ft). Much of Courmayeur's Roman background is reflected in local castles, churches and monuments.

Elevation: Base/Village: 1,224 m (4,068 ft); Top: 3,462 m (11,358 ft)

Vertical: 2,238 m (7,342 ft)

Longest Run: 7 km (4.3 mi)

Terrain: 100 km (62 mi) of downhill runs on 25 trails. Two major ski areas: the Checrouit-Val Veny, and the Mont Blanc slopes; 20% beg., 45% intermed., 25% adv., 10% expert

Skiing Circus: Inter-country skiing; Mont Blanc slopes from Courmayeur, Italy to Chamonix, France

Lifts: 25

Types: 7 Cableways; 1 Gondola; 9 Chairlifts; 8 Surface

Lift Capacity: 23,560 p/h resort

Ski Season: December-April

Cross Country: 25 km (16 mi); Circuits in Val Ferret (4), Val Veny and Dolonne; rentals/instruction available

Ski School: 100 instructors, lessons Dh and XC

Mountain Restaurants: 20

Other Winter Activities: Casino in Chamonix (22 km); fitness center; ice skating/artificial; indoor swimming in Pri St. Didier (5 km); indoor tennis; squash

Shopping/Services: 1 cinema, 1 discotheque, first-aid, many fine shops; bars, cafes, banks, post-office

Credit Cards: AE, MC, VISA, EuroCard, Circus

Child Care: Ski School-Kinderheim;
Tele: 165/846545 (or) 0338/2061307

Lodging: 2,912 beds; 71 hotels, plus apartments

Transportation: Gateway Airport: Geneva 109 km (66 mi); Milan 252 km (159 mi); Turin 150 km

Closest Provincial City: Aosta 36 km (24 mi)

By Auto from airport: Major highways access resort

By Bus from airport: Courmayeur Bus Station (0165/842031)

By Train: Railway station in Pri St. Didier, 5 km from Courmayeur; Train from Milan to St. Didier bus to Courmayeur. Bus Geneva-Courmayeur

Courmayeur is the dominant village on the Italian side of Mount Blanc.

ITALY

CERVINIA/VALTOURNENCHE
BREUIL-CERVINIA
APT
Via Carrel, 29-CAP 11021, Aosta, Italy
Telephone: (39) (166) 949136 Fax: 969730

Elevation: Base/Village: 2,050 m (6,721 ft); Top: 3,492 m (11,449 ft)

Vertical: 1,442 m (4,728 ft)

Longest Run: 8.0 km (4.7 mi)

Terrain: 110 km (62 mi) of downhill runs at Cervinia interconnects with 40 km (25 mi) of runs at Valtournenche; snowmaking equipment

Skiing Circus: International ski: (Cervinia, Italy-Zermatt, Switzerland) Villages: Cervinia-Valtournenche interconnected lift network

Lifts: 33

Types: 4 Cableways; 3 Gondolas; 11 Chairlifts; 15 Surface

Lift Capacity: 25,000 p/h Cervinia/Valtournenche

Ski Season: December-April

Summer Skiing: May to November on Plateau Rosa

Cross Country: 19.5 km total X-C ski trials (6.5 km at Cervinia, 13 km at Valtournenche)

Ski School: Three schools-120 instructors

LA THUILE
LA THUILE-A.P.T.
Via Collomb 4 CAP 11016
Aosta, Italy
Telephone: (39) (165) 884179 Fax: (39) (165) 885196

Elevation: Base/Village: 1,441 m (4,728 ft); Top: 2,650 m (8,694 ft)

Vertical: 1,209 m (3,967 ft)

Terrain: 135 km (85 mi) of downhill slopes with 61 downhill ski runs-for beginner to advanced intermediate skiers; 44% beginner, 36% intermediate; 20% advanced

Skiing Circus: International skiing: La Thuile, Italy-La Rosiere, France

Lifts: 35

Types: 1 Cableway; 16 Chairlifts; 18 Surface

Lift Capacity: 41,299 p/h resort

Ski Season: Dec.-April 25

Summer Skiing: At Plateau Rosa Glacier, Cervinia

Cross Country: 10 km; Excursion and cross country ring

Ski School: 50 instructors

Other Winter Activities: Helicopter skiing; squash; indoor bowling; sauna, two swimming pools, gym; amusement arcade

AOSTA-VALLEY (Languages Italian and French)
A world famous ski resort in the Western Alps, near the Italian-Swiss border. Skiing from Cervinia to Zermatt, Switzerland is popular, as is the return ski from Zermatt via Europe's highest cableway, the "Klein Matterhorn," at 3,820 m (12,533 ft). Cervinia is among the highest resorts in the Alps with good snow/sun conditions.

Mountain Restaurants: 20

Other Winter Activities: Helicopter skiing; ice skating/natural; indoor swimming; paragliding; horses; sauna

Après-Ski: Bars, 6 discos, cafes, cinemas

Shopping/Services: Grocery, services, many shops

Credit Cards: AE, DC, MC, VISA

Child Care: Kindergartens; Kid's ski school; Nursery

Lodging: 3,500 beds; 45 Hotels-Cervinia; 18 Hotels-Valtournenche, plus chalets, apartments, guest houses

Transportation: Gateway Airport: Milan 200 km (125 mi); Turin 120 km (75 mi); Geneva 220 km (137 mi)

Closest Provincial City: Aosta 50 km (31 mi)

By Auto from airport: From Milan or Turin, autostrada to Cervinia exit. From Geneva via the Mont Blanc tunnel and the Aosta motorway

By Train: Italian State Railways (FS) Milan-Turin Intercity train; Turin to Chatillon-27 km to Cervinia by local bus

Best Deal: Ski connection between Cervinia and Zermatt, Switzerland

AOSTA VALLEY (Language Italian and French)
La Thuile is located in the western Alps, south of Courmayeur in the Mont Blanc range, near the French/Italian border at the Little Saint Bernard pass. This modern well equipped resort is in a glen, sheltered by the massif of the Mont Blanc, and enjoys a dry and sunny climate with lots of snow.

Après-Ski: Disco, casino at St. Vincent

Shopping Services: Restaurants, shops, first-aid

Credit Cards: AE, DC, VISA

Lodging: 2,087 beds; 14 hotels/pensions/residences

Transportation: Gateway Airports: Turin; Milan; Geneva

Closest Provincial City: Aosta 40 km (25 mi)

By Auto from Airport: Motorway from gateway airports

By Train: Nearest railway station: Pre-Saint-Didier, 10 km (6 mi), then bus service to La Thuile

Bus service from Pre-Saint-Didier to Milan and Turin

Other Information: Day trip to France or Courmayeur; Interconnected lift system, La Thuile-La Rosiere, France with a unique ski pass

©Publishers Group International, 1998

ITALY

GRESSONEY
GRESSONEY-ST. JEAN-A.P.T.
Villa Margherita-CAP 11025, Aosta, Italy
Telephone: (39) (125) 366143 Fax: (39) (125) 366323
(39) (125) 355185 (39) (125) 355895

Elevation: Base/Village: 4,455 m (1,637 ft); Top: 8,946 m (2,861 ft)

Vertical: 4,491 m (1,224 ft)

Terrain: 90 km (56 mi) of downhill slopes, which provide a good variety of skiing with reliable snow conditions. 35% beginner, 55% intermediate, 10% advanced

Skiing Circus: Three ski areas in the Gressoney valley are linked by bus and lifts, and with neighboring Ayas-the "Monterosa ski" installations complex.

Lifts: 16

Types: 3 Cableways; 4 Chairlifts (4 doubles); 9 Surface

Lift Capacity: 11,240 p/h resort

Ski Season: Dec.-April

Summer Skiing: Nearby-Plateau Rosa (May-Nov.)

Cross Country: 25 km of trails

Ski School: Two schools, 40 instructors (Gressoney-La Trinite, Gressoney-St. Jean)

Other Winter Activities: Fitness center; helicopter skiing; hiking; ice skating/natural; indoor swimming; mono-skiing; sauna; snowboarding

PILA
AOSTA-Regional Tourist Office
3-CAP 11100 Piazza Chanoux 8
Aosta, Italy
Telephone: (39) (165) 236627 Fax: (39) (165) 34657

Elevation: Base/Village: 1,750 m (5,741 ft); Top: 2,703 m (8,868 ft)

Vertical: 953 m (3,127 ft)

Terrain: 70 km (44 mi) of downhill runs with good open skiing and wide wooded glades. Strong intermediate area; 25% beginner, 55% intermediate, 20% advanced

Skiing Circus: Good location for excursions to Courmayeur, Cervina-Zermatt, Chamonix

Lifts: 13

Types: 2 Cableways; 9 Chairlifts; 2 Surface

Lift Capacity: 16,300 p/h resort

Ski Season: Dec.-April

Summer Skiing: Close to plateau Rosa Glaciers

Cross Country: 10 km ski and excursion terrain

Ski School: 110 instructors

Mountain Restaurants: Yes

Other Winter Activities: Ice skating/natural; indoor swimming (Aosta); indoor tennis (Aosta); gliding; snowboarding

AOSTA VALLEY
Gressoney valley has three separate ski areas linked by a network of lifts and by buses. Gressoney-St. Jean is the largest, 5 km further is Gressoney La Trinite and at the head of the valley another 3 km away is Stavel. The valley stretches as far as the slopes of Mont Rosa where glaciers form a stunning background.

Après-Ski: Bars, discos, casino at St. Vincent (40 km), folklore evenings

Shopping Services: First-aid, restaurants, many shops

Credit Cards: AE, VISA; most major American credit cards are honored

Child Care: Contact/call Tourist Office

Lodging: Gressoney-St. Jean—15 hotels/pensions, 488 beds; Gressoney-La Trinte—12 hotels, 728 beds

Transportation: Gateway Airports: Milan; Turin; Geneva

Closest Provincial City: Aosta 85 km (53 mi)

By Auto from Airport: Motorway from airports, exit at Pont St. Martin, local road to Gressoney Valley

By Train: R.R. station in Pont St. Martin-trains from all gateway cities, bus 29 km (18 mi) to Gressoney

Best Deal: Skiing facilities at Gressoney form a single network with those of adjoining Ayas Valley

Other Information: Reliable snow conditions. Ancient German dialect is still spoken in Gressoney, as well as Italian and French. Many German/Swiss traditions

AOSTA VALLEY
Pila is 18 km southwest of Aosta, which is the capital of the region, and is surrounded by the highest peaks of the Alps: Mont Blanc, Mont Rosa, the Matterhorn and the Gran Paradiso range. It is a modern, purpose built resort with excellent facilities, and a fine network of ski lifts and slopes.

Après-Ski: Discos, casino at St. Vincent

Shopping Services: Cinema (Aosta), first-aid, shops

Credit Cards: AE, VISA; Most major American credit cards honored

Lodging: 2,966+ beds; Pila: 16 hotels, 1,338 beds; Aosta: 33 hotels, 1,918 beds

Transportation: Gateway Airport: Turin; Milan, Geneva

Closest Provincial City: Aosta 18 km (11 mi)

By Auto from Airport: Motorway from Gateway airports, cableway from Aosta 18 km (11 mi) to Pila Resort

By Train: Railway station in Aosta, 18 km (11 mi) from resort

Other Information: North facing slopes ensure good snow conditions. Southern location in the province provides mild temperatures. Choice of various ski resorts because of central location. Evening activity in Aosta

ITALY

Downtime in Sestriere. Photo: Italian Government Travel Office

BARDONECCHIA*
BARDONECCHIA-A.P.T.
Viale della Vittoria 44-CAP 10052
Bardonecchia (TO), Italy
Telephone: (39) (122) 99032 Fax: (39) (125) 424084

Elevation: Base/Village: 1,312 m (4,304 ft); Top: 2,747 m (9,022 ft)

Vertical: 1,437 m (4,718 ft)

Terrain: 140 km of downhill slopes; 25% beginner, 55% intermediate, 20% advanced

Lifts: 27

Types: 6 Chairlifts; 21 Surface

Lift Capacity: 22,000 p/h resort

Ski Season: December-April

Summer Skiing: Limited glacier skiing (June-August)

Cross Country: 32 km of cross country ski trails

Ski School: 2 schools-100 instructors

Mountain Restaurants: Yes

Other Winter Activities: Hiking; ice skating/natural; indoor tennis; sauna; ice hockey; horse riding; bowling

PIEDMONT
Bardonecchia is in the southwestern Alps just before the Frejus Tunnel which connects Italy and France. Top level skiing is found on the majestic slalom pistes of this Val di Susa resort.

Après-Ski: Bars, 3 discos, cafes, cinema

Shopping/Services: Shops

Credit Cards: AE, VISA; Most major credit cards honored

Child Care: Kindergartens

Lodging: 1,500 beds; 29 hotels and pensions plus additional 31 chalets/apartments—250 beds

Transportation: Gateway Airports: Turin; Milan

Closest Provincial City: Torino (93 km)

By auto from airport: Milan-Turin-Bardonecchia—via Motorway

By Train: Service from both Turin and Milan

Best Deal: Skiing at nearby Italian resorts using "Milky Way Pass"; 12 km from France

©Publishers Group International, 1998

ITALY

SESTRIERE*
SESTRIERE-A.P.T.
Piazza G. Agnelli, 4-CAP 10058
Sestriere, (TO) Italy
Telephone: (39) (122) 755444 Fax: (39) (122) 755171

Elevation: Base/Village: 2,035 m (6,666 ft); Top: 2,823 m (9,262 ft)

Vertical: 788 m (2,585 ft)

Longest Run: 5-8 km (3.1-5.0 mi)

Terrain: 400 km of downhill slopes; 18% beginner, 25% intermediate, 38% advanced, 19% expert

Skiing Circus: "Milky Way Pass"—Sestriere, Sauze d'Oulx, Sansicario, Cesana and Claviere Resorts

Lifts: 66

Types: 1 Gondola; 25 Chairlifts; 40 T-bars

Lift Capacity: 71,000 p/h resort

Ski Season: 15 November-30 April, 1998
Promotion: 11/1-12/24; 3/24-3/30; 4/14-4/30

Summer Skiing: No

Cross Country: 13 km of cross country trails

Ski School: 130 Instructors

Mountain Restaurants: 21 on the Milky Way

Other Winter Activities: Ice skating/natural; fitness center; sauna; ice hockey; paragliding; helicopter skiing; indoor tennis, mono-skiing; snowboarding; go-karts on ice; ski-doo & motor sled rental; NASTAR course

PIEDMONT
Sestriere, originally created by Fiat, is a modern well designed ski resort in the Val Dí Susa area of the Southwestern Alps near the Italian/French border. Reliable snow, challenging advanced terrain, and a warm sunny climate attract a sophisticated, international clientele.

Après-Ski: 1 disco, 12 bars; 2 piano bars; folklore evenings

Shopping Services: Cinema, first-aid, numerous shops: antique, tailor, sporting goods, jewelry, perfume, confectionery

Credit Cards: AE, MC, VISA, EC, CARTA-SI; Major credit cards honored at hotels; VISA for ski passes

Child Care: Kid's ski school: Yes. Nursery: No

Lodging: 2,000 beds; 1,137 rooms; 15 hotels/pensions; 4,000 chalet/apartments-15,000 beds

Transportation: Gateway Airport: Turin; Milan

Closest Provincial City: Turin 100 km (56 mi)

From Airport: Freyus Motorway-Turin-Sestriere 112 km

Ski Bus: from Oulx 22 km, from Torino 100km

By Train: Svc. from Oulx 22 km. On the line Rome-Paris

Best Deal: "Milky Way" Ski Pass-6 resorts, 66+ lifts, ski from Cesana/Claviere to French area of Montgenevre. Promotion Season—(see Ski Season).

LIMONE PIEMONTE*
CUNEO A.P.T.
Limone Piemonte
Piazza Municipio-CAP 12015-Italy
Telephone: (39) (171) 92101 Fax: (39) (171) 927064

Elevation: Base/Village: 1,010 m (3,305 ft); Top: 2,050 m (6,724 ft)

Vertical: 1,005 m (3,298 ft)

Terrain: 100 km (62 mi) of downhill slopes, suitable for beginners to avanced intermediates

Skiing Circus: "White Reserve Ski Pass"—interconnecting lifts and ski runs—3 resorts: Limone, Colle de Tenda, and Limonetto

Lifts: 29

Types: 5 Chairlifts; 24 Surface

Lift Capacity: 22,000 p/h resort

Ski Season: Dec.-April

Cross Country: 6 km cross country trails/course

Ski School: 120 instructors

Après-Ski: Bars, discos, cafes, 1 cinema

Shopping Services: Good variety of shops, restaurants and bars

PIEDMONT
Limone lies at the foot of the north-west facing slopes of the Maritime Alps in the Southern Alps close to the French border. Lift systems link three valleys and the resorts of Limone, Colle di Tenda and Limonetto.

Credit Cards: Most major American credit cards honored

Lodging: 21 Hotels, 7 residences, 1 camping area

Transportation: Gateway Airport: Turin 110 km (68 mi); Milan 240 km (149 mi)

Closest Provincial City: Cuneo 27 km (17 mi)

By Auto from Airport: Motorway Milan-Turin-Cuneo-Limone (110 km (68 mi)-Turin, 240 km (150 mi)-Milan)

By Train: FS (State Train)-Station in Limone-From Turin and Milan-Genova-Veutimiglio-Nice

Best Deal: 80 km ski tour through the three valleys—"White Reserve"

Other Information: Mild temperatures, plenty of sunshine. 80 km (50 mi) from San Remo (Italian Riveria)

ITALY

SAUZE D'OULX*
SAUZE D'OULX-A.P.T.
Piazza Assietta 18-CAP 10050
Sauze d'Oulx (TO) Italy
Telephone: (39) (122) 858009 Fax: (39) (122) 850497

Elevation: Base/Village: 1,510 m (4,954 ft); Top: 2,601 m (8,532 ft)

Vertical: 1,091 m (3,579 ft)

Longest Run: 12.0 km (7.5 mi)

Terrain: 120 km (75 mi) of downhill slopes; 25% beginner, 55% intermediate, 20% advanced

Skiing Circus: "Milky Way Pass"-Sauze d'Oulx, Sestriere, Sansicario, Cesana-Claviere, and Montgenevre in France

Lifts: 22 (66 in entire Milky Way)

Types: 11 Chairlifts; 11 Surface

Lift Capacity: 24,339 p/h resort

Ski Season: December-April

Cross Country: 3 km of trails

Ski School: 3 ski schools-154 instructors

Mountain Restaurants: 11

Other Winter Activities: Ice skating/artificial; sauna; ice hockey; helicopter skiing; hiking; indoor tennis; mono-skiing; snowboarding; ski touring; ski bike

PIEDMONT
Sauze d'Oulx is situated along the southwestern Alps and is easily accessible. A successful combination of pleasant atmosphere and the alliance with other nearby Italian and French ski resorts provide a variety of skiing opportunities.

Après-Ski: 25 bars, 4 discos, 7 cafes, cinema, piano bars, restaurants, bowling, billiards, massages, flippers

Shopping/Services: Boutiques, handcraft, haberdashery, clothes, sports, jewelry, supermarkets

Credit Cards: AE, MC, VISA, DC, EC

Child Care: Kid's ski school from age 3; Child care ages 0 months - 12 years, L30,000 p/½d; L50,000 p/d; L1,160,000 p/6 days

Lodging: 1,833 Beds; 33 hotels plus chalets/apartments

Transportation: Gateway Airport: Intern. Airport: Milan (Malpensa-Lenate); Torino (Caselle)

Closest Provincial City: Turin 80 km (50 mi)

By Auto from airport: Easy access by motorway-Milan-Turin-Oulx—SS 24 from Oulx to Sauze D'Oulx, 83 km

Ski Bus: Yes—Free village shuttle service

By Train: Service from both Turin and Milan (Torino-Modane-Paris Line) to Oulx

Transfer needed to bus or train to train—yes

Best Deal: "Milky Way" Ski Pass-includes five resorts, more than 66 lifts

MACUGNAGA-MONTE ROSA*
A.P.T. dell'Ossola-Macugnaga
Piazza Municipio-CAP 28030
Macugnaga (VB), Italy
Telephone: (39) (324) 65119 Fax: (39) (324) 65119

Elevation: Base/Village: 1,320 m (4,331 ft.); Top: 2,846 m (9,360 ft)

Vertical: 1,526 m (5,031 ft)

Longest Run: 4.5 km

Terrain: Variety for all levels—beginner to advanced; 50% beginner, 40% intermediate, 10% advanced

Skiing Circus: None; day tour to Saas Fee

Lifts: 12

Types: 2 Cableways; 2 Chairlifts; 8 Surface

Lift Capacity: 7,000 p/h resort

Ski Season: December-April (often November-May)

Summer Skiing: None

Cross Country: 21 km of trails (green trails to red)

Ski School: 2 schools-50 instructors

Mountain Restaurants: Five

Other Winter Activities: Ice skating/natural; ice hockey; paragliding; sauna; snowboarding; mountaineering; hiking: helicopter skiing; fitness center

PIEDMONT
Macugnaga is located in the western Alps, the northwest section of the Italian peninsula. The resort is divided into two ski areas, Staffa and Pecetto. An attractive alpine village with a lot of charm. Close enough to the Italian/Swiss border, so that a day trip to Saas Fee in Switzerland can be enjoyed.

Après-Ski: Discos, cafes, bars

Shopping/Services: Several shopping centers; also close to Switzerland for day trips.

Credit Cards: AE, MC, VISA; Most major credit cards honored

Lodging: 527 beds; 15 hotels and pensions; 350 chalets/apartments with additional 2,580 beds

Transportation: Gateway International Airport: Milan-Malp.; Local Airport: Milano-Linate

Closest Provincial City: Verbania 60 km (36 mi)

By Auto from airport: Motorway from Milan or Turin (3 hrs)—National Route 110 km

By Ski Bus from airport: Same route as auto

Other Information: Feb.-April averages 9 hours sunshine a day; snowmaking on Pecetto ski area

©Publishers Group International, 1998

ITALY

CLAVIERE-CESANA TORINESE*
CLAVIERE-CESANA TORINESE-A.P.T.
Via Nazionale, 30-CAP 10050
Claviere, (TO) Italy
Telephone: (39) (122) 878856

Elevation: Base/Village: Claviere 1,760 m (5,984 ft); Casana: 1350 m Top: 2,708 m (8,886 ft)

Vertical: 948 m (2,902 ft)

Terrain: 85 km of downhill ski terrain for all levels of abilities, but especially for the intermediate to advanced skier; 20% beginner, 50% intermediate, 30% advanced

Skiing Circus: "Milky Way" Pass-six resorts, including linked skiing with Montgenevre in France

Lifts: 12

Types: 4 Chairlifts; 8 Surface

Ski Season: Dec.-April

Summer Skiing: June-August glacier skiing

Cross Country: 27 km of ski trails (Cesana & Clariere)

Ski School: Three Schools/100 Instructors

Mountain Restaurants: Yes

Other Winter Activities: Hiking; ice skating/natural; sauna; ice hockey; bob run

LIVIGNO
TOURIST OFFICE: LIVIGNO
A.P.T.M. Livigno-Via DaLa Gesa 65
23030 Livigno Sondrio, Italy
Telephone: (39) (342) 996379 Fax: (39) (342) 996881

Elevation: Base/Village: 1,816 m (5,958 ft); Top: 3,000 m (9,842 ft)

Vertical: 1,184 m (3,884 ft)

Longest Run: 7 km (5 mi) ("Bellavista")

Terrain: 100 km of runs; skiable area 70 square km; 40% beginner, 50% intermediate, 10% advanced

Skiing Circus: The "Alta Valtellina Ski Pass" is valid for the lifts of: Bormio S. Caterina-Valfurva, Livigno, Val Di Dentro, Val Di Sotto

Lifts: 30

Types: 3 Gondolas; 11 Chairlifts (6 h-s quads, 2 triple, 3 doubles); 16 Skilifts

Lift Capacity: 40,000 p/h resort

Ski Season: End of Nov.-beginning of May

Summer Skiing: Diavolezza-Stelvio; Season: End of May-beginning of November

Cross Country: 42 km (26 mi) trails

Ski School: Five; 100-120 Instructors (4 Alpine, 1 X/C)

Mountain Restaurants: Yes-five

Other Winter Activities: Fitness center; horse drawn sleigh; ice skating; mono-skiing; sauna; snowboarding; sleigh riding; horse riding; mountaineering; paragliding; telemark; curling; walks on the snow; motorscooters

PIEDMONT
Claviere-Cesana Torinese are two mountain villages situated high in the Susa valley in the Southwestern Alps on the Italian/French border. The resort is very accessible, only 1½ hours from the Turin airport. It has challenging ski terrain, good facilities, and direct acess to the facilities of the linked resorts around it.

Après-Ski: Bars, pubs, discos, cafes, cinema in Sansicario

Shopping Services: Shops, first-aid, night club

Credit Cards: AE, EC, MC, VISA; Most major American credit cards honored

Child Care: Kindergarten (in Sansicario)

Lodging: 1,050 beds; 18 hotels/pensions (Claviere & Cesana)

Transportation: Gateway Airport: Turin; Milan

Closest Provincial City: Torino 93 km (58 mi)

By Auto from Airport: Motorway-Milan or Turin to Claviere-Cesana Torinese

By Train: Service from both Torino and Milan

Best Deal: "Milky Way" ski pass—includes six resorts, including interconnected lifts with Montgenevre Resort in France

LOMBARDY
Livigno is in the central Alps near the Italian-Swiss border in the Po Valley, heart of the "Italian Tibet" Valley. The modern hotels, facilities and residences of this popular resort blend well with buildings dating back to the sixteenth century.

Après-Ski: Discos, cafes, cinema, piano bar, video games

Shopping/Services: First aid; mountain dining; 250 duty free shops in Livigno

Credit Cards: AE, DC, MC, VISA

Child Care: Yes

Lodging: 4,800 beds; 100 hotels, plus 922 extra hotel facilities with over 3,800 beds nearby. Total 8,600

Transportation: Gateway Airport: Milan (3½-4 hrs)

Closest Provincial City: Sondrio 95 km (60 mi)

By Auto from airport: 3½-4 hrs-Milano-Lecco-Colico-Sondrio-Tirano-Bormio-Livigno

By Bus from airport: 4 hrs

By Train: To Tirano-fast 2½ hrs

Train or Bus Information: Write/call tourist office

Best Deal: With a ski pass for more than 6 days it is possible to ski one day in St. Moritz, Switzerland (Pool Agob ski lifts) against reimbursement for one day. "Ski Pass Alta Valtellina" includes Bormio, S. Caterina Valfurva, Valdidentro and Valdisotto.

Other Information: From January-April the village area averages 9 hours of sunshine a day. Duty free area

ITALY

BORMIO
APT-VALTELLINA-OFFICE of BORMIO
Via Roma 131/B
23032 Bormio (So) Italy (Regional Capital: Milan)
Telephone: (39) (342) 903300 Fax: (39) (342) 904696

Elevation: Base/Village: 1,225 m (4,019 ft); Top: 3,012 m (9,882 ft)

Vertical: 1,787 m (5,862 ft)

Longest Run: 6 km (3.7 mi)

Terrain: 33 km (20 mi) of marked runs—variety of terrain; 30% beginner, 40% intermed., 30% advanced

Skiing Circus: The "Alta Valtellina Ski Pass" is valid for the lifts of: Bormio, Santa Caterina Valfurva, Livigno, S. Colombano (Valdidentro & Valdisotto) ski areas

Lifts: 16

Types: 2 Cable Cars; 1 Gondola; 7 Chairlifts (1 triple, 5 doubles, 1 single); 7 Surface

Lift Capacity: 15,724 p/h, Bormio

Ski Season: December through April
High Season: 12/19-1/6, 1/30-4/9
Low Season: until 12/18, 1/7-1/29, 4/9-closing

Summer Skiing: Passo Stelvio (20 km from Bormio) End May-Beg. Nov.

Cross Country: 12.5 km (8 mi).

Ski School: 6 alpine, 1 X-C—80/100 instructors

S. CATERINA VALFURVA
SONDRIO-A.P.T.
Via C. Battisti, 12-CAP 23100
Sondrio, Italy
Telephone: (39) (342) 512500

Elevation: Base/Village: 1,738 m (5,699 ft); Top: 2,725 m (8,938 ft)

Vertical: 987 m (3,237 ft)

Terrain: Reliable snow; terrain for all levels of skier ability, good for beginners to intermediates

Skiing Circus: "Alta Valtellina Ski Pass" valid for the lifts of: S. Caterina, Bormio, Livigno, Valdidento, Val Di Sotto

Lifts: 8

Types: 7 Chairlifts; 1 Surface

Lift Capacity: 7,065 p/h resort

Ski Season: December-April

Summer Skiing: May-November at Passo Stelvio 30 km (19 mi)

Cross Country: 18 km of trails, good high mountain touring; good cross country facilities

Ski School: One school-50 instructors

Mountain Restaurants: Five

LOMBARDY (Central Alps)
Bormio has been an internationally renowned resort since hosting the 1985 Alpine Ski World Championship. It is widely recognized for its spa/thermal treatments. Much of Bormio's Romanesque architecture and history have been preserved in local museums, churches, and palaces.

Mountain Restaurants: Yes

Other Winter Activities: Ice skating/artificial; mono-skiing; snowboarding; fitness center; indoor swimming; sauna; squash; horse riding; climbing; indoor tennis

Après-Ski: Discos, cafes, restaurants; sauna

Shopping/Services: Many shops, drug stores, cinema, first-aid, thermal-treatments, folklore evenings

Credit Cards: Most major credit cards accepted

Lodging: 3,491 beds; 54 hotels from one to four stars plus apartments and private homes

Transportation: Gateway Airport: Milan 200 km

Closest Provincial City: Sondrio 64 km (40 mi)

By Auto from airport: 200 km (125 mi), Milan-Lecco-Colico (motorway) Sondrio-Bormio (Provincial rd.)

By Ski Bus from airport: Yes; bus information: Tele: Bormio (342) 910105 & 905090 Milan: (286) 464854

Other Information: Snowmaking. The alpine range protects Bormio from the cold northern wind - clear, dry weather

LOMBARDY
This charming ski resort in the central Alps-Tresero range, lies about 12 km south-east of Bormio. S. Caterina gained international attention when it hosted the Women's Downhill Race in the 1985 Alpine World Championships.

Other Winter Activities: Hiking; ice skating/natural; indoor swimming; sauna; sleigh riding; ice hockey

Après-Ski: Bars, discos, night clubs/bands

Shopping/Services: First-Aid, shops

Credit Cards: AE, MC, VISA; most major credit cards honored

Lodging: 1,206 beds in 23 hotels and pensions plus additional 12 Holiday Houses with 534 beds

Transportation: Gateway Airport: Milan

Closest Provincial City: Sondrio 76 km (47 mi)

By Auto from airport: 190 km (118 mi); Milan-Lecco-Colico-Sondrio-S. Caterina Highway

By Train from Milan: Milan-Sondrio-Tirano

By Bus from Tirano: Tirano-Bormio-S. Caterina

Best Deal: Ski circus; Bormio's skiing is close; convenient bus service between the two resorts

Other Information: Long lasting snow on the mainly north facing slopes

©Publishers Group International, 1998

ITALY

ALTOPIANO DI ASIAGO 7 COMUNI*
A.P.T. "ASIAGO 7 COMUNI" Via Stazione, 5
36012 Asiago (VI) Italy
Telephone: (39) (424) 462221 Fax: (39) (424) 462445

VENETO
Asiago is close to the Trentino Region and the Dolomites. The seven member comuni association are: Asiago, Conco, Enego, Foza Gallio, Lusiana, Roana and Rotzo.

Elevation: Base/Village: 1,000 m (3,181 ft); Top: 2,336 m (7,664 ft)
Vertical: 1,336 m (4,383 ft)
Longest Run: 2.5 km (1.6 mi)
Terrain: 100 km of downhill slopes; Beginner-intermediates; Good novice terrain for learning
Lifts: 69
Types: 5 Chairlifts (4 doubles, 1 single); 64 Surface (2 T-bars, 62 platters)
Lift Capacity: 50,500 p/h resort
Ski Season: Dec. 8-April 30
Cross Country: 250 km of cross country trails and excursion terrain
Ski School: Nine ski schools
Mountain Restaurants: 15
Other Winter Activities: Ice skating/natural; 3 indoor swimming; indoor tennis; tourist airport; tobogganing

Après-Ski: 10 Discos, 10 cafes, 140 bars, 2 ice bars
Shopping Services: Shops-complete variety, first-aid, cinema
Credit Cards: AE, DC, MC, VISA, Euro Card
Child Care: Contact tourist office (424) 462221
Lodging: The Asiago table-land has 100 hotels; 9,761 rooms; 22,000 beds in all categories—flats, camps, etc.
Transportation: Gateway Airport: Venice
Local Airport: Asiago
Closest Provincial City: Vicenza 55 km (34 mi)
By Auto from Airport: Motorway: Venezia-Vicenza-Asiago
By Train: Venice to Vicenza, then bus: Vicenza to Asiago
Best Deal: Reduced rates in January (White Week) and March

ARABBA
A.P.T. Dolomite
Piazzetta S. Francesco 8-CAP 32043
Cortina d'Ampezzo (BL) Italy
Telephone: (39) (436) 79130 Fax: (39) (436) 79300

VENETO
Arabba is located in the Eastern alpine range, near the Sella Massif on its south-eastern side, and where the Dolomite passes of Falzarego, Pordoi, Campolongo and Fedaia meet. It is a splendid resort with good facilities for skiers, and provides excellent skiing on challenging runs.

Elevation: Base/Village: 1,600 m (5,249 ft); Top: 2,500 m (8,302 ft)
Vertical: 900 m (2,953 ft)
Terrain: 50 km (31 mi) of downhill runs providing excellent skiing for all ability levels; 25% beginner, 55% intermediate, 20% advanced
Skiing Circus: Sella Ronda—4 valleys, 30 km (Fassa, Livinallongo, Badia and Gardena); Dolomite Super Ski Pass
Lifts: 27
Types: 2 Cableways; 9 Chairlifts; 15 Surface
Lift Capacity: 23,000 p/h resort
Ski Season: December-May
Cross Country: 2 km. of cross-country trails
Ski School: 25 Instructors
Mountain Restaurants: Yes
Other Winter Activities: Hiking; ice skating/natural; indoor swimming; sauna; ice hockey

Après-Ski: Discos, cafes
Shopping/Services: First-Aid, various shops
Credit Cards: AE, MC, VISA
Lodging: 3,553 beds; 19 hotels and pensions plus some chalets/apartments
Transportation: Gateway Airport: Venice
Closest Provincial City: Belluno 65 km (40 mi)
By Auto from airport: Motorway-approx. 150 km (93 mi) Venice to Arabba; Arabba is approximately 20 km southwest of Cortina in the Dolomite mountains
By Train: Requires transfer to bus for trip to Arabba
Best Deal: Dolomite Super Ski Pass
Other Information: During December and January the sun is limited to 3-4 hours per day, but from February on, the hours of sunshine are much longer; a "must" is the cable car ride up to Porta Vescovo for its superb view of the Marmolada

ITALY

CORTINA D'AMPEZZO

A.P.T. Dolomite, Piazzetta S. Francesco 8-CAP 32043
Cortina d'Ampezzo (BL) Italy
Telephone: (39) (436) 3231 Fax: (39) (436) 3235

Elevation: Base/Village: 1,224 m (4,015 ft);
Top: 3,243 m (10,640 ft)

Vertical: 2,019 m (6,624 ft)

Terrain: 110 km (60 mi) (60 km-38 mi snowmaking) of downhill slopes with a wide variety of terrain. 50% beginner, 40% intermediate, 10% advanced

Skiing Circus: Dolomite Superski Pass-biggest ski circuit in the world, 464 lifts, 1,180 km (737 mi) ski runs, in 12 valleys with 43 ski centers and 491 km (306 mi)

Lifts: 39

Types: 5 Cableways; 22 Chairlifts; 10 Surface

Lift Capacity: 45,057 p/h resort

Ski Season: December-April

Cross Country: 58 km (36 mi) of cross country trails and loops plus a wide variety of off-piste terrain

Ski School: 3 schools—250 Dh and 24 X-C instructors

Mountain Restaurants: 20

Other Winter Activities: Curling; hiking; horse drawn sleigh; ice skating/at the Olympic Stadium (2); indoor swimming; indoor tennis; sauna; sleigh riding; sports center; ice hockey; bobsled run; tobogganing; taxi-bob; snowrafting; fitness; sleddog and dog-trekking school;

VENETO (Capital-Venice)
Host of the 1956 Winter Olympics, Cortina attained international recognition as an elegant ski resort. Four Dolomite mtn. peaks shield Cortina while providing a world class ski area. A cosmopolitan atmosphere combined with great skiing plus artistic and cultural events make the resort a mecca ski destination.

polo tournament and horse-show on snow; Women Ski World Cup

Après-Ski: Bars, discos, cafes, concerts, cinema

Shopping/Services: 250 fine shops, boutiques rival those in Milan and Rome; cultural activities, art exhibits, 70 restaurants, 6 banks; Orthopedic Hospital

Credit Cards: AE, DC, MC, VISA

Child Care: Private child care at hotels is available

Lodging: 65 Hotels/4,800 beds from five-star to small pensions—18,000 beds in apartments and pvt. homes

Transportation: Gateway Airport: Venice; Milan

Closest Provincial City: Belluno 71 km (44 mi)

By Auto from airport: Motorway, approx. 160 km (99 mi) to Cortina from Venice (2½ hrs.)

By Bus from airport: Bus from Venice (3 hrs.) or Milan

By Train: Requires transfer to bus for trip to Cortina

Best Deal: Dolomite Superski Pass. The "White Weeks," Jan. 9-Feb. 3, lower rates/special facilities

Other Information: Complimentary shuttle service. Dry climate with long hours of sunshine and plentiful snow. Electronic remote skipass, key-watch and key-card

Not everybody can jump off a cornice in Cortina.   Photo: Best of the Alps

ITALY

Skiers on Marmolada have this view of the Dolomites.

Photo: Italian Government Travel Office

ALPE SIUSI-SCHILIAR*
ALPE DI SIUSI-A.A.S.T.
Wegscheid, 2-CAP 39040
Bolzano, Italy
Telephone: (39) (471) 706333 Fax: (39) (471) 705188

ALTO ADIGE (SOUTH TIROL) *(German and Italian) The stupendous Alpe Siusi and the fabulous rock scenery of the Sciliar which stands above it are located in the western Dolomites close to Val Gardena. This area may be the most characteristic of the Dolomites with its variety of ski terrain.*

Elevation: Base/Village: 900 m (2,953 ft); Top: 2,300 m (7,546 ft)

Vertical: 1,400 m (4,593 ft)

Terrain: 70 km of downhill slopes and snowfields, can accommodate skiers of all ability levels; part of a skiing district of 50 sq. kilometers; 30% beginner, 55% intermediate, 15% advanced

Skiing Circus: Dolomite Super Ski is the biggest ski circuit in the world, 464 cableways and lifts; 1,180 km of ski runs, 12 valleys

Lifts: 23

Lift Capacity: 23,000 p/h resort

Ski Season: Dec.-April

Cross Country: 70 km of trails

Ski School: 4 Schools & snowboarding/125 Instructors

Mountain Restaurants: Yes

Other Winter Activities: Horse drawn sleigh; ice skating/artificial; indoor swimming; indoor tennis; mono-skiing; sauna; snowboarding

Après-Ski: Bars, discos, cafes

Shopping Services: Variety of shops, first-aid

Credit Cards: AE, MC, VISA; Most major American credit cards accepted

Child Care: Kindergarten

Lodging: 116 Hotels, pensions-chalets, apartments, private homes

Transportation: Gateway Airport: Milan; Munich; Venice

Closest Provincial City: Bolzano 28 km (17 mi)

By Auto from Airport: Motorway to Bolzano-Chuisa-Alpe Siusi

By Bus from Airport: Same as car

By Train: Railway to Bolzano, from Bolzano several bus transfers to resort

Best Deal: Dolomite Super Ski Pass White Season (1/7-2/1/97). Low Season: 11/24-12/21/96 and 3/16-4/18/97. Ski Pass: Val Gardena/Alpe DiSiusi

Other Information: Beautiful scenery with unequalled Dolomite landscapes; language and traditions are mainly German

ITALY

FOLGARIDA-MARILLEVA*
A.P.T. VAL DI SOLE PEJO RABBI
Via Marconi, 7
CAPI-38027 Malè (Trentino) Italy
Telephone: (39) (463) 901280 Fax: (39) (463) 901563

Elevation: Base/Village: 900 m (2,953 ft); Top: 2,179 m (7,149 ft)

Vertical: 1,279 m (4,196 ft)

Longest Run: 7 km (4.4 mi)

Terrain: 45 km (32 mi) of marked slopes (29 km snowmaking); 60% beginner, 25% intermediate, 15% advanced

Skiing Circus: Skirama Dolomiti Di Brenta from Marilleva-Folgarida to M. Di Campiglio

Lifts: 24

Types: 4 Gondolas; 15 Chairlifts (1 h-s quad, 4 triples, 10 doubles); 5 Surface

Lift Capacity: 29,000 p/h resort

Ski Season: December-April

Summer Skiing: Passo Tonale/Presena Glacier, 30 km

Cross Country: 120 km (75 mi); Mezzana X-C center

Ski School: 160 Instructors, three schools

Mountain Restaurants: Yes

Other Winter Activities: Fitness center; ice skating; indoor swimming; sauna; snowboarding; telemark

MONTE BONDONE
A.P.T. OF TRENTO
Via Alfieri 4-38100, Trento, Italy
Telephone: (39) (461) 983880
Fax: (39) (461) 984508

Elevation: Base/Village: 1,300 m (4,265 ft); Top: 2,090 m (6,857 ft)

Vertical: 790 m (2,592 ft)

Terrain: 15 km—10 slopes; 40% novice, 50% intermediate, 10% advanced

Skiing Circus: No

Lifts: 9

Types: 1 Gondola; 7 Chairlifts (2 Triples, 4 Doubles, 1 Single); 1 Drag Lift

Lift Capacity: 8,500 p/h resort

Ski Season: December-April

Summer Skiing: No

Cross Country: 26 km, X-C Center - Viote

Ski School: Two—1 downhill with 20 instructors, 1 cross country with 5 instructors

Other Winter Activities: Folklore evenings; ice skating/artificial; mono-skiing; paragliding; snowboarding; horseback riding; horse drawn sleighs

Après-Ski: Bars, discos, ice bar; cafes, concerts

TRENTINO-ALTO-ADIGE
The Folgarida-Marilleva resorts are located in the central Alps-Brenta Dolomite range a part of Val di Sole. Modern ski area in traditional surroundings.

Shopping/Services: Doctor for tourists, discos, cinema, pharmacy, shops

Credit Cards: AE, DC, MC, VISA

Lodging: 35 hotels/3,500 beds; 15,000 apartment beds

Transportation: Gateway Airport: Milan

Closest Provincial city: Trento 66 km (41 mi)

By Auto from airport: Motorway A22 Verona-Brennero to S. Michele-Alto Adige, then National Road N.42 to Val di Sole: Folgarida and Marilleva

By Ski Bus from airport: On Saturdays and Sundays, Jan. 6-March 3; daily during Christmas, bus from Milan

By Train: Milano-Trento on the Italian State Railways (FS), then local train service Trento-Male, then local bus to resorts
Train: FS-Trento 0461/234545; Bus: Atesina 0461/983627; Trento-Male 0461/822725

Best Deal: Skirama: Folgarida-Marilleva-Madonna di Campiglio-Mezzana by a single circuit of cable lifts

Other Information: In Trentino the principal language is Italian, in Alto-Adige language and traditions are German

TRENTINO—ALTO ADIGE
A well known winter resort 15 km from Trento, capitol of the province of Trentino. It is one of the oldest winter sports centers in Italy. Affords a wonderful view of the Adige Valley, Brenta Dolomites, Adamello Glacier, Garda Lake and the Austrian Alps.

Shopping Services: Various shops, markets, drug stores, banks, hospital, etc. in nearby villages & in Trento

Credit Cards: Yes—AE; DC, EC; MC; Visa; Access Card

Child Care: Children's Ski School; Nursery—yes

Lodging: 1,623 beds; 663 rooms; 18 apartments. At Resort: 18 hotels and residence hotels

Transportation: Gateway Airport: Verona; Milan

Closest Provincial City: Trento 15 km

By Auto from Airport: Routes A22 Motorway to Trento, 100 km from Verona, 219 km from Milan

By Train: Venezia, Verona, Milano; Brennero Railway to Trento. Transfer by bus needed from Trenton to resort

Best Deal: Special weekly ticket including: Folgarida, Marilleva, Pejo, Pinzolo, Passo Tonale and Madonna di Campiglio

Other Information: Variety of slopes with snowmaking—many ski competitions. Town of Trento with 102,000 population half-hour by car, beautiful art, Romanesque, Gothic Renaissance monuments and buildings

ITALY

MADONNA DI CAMPIGLIO
Tourist Office: A.P.T.-M. Di Campiglio-
Pinzolo-Val Rendena, Via Pradalago 4
38084 M. Di Campiglio (Trento) Italy
Telephone: (39) (465) 42000 Fax: (39) (465) 40404

TRENTINO-ALTO-ADIGE
Madonna di Campiglio lies in a beautiful, sunny, protected position in the Brenta Dolomites, surrounded by pine forests and lakes in a mountain background. A great variety of skiing in a beautiful setting for all levels of skier ability.

Elevation: Base/Village: 1,550 m (5,085 ft); Top: 2,450 m (8,038 ft)

Vertical: 900 m (2,953 ft)

Longest Run: 7 km (4.4 mi)

Terrain: 90 km (56 mi) slopes in M. di Campiglio, 150 km (93 mi) with Folgarida and Marilleva. Great variety of terrain; 44% beginner, 40% intermediate, 16% advanced

Skiing Circus: Ski circuit-Madonna Di Campiglio-Folgarida-Marilleva

Lifts: 30

Types: 1 Cable car, plus 4 with automatic linking; 15 Chairlifts (2 triples, 11 doubles, 2 four-seats (quads) with automatic linking); 7 Surface

Lift Capacity: 30,700 p/h resort

Ski Season: December-April

Cross Country: 30 km; Cross country center-Campo Carlo Magno

Ski School: 150 Instructors/6 schools

Mountain Restaurants: Good selection

Other Winter Activities: Snowboarding; ice skating/natural; indoor swimming; mono-skiing; squash; sauna

Après-Ski: Discos, cafes, folklore evenings, cinema

Shopping/Services: Many boutiques, variety of shops, fine restaurants, first aid, active nightlife, pharmacy

Credit Cards: AE, DC, MC, VISA

Lodging: 27,037 beds; 66 hotels with 5,037 beds; plus 22,000 beds in apartments

Transportation: Gateway Airport: Milan International Airport. Local Airport: Verona

Closest Provincial City: Trento 75 km (47 mi)

By Auto from airport: Highway Milano-Brescia-Tione-M di. Campiglio (4½ hrs)

By Bus from Trento: Tele: 0461-983627

By Train: F.S. Trento-Train station Tele: 0461/234545

Best Deal: Low season (Jan. 10-24, 1999, March 21-28, 1999)

Other Information: Sunny, sheltered location

A great name to drop is Madonna di Campiglio; it rolls off the tongue.
Photo: Italian Government Travel Office

ITALY

SOLDA-TRA FOI*
BOLZANO/BOZEN-A.A.S.T.
Piazza Walter, 8-CAP 39100
Bolzano, Italy
Telephone: (39) (471) 975656 Telex: 400444

TRENTINO ALTO ADIGE
Solda-Tra Foi is situated in the heart of the alpine circle, the most northern region in Italy, in the mountainous zone of the Ort Les-Cevedale range. High Alpine village is close to the Swiss and Austrian borders.

Elevation: Base/Village: 1,850 m (6,068 ft); Top: 2,499 m (8,200 ft)

Vertical: 650 m (2,132 ft)

Terrain: 30% beginner, 60% intermediate, 10% advanced

Skiing Circus: Close to Dolomite Areas

Lifts: 14

Types: 1 Cableway; 2 Chairlifts; 11 Surface

Ski Season: Dec.-April

Summer Skiing: Stelvio (close-19 mi) May-Nov.; also Cima Solda/Cevedale Glaciers

Cross Country: 12 km of trails—very good touring area

Ski School: Three

Mountain Restaurants: Yes

Other Winter Activities: Hiking; ice skating/natural; indoor swimming; sauna

Après-Ski: Bars, discos, cafes

Shopping Services: Shops, first-aid

Credit Cards: AE, MC, VISA; Most major American credit cards honored

Lodging: 90 hotels and pensions

Transportation: Gateway Airport: Venice; Milan

Closest Provincial City: Bolzano 96 km (60 mi)

By Auto from Airport: Approx. 3½-4 hours drive, via motorway from Venice or Milan

Easily accessible from every part of Europe by road and railway through the Brenner Pass, and in direct link with all the rest of Italy

Best Deal: A lot to chose from, between the Ortles and the western Dolomites

Other Information: German and Italian spoken

"The sunny side of the Alps" is an ideal place to relax after lunch, before returning to the slopes.
Photo: Italian Government Travel Office

ITALY

VAL DI FASSA
A.P.T. VALLE di FASSA
Via Costa-CAP 38032
Canazei (Trento), Italy
Telephone: (39) (462) 602466 Fax: (39) (462) 602278

Elevation: Canazei: Base 1,460 m (4,790 ft); Top: Marmolada 3,343 m (10,968 ft)

Vertical: 1,883 m (6,178 ft)

Longest Run: 6.2 km (3.8 mi)

Terrain: 193 km (120 mi) of marked runs; 30% beginner, 62% intermediate, 8% advanced

Skiing Circus: Part of the Sella Ronda ski carousel encompassing four passes and as many valleys: Fassa, Livinallongo, Badia and Gardena. Ski carousel: Tre Valli

Lifts: 80

Types: 2 Gondolas plus 2 high speed gondolas; 7 Funiculars; 38 Chairlifts (8 h-s quads, 8 triples, 22 doubles); 31 Surface

Lift Capacity: 96,000 p/h Valle di Fassa

Ski Season: December-April

Summer Skiing: Marmolada Glacier (June-Sept.)

Cross Country: 85 km (57 mi); 11 Trails: 2 schools

Ski School: 265 Instructors-9 schools

Mountain Restaurants: Each area—good selection

Other Winter Activities: Horse drawn sleigh; ice skating/natural; indoor swimming; fitness center; mono-

VAL DI FIEMME
A.P.T. VALLE DI FIEMME
Via F. Ilí Bronzettí, 60-I 38033, Cavalese (TN), Italy
Telephone: (39) (462) 241111
Fax: (39) (462) 230649

Elevation: Base/Village: 1,000 m (3,281 ft); Top: 2,415 m (7,923 ft)

Vertical: 1,415 m (4,642 ft)

Longest Run: 4.5 km—Piste Olympia—Alpe Cermis

Terrain: 140 km of marked runs with a variety of challenging terrain, 40% novice, 40% intermediate, 20% advanced

Skiing Circus: Fiemme resorts of Cermis, Pampeago form a single carousel with Obereggen

Lifts: 51

Types: 2 Gondolas; 3 Funiculars; 26 Chairlifts: (10 high speed quads; 1 Fixed grip quad; 2 triples; 13 doubles); 20 Platter

Lift Capacity: 5,400 p/h resort

Ski Season: 1 December-end of April

Summer Skiing: No

Cross Country: 150 km, 4 km slopes-lighted for evening X-C; 20 km of slopes w/ snow-making

Ski School: 7 ski schools—130 instructors

Mountain Restaurants: Yes—good quality cuisine

TRENTINO
Val di Fassa located in the central Alps is a beautiful valley in the province of Trento and is included in the "Sella Ronda" ski pass. The valley winds its way through the ragged peaks of the Dolomite Mountains. The "Marcialonga" cross country marathon is held here every year. High plateau mountain skiing.

skiing; sauna; snowboarding; squash; bowling; telemark; hiking; mountaineering; paragliding; sleigh riding

Après-Ski: Folklore evenings; 20 bars; 8 discos; 20 cafes; 5 coffee houses; 2 cinemas, torchlight skiing

Shopping/Services: Shopping (170+ shops and boutiques); alpine guides, taxis, 65 restaurants, first aid

Credit Cards: AE, DC, MC, VISA

Child Care: Contact ski schools; nursery: kindergarten

Lodging: 320 hotels-16,000 beds; 4,500 apartments-22,000 beds; Total capacity-49,000 beds

Transportation: Gateway Airport: Venice (3 hrs), and Milano; Verona, 2½ hours

Closest Provincial City: Trento 85 km, Bolzano 40 km

By Auto from Airport: Motorway A22 through Verona-Trento-exit Ora (60 km) or Bolzano-Costalunga Pass

By Train: FS-Trento Tele: (461) 234545-From Bolzano, or Trento international trains

Ski Bus Available: Free service from every town in the valley to ski areas; (461) 983627 & (471) 450111

Best Deal: Sella "Ski Carousel"; or "Superski Pass"

TRENTINO—DOLOMITES
The Fiemme Valley is one of the most important and well known winter areas of the Dolomites in the Alpine arc. There are excellent facilities at the resorts of: Cavalese-Cermis, Ski Center Latemar, Bellamonte, Predazzo, and Ziano. A splendid family area.

Other Winter Activities: Fitness center; folklore evenings; hiking; ice skating/natural; ice skating/artificial; indoor swimming; indoor tennis; mono-skiing; mountaineering; paragliding; sauna; snowboarding

Après-Ski: 15 Bars, 2 discos, 8 cafes, many concerts

Shopping Services: many boutiques and shops; pharmacies, food markets, hand crafts

Credit Cards: AE; DC; EC; MC; Visa; Accepted in most shops and banks

Child Care: Kid's Ski School; nursery in Ski Center

Lodging: Beds—33,350—115 Hotels—6,000 Beds and 28,000 beds in apartments and private rooms

Transportation: Gateway Airport: Milan—280 km

Closest Provincial City: Trento 62 km; Bolzano 42 km

By Auto from Airport: Routes—Autobrennero and SS 48

Ski Bus: Available from all of the valley

By Train: from Ora/BZ, Transfer needed to bus

Best Deal: Dolomite Superski Pass

Other Information: Sunny, dry climate; snowmaking

ITALY

Val Senales in South Tirol is noted for its scenery.

Photo: Italian Government Travel Office

VAL SENALES/SCHNALSTAL

Tourist Board Val Senales
Bolzano, Italy
Telephone: (39) (473) 679148 Telex: (473) 679177

Elevation: Base/Village: 2,000 m (6,562 ft); Top: 3,212 m (10,538 ft)

Vertical: 1,212 m (3,976 ft)

Terrain: 25 km (16 mi) of downhill slopes, with snowfields and ski runs for all ability levels; 23% beginner, 47% intermediate, 30% expert

Skiing Circus: Many resorts and villages close by with excellent skiing resources

Lifts: 10

Types: 1 Cableway; 9 Chairlifts/Surface

Lift Capacity: 8,600 p/h resort

Ski Season: Dec.-April

Summer Skiing: May-Nov. Glaciers (Cima Solda and Cevedale) also Stelvio (1 hr. by car)

Cross Country: 30 km of trails/slopes

Ski School: One

Mountain Restaurants: Yes

Other Winter Activities: Curling; hiking; ice skating/artificial; indoor swimming; sauna

ALTO ADIGE (SOUTH TIROL) *(German speaking region)*
A beautiful resort near the Italian-Austrian border, in the midst of the Alpine circle. A mass of mountains which rise to 3,950 m amongst the Ortles-Venosta range. Near the principal city of Merano, which is a health resort of world fame.

Après-Ski: Bars, discos, cafes, folklore evenings

Shopping Services: Shopping locally and day tour to Austria; first-aid

Credit Cards: AE; Most major American credit cards honored

Lodging: 1,600 beds; 38 hotels/pensions

Transportation: Gateway Airport: Venice; Milan; Munich; Innsbruck

Closest Provincial City: Bozen 55 km (34 mi)

By Auto from Airport: Approx. 3½ hrs drive via motorway from Venice or Milan and Munich

Easily accessible from northern Europe by road and railway through the Brenner Pass

Best Deal: Many resorts/villages close by, as are the Dolomites. Austria via Brenner Pass within 1 hr drive

Other Information: German language and traditions. Val Senales offers a highly developed network of facilities and is accessible from major airports

©Publishers Group International, 1998

ITALY

**VAL GARDENA: SELVA GARDENA/
S. CRISTINA/ORTISEI**
SELVA GARDENA
39048 Selva "1" (BZ), Italy
Telephone: (39) (71) 795122 FAX: (39) (71) 794245

Elevation: Base/Village: 1,200 m (3,937 ft); Top: 2,681 m (8,796 ft)

Vertical: 1,481 m (4,859 ft); Resort: Ortisei-1,236 m; Villages: S. Cristina-1,428 m, Selva Gardena-1,563 m

Longest Run: 8 km (5 mi), Nogler

Terrain: Wooded glades; 175 km (109 mi) (52.5 km, blue, 105 km red, 17.5 km black); snowmaking 90 km of slopes

Skiing Circus: See Best Deal

Lifts: 81

Types: 4 Gondolas; 4 Funiculars; 28 Chairlifts; 42 Surface

Lift Capacity: 83,700 p/h resorts

Ski Season: December-April

Cross Country: 98 km (60 mi)

Ski School: Three ski schools; 280 ski instructors

Mountain Restaurants: Yes

Other Winter Activities: Horse drawn sleigh; curling; horse riding; shooting; free-climbing; ice skating/artificial (2); indoor swimming; indoor tennis (2); mono-skiing; paragliding; snowboarding; squash; billiards; bowling; winter walks (105 km); sports center; climbing wall

Après-Ski: Bars, discos, cafes, coffee houses, folklore evenings; sauna

Shopping/Services: Massages, variety of shops

Credit Cards: AE, DC, MC, VISA

Child Care: 3 Kid's Ski Schools; 3 Nurseries

Lodging: 16,500 beds all categories; hotels, chalets, apartments, private homes

Transportation: Gateway Airport: Milan; Munich

Closest Provincial City: Bolzano 40 km (25 mi)

By Auto: Bolzano-Chiusa/Brenner-Chiusa

By Train: Railway to Bolzano or to Bressanone (35 km), bus to Val Gardena

Best Deal: "Sella Ronda"-ski pass-4 Valleys-50 km of daytrips. Dolomite Superski Pass, 464 lifts, 1,180 km slopes in 12 valleys

Other Information: Dramatic skiing - lovely scenery

VAL GARD
Val Gardena is in the heart of the Sella mountain range, Italian Dolomites. It is comprised of three villages: Ortisel, S. Cristina and Selva Gardena. A wide variety of skiing on open slopes. The language and traditions of Val Gardena are Italian, although German and "Ladin" are also spoken.

"A jug of wine, a bowl of fruit and thou, sitting beside me in the snow, were paradise enow."
Photo: Italian Government Travel Office

ITALY

PIANCAVALLO*
PIANCAVALLO (AVIANO) A.A.S.T.
Viale S. Giorgio-CAP 33081
Pordenone, Italy
Telephone: (39) (434) 655191 Telex: 450816 ENTUR-1

FRIULI VENEZIA GIULIA
Piancavallo resort is situated on a plateau in the Carnic and Julian ranges of the Eastern Alps. This region rises from east to north along the former Yugoslavian border. From the summit the views stretch to the sea and the craggy peaks of the border.

Elevation: Base/Village: 1,300 m (4,264 ft); Top: 2,000 m (6,562 ft)
Vertical: 700 m (2,298 ft)
Terrain: Mostly for beginners-intermediates; 40% beginner, 50% intermediate, 10% advanced
Lifts: 30
Types: 15 Chairlifts; 15 Surface
Lift Capacity: December-April
Cross Country: 25 km of trails
Ski School: Two schools; 20 Instructors
Mountain Restaurants: Five
Other Winter Activities: Ice skating/artificial; indoor swimming (2 at hotels); sauna, sleigh riding; ice hockey; tobogganing
Après-Ski: Bars, discos, cafes, night club/band

Shopping Services: Cinema, shopping, first-aid
Credit Cards: Most major American credit cards honored
Child Care: Kindergartens; kid's ski school; nursery
Lodging: 800 Beds, 5 Hotels, 1,300 chalets/apartments with 6,480 additional beds
Transportation: Gateway Airport: Venice (1½ hr drive); Milan
Closest Provincial City: Pordenone 15 km (9 mi)
By Auto from Airport: Motorway from Venice to Pordenone, local road to Piancavallo
Best Deal: Close to Venice (1½ hr drive) or Trieste
Other Information: Attracts many young skiers—has hosted World Cup Freestyle competitions

Skiers rest below one of the impressive Dolomite peaks.

Photo: Trentino Tourist Office

©Publishers Group International, 1998

Italian Delight

by Richard J. Muello

Skiers constantly yearn for new and exciting experiences. They can be unbearable name-droppers, eager to talk about European resorts they have visited and their challenging mountain adventures.

Many Americans used to think the Alps were only Swiss and Austrian with fascinating, yet quite difficult to pronounce Germanic sounding names. Skiers who want to stay ahead of the curve, and are seeking new names to lay on their neighbors should consider Italy, on the sunny side of the Alps.

Italy is Big in skiing. It has some of the best terrain on the continent, as well as marvelous après-ski activities. And, the resorts have romantic, melodically sounding names that roll off the tongue, such as Cortina d'Ampezzo, Madonna di Campiglio, and Sestriere.

More than 100 major resorts in Italy offer terrific skiing, incredible ambiance and a touch of history with a different accent. Three of the more popular resorts for many U.S. skiers and *The Blue Book* editors, are Bormio, Cervinia, and Courmayeur.

The last two are close to national borders, where a passport tucked in your parka is advisable. Border guards are gone, but you may still need the document for identification or to cash traveler's checks.

From Cervina it is possible, make that desirable, to ski into Zermatt, Switzerland, swinging on a glacier past the Matterhorn, the world's most photogenic rock. Courmayeur is on the south side of Mont Blanc, the highest peak in western Europe. It is a starting point for a memorable ski journey down another glacier into Chamonix, France.

In these resorts the skiers are mostly Italian, but other nationalities are found in every lift line. They are a mixed bag of budget-minded skiers and elegant shoppers who double park their Maseratis in front of fur and leather shops.

BORMIO

In the Rhaetian Alps, 35 miles due east of the Swiss glamour spot of St. Moritz, is the popular Italian resort of Bormio. It is about a four-hour drive from Malpensa airport above Milan; part of the drive is along semi-tropical Lake Como.

The 4,000-plus inhabitants of this old Roman village are proud of their history. The scholar Pliny wrote in the first century about the therapeutic mineral baths. The town was politically and militarily important in the Middle Ages. Napoleon slept here. World War I battles described by Ernest Hemingway were fought in surrounding mountains.

Skiing is as challenging as skiers care to make it. . . . on wide-open snowfields draped on 10,000-feet-high Monte Vallecetta. Experts can stay in the fall line and yet run miles at a time. Novices and intermediates use easier slopes and wider traverses to log 50 miles of downhill a day. The 5,500-foot vertical drop is higher than that of any resort in North America.

For après-ski adventure there is an indoor thermal pool, with a coed sauna, massage room and mud baths. Shops stay open late in the old part of town with bargains in leather, clothing and ski equipment. A medieval tower helps as a reference point in locating restaurants and discos.

Accommodations range from rooms in modest pensions to suites in regal hotels. A typical three-star hotel will offer lodging, breakfast and dinner for reasonable prices, but more important will be the treatment. Skiers become part of the family. At dinner the owner may personally uncork a chilled local wine to temper the piping-hot pasta. Later he may join the group in the disco. Often there is a hiss of steam in the lounge as cappuccino and espresso are prepared for guests coming in from a moonlight walk along the Roman walls.

CERVINIA

Northwest of Milan, 110 miiles away in another part of the Alps, is Cervinia, the Italian village that shares the Matterhorn with Switzerland's Zermatt. From the Swiss side the mountain is a sharp jagged pyramid. From the Italian side, where it is known as Monte Cervin, it is rounded and less dramatic. But ski instructors who are mountain guides in summer insist this is the more challenging side to climb.

Cervina does not have the charm of Bormio; it is still young, born in the

A festive Trentino table.

ITALY

20th century. But no one can fault the skiing. From the village up to the top of lift-served terrain are billowing expanses of snow, looking like endless formations of cumulus clouds. The slopes are south facing and in the sun all day.

For a description of how much fun they can be, see "The run to Cervina" account in the Swiss section, which talks about a day trip from Zermatt to Cervinia. Skiers who have Cervinia as home base can reverse the procedure and drop into Switzerland for lunch and a bit of sightseeing.

Cervinia, like most modern ski resorts, has miles of cross country trails woven into the landscape.

COURMAYEUR

This popular resort is in northwest Italy, just below the Mont Blanc tunnel, on the main road to Chamonix, France.

Like Cervinia, it is less than an hour's drive from Aosta, the major city in the province of Valle d'Aosta. The city of Aosta traces its origins back to Roman times; its ruins are worthy of mention in any guidebook. The massive Arch of Augustus predates Columbus by 1517 years.

Throughout the Aosta valley dozens of medieval castles stand on hilltops like sentinels guarding the old Roman road. Visiting some of them is a good way to spend a day off the slopes when the weather is bad.

Courmayeur itself is a colorful town in which you will hear a lot of Italian and French, but also much English.

Into the Vallée Blanche from Courmayer.

The village has long been a favorite with folks from the British Isles and they are everywhere in the lively après-ski scene.

Compagne des Alpes, one of the sponsors of *The Blue Book*, is the premier lift company in the Alps. You will notice their logo in the tourist office boxes in the France sections; it signifies that they are a major owner of lifts in those particular resorts. CDA is now in Italy with facilities in Courmayeur, offering skiers speedy rides up the mountains.

Courmayeur offers skiing for everybody, including some daring, off-piste stuff on several mountains that surround the town. But on a sunny day in late winter, adventurous skiers leave their chalets to ski the Vallee Blanche from the hip of the Mont Blanc massif down into France. One of the world's most scenic runs, it is not reserved for experts. Intermediate skiers can handle it, if they heed their guide.

(Refer to the account in the French section of the exciting access to the Vallee Blanche that causes goosebumps for skiers starting the trip in Chamonix, France.)

On the Italian side, skiers meet their guide at the La Palud cable car station for the first of two trams up to Pont Heilbronner. After coffee and a final rest stop in the mountain res-

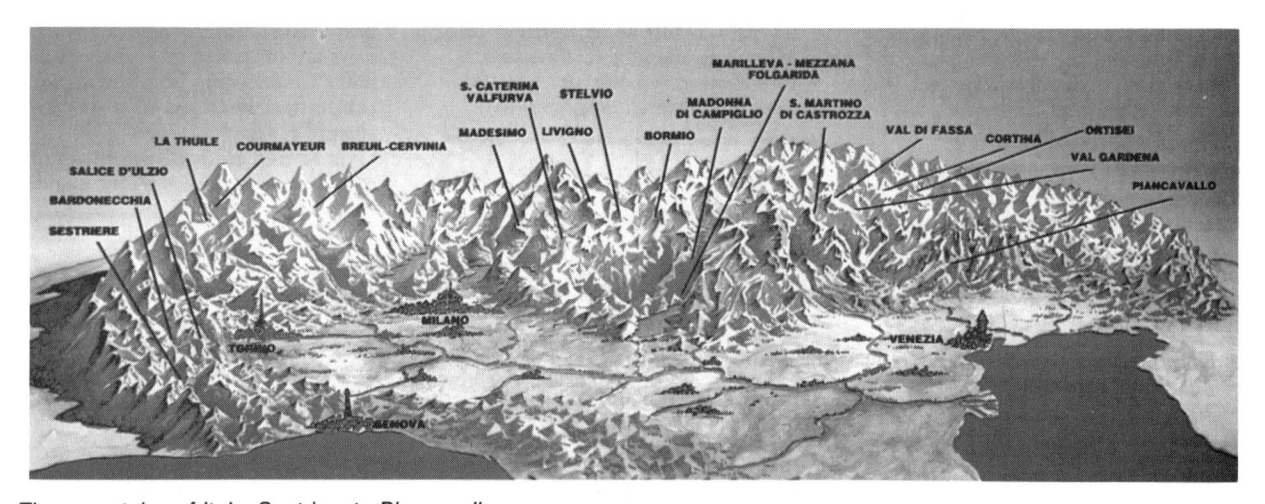

The mountains of Italy: Sestriere to Piancavallo.

©Publishers Group International, 1998

ITALY

taurant, skiers saddle up for the trip through massive canyons. It will take four or five hours, depending on how often skiers stop to take pictures, and how long they linger over the picnic lunch in the snow. The guide carries the hotel-packed snacks in his rucksack.

The guide leads the way and tells his group when it is O.K. to leave the track and venture into untouched powder. But there will be stretches where he sternly forbids anyone to ski. He does not want to be embarrassed by having lost someone on the mountain. He stops for a demonstration and pokes his pole around a small hole in the snow. The hole grows with each stab, until it becomes a wide crevasse with an invisible bottom. It makes believers of skiers. They follow him, very carefully, around other fissures and through strange new formations. It is a fairyland, but not the place to spend eternity.

As they come down the valley, skiers sometimes find the snow changing from powder to corn snow. Suddenly they are upon the Mer de Glace, a sea of ice. Huge, blue-grey blocks of ice, shifting with the glacier throughout thousands of years, look like capsized destroyers. As skiers work their way through them, there are frequent pauses to look back in disbelief: "Did we really come through that?"

The last hour is in an evergreen forest on a narrow trail that may be the most difficult part of the journey. And then the group is in Chamonix, sitting in a sidewalk cafe' and babbling about their day. The guide smiles and sips his Pernod.

The group hails a couple of taxis for the return to Courmayeur through the seven-mile-long Mont Blanc tunnel. Usually, a tunnel ride seems long and dark. But no one notices; the cabs glow with shared memories.

CORTINA AND VAL GARDENA

Any article spotlighting Italian skiing certainly should include Cortina d'Ampezzo and Val Gardena as among the finest resorts in the world. Both resorts are located in the beautiful, rugged, ragged Dolomite mountains, and are annual hosts for World Cup events.

Cortina rests below the beautiful Dolomites.
Photo: Italian Government Travel Office

Cortina lies nestled in the Ampezzo valley, surrounded by the jutting mountain peaks of: Tofana, Pomagagnon, Cristallo, Sorapis and Croda. It is located 110 miles north of Venice in the eastern Dolomites, and only 25 miles from the Austrain border.

These mountains, with their vast snowfields, provide skiers and riders with more than 70 miiles of runs on diverse, challenging terrain. From the highest skiable point, at 10,640 feet, skiers enjoy a 6,624 foot vertical drop to the base area. The vistas are superb and the skiing is phenomenal.

Hang gliding around Arosa.
Photo: Italian Government Travel Office

Alberto Tomba, the ever-popular, flamboyant, former Olympic and World Cup champion had his initial ski lessons at the famous Cortina Ski School.

Cortina is renowned for its latest amenities, excellent accommodations, variety of fine restaurants, a lively après-ski atmosphere, numerous sporting events and entertainment facilities, as well as many cultural opportunities. The pedestrian shopping mall in the center of town includes hundreds of specialty shops and stylish boutiques.

Cortina is an upscale, elegant resort that attracts a wealthy clientele including many celebrities. It is a great place to view fabulous fashions, furs, glamorous people and of course, to ski.

Val Gardena, in South Tirol, is one of the most popular ski areas in the magnificent Dolomites. It is about 75 miles from Innsbruck, in the Sella mountain range, and reflects its Austrian culture and traditions.

The valley offers a network of 110 miles of runs on a variety of spectacular terrain, with breathe taking scenery, and many off-mountain activities and options. Gardena is an important part of the "Dolomite Superski" pass, and offers the "Sella Ronda" pass, a 16 mile ski tour around the impressive Sella Massif.

Val Gardena is composed of three village resorts: Ortisei, S. Cristina and Selva Gardena.

Ortisei is the largest village and the main resort in the valley. It is the cultural center, has the most amenities, and the widest selection of non-ski activities. A lively town pedestrian center has many shops displaying traditional handcrafts specializing in local woodcarving.

Several cable cars connect Ortisei with the skiing areas, including the Alpe di Siusi, a real sunny paradise.

S. Cristina lies between Selva Gardena and Ortisei. It provides the most challenging terrain in the valley and is in the mainstream of the Sella Ronda. This is the location of the famous valley based World Cup downhill races. It is the preferred family resort with a quiet, comfortable, relaxed atmosphere.

Selva Gardena may be the best known of the three valley resorts,

ITALY

and is one of the leading ski resorts in the Alps, It is located at the east end of the valley, at an altitude of 5126 feet, at the foot of the Sella Massif. It offers some of Europe's finest skiing terrain, and is convenient to lifts and cable cars.

Selva Gardena enjoys a fun atmosphere, plenty of après-ski activities, and a reputation for the best nightlife in the valley.

THE DOLOMITÉS

Other recommendations—Trentino

The province of Trentino bordered by the majestic Dolomite mountain range contains more than 40 ski resorts and ski centers offering a variety of ski experiences and excellent accommodations.

Among them are: Valle Di Fassa, Valle Di Fiemme, and Madonna di Campiglio.

Trentino a winter wonderland, has more than 300 lifts, capable of moving 310,000 skiers per hour. They include cable cars, gondolas, chair lifts, and surface lifts. The uphill system accesses 373 miles of downhill runs, with non-stop skiing from valley to valley. An electronic "ski-pass," which is now in use at 22 of the leading ski areas in Trentino, gives skiers a quick, comfortable entry system. No delays or fumbling for a card. The skier simply tucks the pass into an outside pocket of his or her ski clothes and forgets about it. Within a couple of yards of the checkpoint, an electronic beam approves the skier's credential and he or she is cleared to pass through.

Trentino has 1,741 hotels that can accommodate 88,900 guests, with many of them offering attractive packages. In the major resort of Madonna di Campiglio, a week's vacation in a four-star hotel with two meals daily costs approximately $750 per person in high season and $500 in low. A six day ski-pass costs approximately $144 in high season and $132 in low. A three-star or two-star hotel costs 30 to 40 percent less.

We encourage readers to visit the Internet at [http://www.skiItaly.com] for current lodging information and resort photos.

As Swiss *Blue Book* editor, Ted Heck, recently said, "My feeling about Italian skiing is that you can throw a dart or a boccie ball and go where it lands. It's that good! Plus, Renaissance palaces, stunning cathedrals and museums are along the way. Few countries can match the art, architecture and colorful history of Italy."

Have Fun—while schussing the great slopes in sunny Italy.

Cross country enthusiasts enjoy the solitude of the Trentino Valley.
Photo: Trentino Tourist Office

©Publishers Group International, 1998

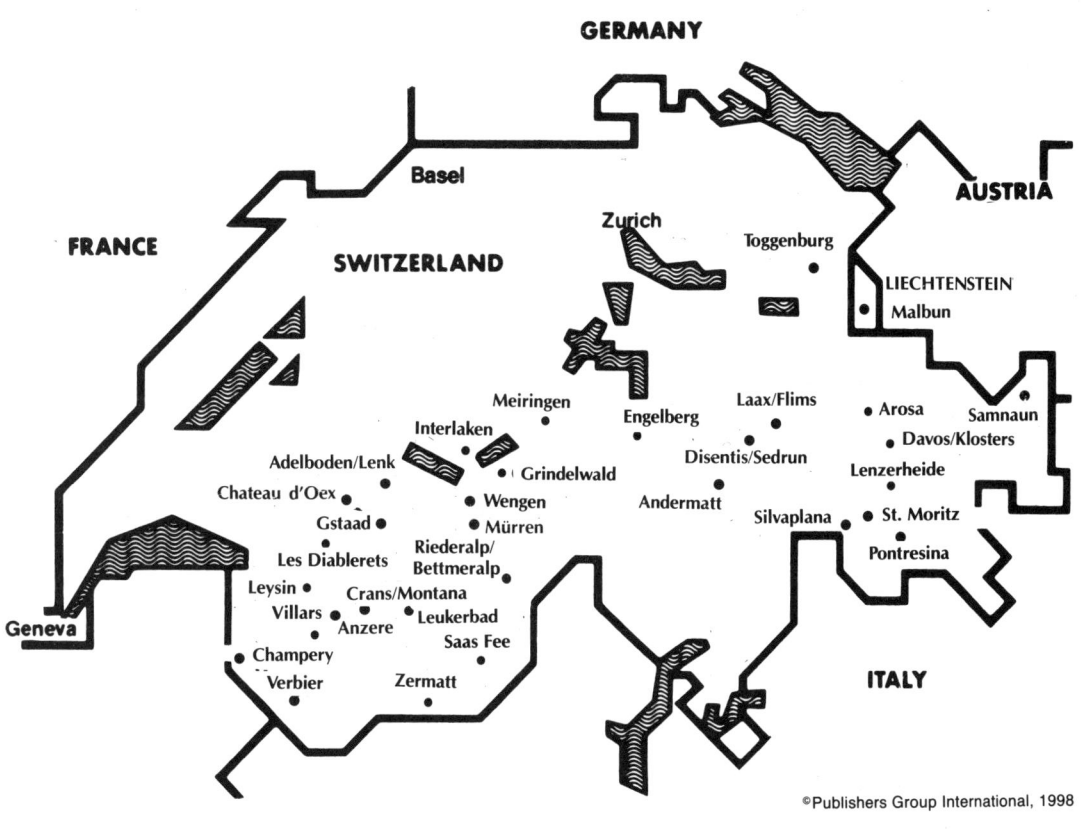

SWITZERLAND

GERMANY
FRANCE
SWITZERLAND
Basel
Zurich
Toggenburg
AUSTRIA
LIECHTENSTEIN
Malbun
Meiringen
Laax/Flims
Arosa
Samnaun
Interlaken
Engelberg
Davos/Klosters
Adelboden/Lenk
Grindelwald
Disentis/Sedrun
Lenzerheide
Chateau d'Oex
Wengen
Andermatt
Gstaad
Mürren
Silvaplana
St. Moritz
Les Diablerets
Riederalp/Bettmeralp
Pontresina
Leysin
Crans/Montana
Villars
Anzere
Leukerbad
Saas Fee
Champery
Verbier
Zermatt
ITALY
Geneva

©Publishers Group International, 1998

SWITZERLAND	Page No.		Page No.
Adelboden/Lenk	101	Leukerbad*	98
Andermatt*	107	Leysin	95
Anzère	96	Malbun/Steg (Liechtenstein)*	116
Arosa	110	Meiringen/Hasliberg	106
Champéry	96	Mürren	105
Chateau-d'Oex	94	Pontresina	113
Crans-Montana	98	Riederalp/Bettmeralp	99
Davos	108	**St. Moritz**	**115**
Disentis/Sedrun	111	Samnaun	112
Engelberg	107	Saas-Fee	99
Flims-Laax-Falera	112	Silvaplana	114
Grindelwald	102	Toggenburg	116
Gstaad	101	Verbier	97
Interlaken	106	Villars	95
Klosters	109	Wengen	103
Lenzerheide/Valbella	111	Zermatt	100
Les Diablerets	94		

*Areas marked with an asterisk in the text did not update their information for this edition.

SWITZERLAND

by Ted Heck

The mountainous country of Switzerland evokes images of scenic grandeur, charm and adventure. But it is also noted for commerce and efficient service. Its people cater to visitors and answer requests with "No problem."

Winter fun is a top entry on the adventure menu and ski resorts are among the best in the world. But there are 160 ski areas in a small nation that would fit into Vermont and New Hampshire combined. So your editors have a dilemma about which resorts to include in a guide read primarily by North American skiers. They range in size from alpine pastures served by modest lifts to world class resorts with vast snowfields above the tree line and reached by high tech conveyances. Major resorts have more skiing terrain than nearly anything in the American Rockies; their long runs and vertical drops dwarf those of ski areas in New England.

To list particulars on all 160 areas is beyond the scope of this reference book. Most skiers from the United States and Canada will choose a resort from the more than 40 described or mentioned here. We include such popular resorts as Zermatt, St. Moritz, Davos, Klosters, Verbier and the Jungfrau Region and many others that we feel have important attributes for skiers to evaluate, such as location, terrain, facilities and apres-ski amenities.

On the previous page resorts are listed alphabetically, but in the descriptions that follow they are grouped by regions, from west to east: Lake of Geneva, Valais, Bernese Oberland, Central Switzerland, Graubünden, Eastern Switzerland and Liechtenstein.

To rhapsodize about skiing in Switzerland is easy. Skiers of all levels of ability can find something to their liking. Comfortable groomed pistes for cruising or challenging powder chutes where adrenal glands work overtime. Long runs that begin on open snowfields, drop down into the trees, past farm houses hanging on sides of steep pastures, to remote villages from which skiers return by a train in the valley. Memorable slopes alongside awesome glaciers. Opportunities to cross over borders into other countries.

Mountain restaurants with sunlit decks for refreshing breaks in the action.

There is always snow in Switzerland, even in years of less snowfall—if you go high enough. Above 6,000 feet skiers find plenty of snow to cavort on, even though valleys below may be green and temperatures feel more like those of tennis time.

Switzerland thrives on tourism and therefore has a high percentage of English-speaking residents. But the alpine experience is enhanced by listening to conversations in four different languages, all of them official. German is spoken most often in the north and east, French and Italian are heard the closer one gets to neighboring countries. And also in the east is Romansch, an incomprehensible tongue that sounds like someone reading a cryptogram.

Lift ticket, ski school and equipment rental rates are listed in a special section on page 145.

Hotel rates are not included. In surveying resorts we find a universal range of prices. In almost every resort a budget-minded skier can stay in a comfortable pension for U.S. $50 to $60 a day. Two and three star hotels run from $80 to $120, but a skier with a mink parka can spend hundred of dollars a day for a suite in a five star luxury hotel. Travel agents and tour operators in America and local tourist offices in Switzerland are prepared to match accommodations with skiers' pocketbooks.

A note about statistics on terrain and lift facilities: some resorts are near others and share the same mountains. The Jungfrau Region is a good example of how areas promote jointly and lay claim to the same territory. But this highlights the fact that this small country offers an amazing number of options. Choice makes Switzerland special.

Skiing is what *The Blue Book* is all about. But vacationers in Switzerland will want to take advantage of other startling panoramas. There are beautiful lakes on which steamships operate throughout the winter. And legendary rivers, including the Rhine and Rhone, usually thought of as major arteries in other countries, but originating in Switzerland.

The Glacier Express, one of the world's great train rides, runs along the Rhine for a while on a spectacular eight-hour journey from Zermatt to St. Moritz, crossing 300 bridges and entering 91 tunnels.

The gateway cities of Zürich and Geneva are often given short shrift by arriving skiers eager to get to

SWITZERLAND

the mountains. But on the way home they offer urban sightseeing and cultural bonuses to a skiing holiday.

Because the travel industry is so highly organized, assistance is available long before a skier steps off his Swissair flight. Switzerland Tourism offices in the cities listed here have brochures, trail maps, and hotel information on many areas, plus general literature about skiing. Faxed snow reports are available at 212-757-4733. From December to April a daily snow report can be found on the Internet at www.switzerlandtourism.com

SWITZERLAND TOURISM OFFICES
New York
608 Fifth Avenue
New York, NY 10020
Phone: 212-757-5944
Fax: 212-262-6116

Los Angeles
222 North Sepulveda Blvd, Suite 1570
El Segundo, CA 90245
Phone: 310-640-8900
Fax: 310-335-0131

Ontario
926 The East Mall
Etobicoke, ON M9B 6K1
Phone: 416-695-2090
Fax: 416-695-2774

SWISSAIR INFORMATION

Swissair carries skiers to the Alps from Atlanta, Boston, Chicago, Cincinnati, Los Angeles, Montreal, Newark, New York, San Francisco, and Washington, D.C., with connecting service from 21 other U.S. cities.

Swissair offers a brochure called "The Alpine Experience." It includes additional descriptions of major Swiss resorts, as well as popular resorts in Austria, France, Germany and Italy. The colorful brochure contains photos, trail maps, hotel listings and prices for package deals.

For a free copy of "The Alpine Experience" call 800-662-0021 or write to Swissair, P.O. Box 26028, Tampa, FL 33623-6028.

To book one of their exciting adventures call Swissair Vacations at 800-688-7947.

An international ice sculpting contest in front of the 5-star Grand Hotel Regina in Grindelwald. Photo: Fred McKinney

SWITZERLAND

CHATEAUX-d'OEX
TOURIST OFFICE:
Chateau-d'Oex CH-1837
Telephone: (41) (26) 924 2525
Fax: (41) (26) 924 2526

Elevation: Village: 1,000 m (3,280 ft); Top: 1,800 m (5,904 ft)

Vertical: 800 m (2,624 ft)

Longest Run: 8 km (5 mi)

Terrain: 50 km (31 mi) of local pistes, 250 km (155 mi) in region

Lifts: 16

Types: 1 Tram; 2 Chairlifts; 13 Surface lifts

Ski Season: December-April. Summer skiing on glacier at Les Diablerets

Cross Country: 30 km (19 mi); 50 km (31 mi) of winter walking trails

Ski School: All disciplines

Mountain Restaurants: 3

Other Winter Activities: Curling; ice skating/artificial; sleigh riding; ballooning; riding; bowling; paragliding; mono-skiing; snowboarding; helicopter skiing; sports center; sauna

LES DIABLERETS
TOURIST OFFICE:
Les Diablerets CH-1865

Telephone: (41) (25) 53 13 58 Fax: (41) (25) 53 23 48

Elevation: Base: 1,200 m (3,936 ft); Top: 3,000 m (9840 ft)

Vertical: 1,800 m (5,904 ft)

Terrain: 60 km (37 mi) of local downhill runs; 120 km (74 mi) when combined with Villars. 70% intermediate, 10 km of glacier skiing

Skiing Circus: Connects with Villars and Gryon

Lifts: 47 in region; 25 in resort

Types: 4 Trams; 2 Gondolas; 4 Chairlifts; 15 Surface lifts

Lift Capacity: 16,200 p/h resort; 28,000 p/h region

Ski Season: December-April

Summer Skiing: On the glacier

Cross Country: 74 km (46 mi) in region, including skating tracks and ski hiking trails; 30 km (19 mi) of winter walking trails

Ski School: 35 instructors, all disciplines

Mountain Restaurants: 8

Other Winter Activities: Fitness center; hiking; ice skating/artificial; mountaineering; paragliding; snowboarding; sleigh riding; riding; torchlight skiing; curling; helicopter skiing; snowscoot, snowshoes; sauna

LAKE OF GENEVA *(French speaking region)*
This small resort in a wide valley near Gstaad appeals to skiers looking for relaxed charm and not searching too hard for challenging slopes. But tougher stuff is within comfortable bus or car distance.

Après-Ski: Bars, discos, folklore evenings, concerts, museums, cinema, cheese making center

Lodging: 1,000 hotel beds; 20 hotels and pensions; 3,000 beds in chalets and apts; youth hostel

Transportation: Gateway Airport: Geneva (1½ hrs)

Closest Provincial City: Aigle (35 km)

By Auto: Via Lausanne-Montreux-Aigle, Via Lausanne-Vevey-Bulle

By Train: Simplon Route, but also accessible on Montreux-Bernese Oberland route

Best Deal: Bed and breakfast in low season available for 35-40 SF a day

Other Information: Better-known Gstaad is only 20 minutes away for shopping and additional après-ski adventure. Ski pass connected with Gstaad Super Ski Region

LAKE OF GENEVA, Alpes Vaudoises
(French speaking region)
Les Diablerets combines cruising terrain on a glacier, nearly two miles high, with some ebony-black routes down to the village.

Après-Ski: Bars, disco, cafes, concerts, ice bar, folklore evenings

Shopping/Services: Various shops

Credit Cards: MC, VISA, American Express

Child Care: Nursery: Kindergarten; Telephone: (25)/53 20 02

Lodging: 1,000 hotel beds; 10 hotels; 4,000 other beds in chalets and apartments

Transportation: Gateway Airport: Geneva (2½ hrs; 120 km/74 mi)

Closest Provincial City: Aigle (23 km)

By Auto: Lausanne to Aigle to Diablerets

By Train: Geneva-Lausanne-Aigle on the international Simplon line, then ASD mountain railway to Les Diablerets

Best Deal: Pension-type bed and breakfast can be as low as 22 SF in low season. Weeklong packages with half-board and lifts are from 871 SF in a 2-star to 1,234 in a 4-star hotel. Reservations through tourist office

Other Information: See also Villars and Leysin listings for other nearby skiing

©Publishers Group International, 1998

SWITZERLAND

LEYSIN
TOURISM:
Leysin CH-1854
Telephone: (41) (24) 494 2244
Fax: (41) (24) 494 1616

Elevation: Village: 1,200 m (3,936 ft); Top: 2,300 m (7,544 ft)

Vertical: 1,100 m (3,608 ft)

Longest Run: 5 km (3 mi)

Terrain: 60 km (37 mi) of downhill runs locally; 110 km (68 mi) when combined with nearby Les Mosses. Most prepared slopes are easy or intermediate

Lifts: 19

Types: 2 Gondolas; 8 Chairlifts; 9 Surface

Lift Capacity: 12,400 p/h

Ski Season: December-April

Cross Country: 9 km (5.6 mi); 58 km (36 mi) of ski hiking trails; 30 km (19 mi) of winter walking trails

Ski School: All disciplines, 2 schools, 80 instructors

Mountain Restaurants: Panorama revolving restaurant atop Mt. Berneuse; several restaurants on other mountains

Other Winter Activities: Curling; fitness center; hiking; ice skating/artificial; squash; mountaineering;

VILLARS
TOURIST OFFICE:
Villars CH-1884
Telephone: (41) (24) 495 32 32
Fax: (41) (24) 495 27 94

Elevation: Base: 1,300 m (4,264 ft); Top: 2,200 m (7,216 ft)

Vertical: 900 m (2,952 ft)

Longest Run: 4 km (2.5 mi)

Terrain: 60 km (37 mi) of downhill runs; 120 km (74 mi) when combined with other nearby resorts; 35% beginner, 50% intermediate, 15% advanced

Skiing Circus: Skiing several ridges, it is possible to connect with Les Diablerets resort 10 miles away

Lifts: 23 local, 47 with Les Diablerets

Lift Capacity: 23,000 p/h Villars; 35,000 p/h region

Ski Season: Mid-December–Mid-April

Summer Skiing: On the glacier at Les Diablerets

Cross Country: 44 km (27 mi) in the region

Ski School: 100 instructors for all skiing disciplines

Mountain Restaurants: 8 in attractive settings

Other Winter Activities: Curling; fitness center; hiking; ice skating/artificial; indoor tennis; indoor swimming; mono-skiing; mountaineering; paragliding; sauna; snowboarding; sleigh riding; bowling

LAKE OF GENEVA *(French speaking region)*
Leysin, one of the closest ski resorts to the Geneva gateway, is a year-round resort for the vigorous, but offers mountain-air relaxation, too.

paragliding; hang-gliding; snowboarding; sports center with indoor tennis courts & swimming pool; mt. biking; horse riding; guided mountain tours; torchlight descents

Après-Ski: Concerts, bars, discos, restaurants

Shopping/Services: Good shopping variety

Child Care: Nursery ski school for 2-yr. olds plus

Lodging: 1,900 hotel beds; 12 hotels; 6,500 beds in chalets and apartments

Transportation: Gateway Airport: Geneva (1½ hrs)

Closest Provincial City: Aigle (20 min)

By Auto: Geneva-Lausanne-Montreux-Aigle-Leysin

By Train: From airport take train (downstairs) to Aigle, then take cog-rail direct to Leysin Village; Vermont; and Leysin-Feydey; bus also available

Best Deal: 10 to 40% off all sports activities for holders of holiday pass

Other Information: Leysin is a popular convention center

LAKE OF GENEVA *(French speaking region)*
Villars is a smaller resort than some of its neighbors in southwestern Switzerland, but it offers a full range of winter sports, including off-piste skiing as well as tree skiing.

Après-Ski: Bars, concerts, discos, cinema, folklore

Shopping/Services: Full range of facilities, stores, banks, churches

Credit Cards: AE, DC, MC, VISA

Child Care: Nursery: Kindergarten includes skiing and lunch for 55 SF; Telephone: 35 20 43 or 35 22 10

Lodging: 1,800 hotel beds; 15 hotels; 8,000 other beds in chalets and apartments

Transportation: Gateway Airport: Geneva; 120 km (74 mi; 1½ hrs)

Closest Provincial City: Aigle (15 km)

By Auto: Motorway via Lausanne, Montreux, Aigle

By Train: Geneva to Lausanne to Montreux to Aigle

Post bus from Aigle to resort

Best Deal: Special pass for non-skiers (6 days for 80 SF) offers cable car and train sightseeing, plus admission to pool and rink

Other Information: "Super Saver" is also a good deal: 7 nights, two meals, lift tickets from 441 SF. Refer also to Les Diablerets and Leysin descriptions

swissair SWITZERLAND

CHAMPÉRY
TOURIST OFFICE:
Champéry CH-1874
Telephone: (41) (24) 479 2020
Fax: (41) (24) 479 2021

Elevation: Base: 1,055 m (3,460 ft); Top: 2,300 m (7,544 ft)

Vertical: 1245 m (4,084 ft)

Longest Run: 7 km (4.3 mi)

Terrain: 30 km (19 mi) of prepared runs, 650 km (403 mi) in region. Such vast terrain is everybody's cup of tea, but experts here will have a blast. 16% beginner, 35% intermediate, 40% advanced, 9% expert

Skiing Circus: There are so many interconnects that it is advisable to carry a "Ski Links" map in the pocket

Lifts: 35 local, 330 in Portes du Soleil region

Lift Capacity: 10,000 p/h resort, 229,000 p/h in region

Ski Season: Mid-December to Mid-April

Cross Country: 7 km; 2 km skating tracks; 10 km of winter walking trails; 250 km in Portes du Soleil

Ski School: 40 instructors; 650 in region

VALAIS *(French speaking region)*
Champéry is an old mountain village of wooden chalets. It is one of several Swiss resorts that link up with French villages to comprise the Portes du Soleil, one of the largest ski areas in the world. Other Swiss villages include Les Crosets, Champoussin, Val-d'Illiez, Morgins, Chatel and Torgon.

Mountain Restaurants: 6 restaurants and cafeterias

Other Winter Activities: Curling; fitness; ice skating/ artificial; indoor swimming; sauna in sports center; mountaineering; paragliding; snowboarding; bungee

Après-Ski: Bars, discos, cafes, concerts, folklore

Shopping/Services: Sport, clothing, souvenirs

Credit Cards: AE, DC, MC, VISA

Child Care: Contact tourist office 11 hotels

Lodging: 630 hotel beds; 11 hotels; 6,100 chalet and apartment beds. Region has 160 hotels, 93,000 beds

Transportation: Gateway Airport: Geneva (2 hrs)

Closest Provincial City: Montreux is closest big city

By Auto or Bus: Geneva-Lausanne-Aigle-Champéry

Other Information: See listings in France section for Avoriaz and Morzine—only one lift pass needed

---

Portes du Soleil
In addition to Champéry in this French-speaking section of the Valais, skiers may want to explore the following resorts. See Portes du Soleil map in French section (page 31) for location:
Morgins, CH-1875; Tel: (24) 477 23 61; Fax: (24) 477 37 08; Torgon, CH-1891; Tel: (24) 481 31 31; Fax: (24) 481 4620; Val-d'Illiez, CH-1873; Tel: (24) 477 20 77; Fax: (24) 477 37 73

ANZÈRE
TOURIST OFFICE:
Anzere CH-1972
Telephone: (41) (27) 399 28 00
Fax: (41) (27) 399 28 05

Elevation: Base: 1,500 m (4,920 ft); Top: 2,462 m (8,075 ft)

Vertical: 962 m (3,155 ft)

Longest Run: 5 km (3.1 mi)

Terrain: 45 km (28 mi) of downhill runs; 25% beginner, 50% intermediate, 25% advanced

Lifts: 11

Types: 1 Gondola; 4 Chairlifts (1 triple, 3 doubles); 6 Surface (4 T-bars, 2 platters)

Lift Capacity: 9,500 p/h

Ski Season: December to April

Cross Country: 13 km (8 mi); Also 10 km (6 mi) of walking trails

Ski School: Up to 60 instructors in peak season

Mountain Restaurants: 3

Other Winter Activities: Hiking; ice skating/artificial; indoor swimming; mountaineering; paragliding; bowling; curling; sledding; snowshoes; Delta flying

VALAIS *(French speaking region)*
Anzère has open snowfields, facing south and overlooking the Rhone River that flows through the Valais region. Strict construction planning gives even tiered hotels a chalet look.

Après-Ski: Bars, discos, cafes

Credit Cards: AE, DC, MC, VISA

Child Care: Kid's Ski School: Tele.: 027/398 27 44

Lodging: 500 beds in 4 hotels; 7,000 beds in chalets and apartments

Transportation: Airport: Geneva; 1½ hours away

Closest Provincial City: Sion (9 mi)

By Auto: Motorway to Sion (N-1, N-9, N-62)

By Train: To Sion, then Post bus or taxi to resort

Other information: Part of the same high plateau, Anzère is close to Crans-Montana

---

*On parle français — Man spricht Deutsch
Readers will note that the predominant language changes from French to German as you move eastward from Lake Geneva toward Zermatt and Saas-Fee. The large canton of Valais in southern Switzerland is called Wallis in German*

©Publishers Group International, 1998

SWITZERLAND

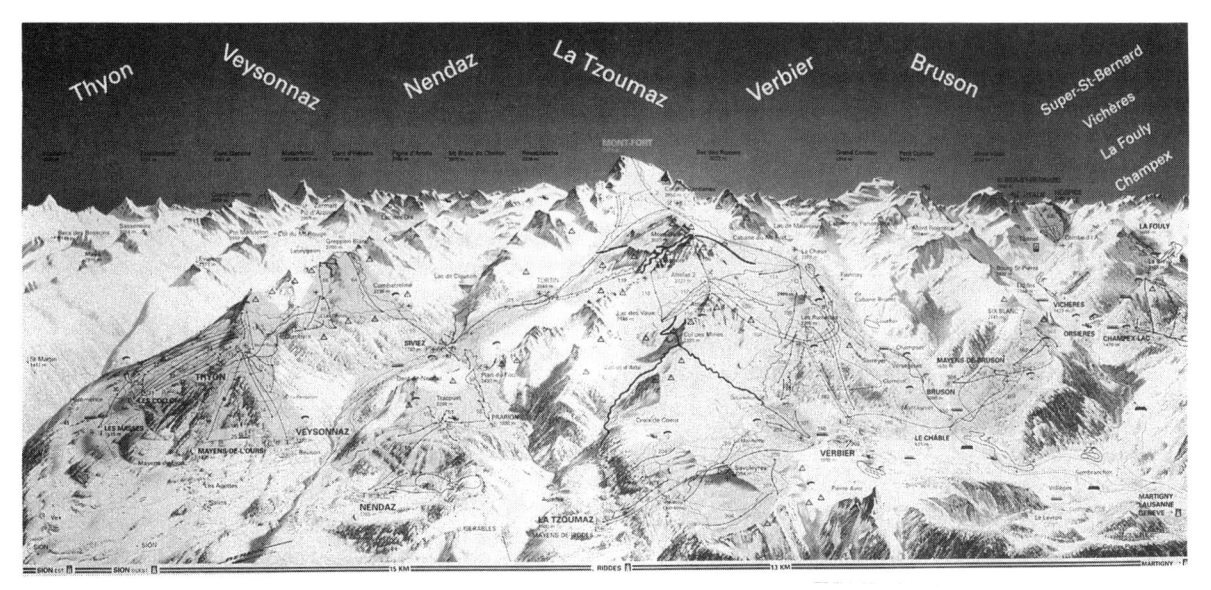

Verbier is centrally located in one of the world's major ski arenas—the 4 Vallees. Skiers have a choice among over 100 ski lifts and 400 km of slopes stretching 28 km across the valleys.

VERBIER
TOURIST OFFICE:
Verbier CH-1936
Telephone: (41) (27) 775 38 88
Fax: (41) (27) 775 38 89

VALAIS *(French speaking region)*
Verbier is centrally-located in one of the world's largest ski areas-the "4 Valleys." The high mountain village near the French and Italian borders has chalet-style hotels and public buildings.

Elevation: Village: 1,500 m (4,921 ft); Top: 3,330 m (10,922 ft)

Vertical: 1,830 m (6,002 ft)

Longest Run: 13 km (8 mi)

Terrain: 114 km (71 mi) of downhill runs locally; 410 km (254 mi) on interconnected mountains. Boulevards for cruisers, steep black for experts; 32% beginner, 42% intermediate, 26% advanced

Skiing Circus: From 3,330 meter-high Mont Fort the skier overlooks a seemingly endless number of interconnected runs and lifts

Lifts: 100 region; 34 Chairlifts; 47 Surface; 19 Trams and Gondolas. 30-passenger Funitel

Lift Capacity: 70,768 p/h in region

Ski Season: November-April

Summer Skiing: Mont Fort glacier

Cross Country: 59 km (37 mi) in Verbier; 30 km (24 mi) additional in region; 20 km (12 mi) of walking trails

Ski School: 180 instructors, teaching every snowsport

Mountain Restaurants: 25

Other Winter Activities: Curling; fitness center; helicopter skiing; ice skating/articifial; indoor swimming; mountaineering; paragliding; sauna; sleigh riding; Sports Centre; riding; hang-gliding; citizen races; torchlight descents

Après-Ski: Bars, discos, cafes, concerts, cinema

Shopping/Services: Full range of facilities

Child Care: Nursery: Baby sitting—check with tourist office

Lodging: 1,500 hotel beds; 27 hotels; 25,000 beds overall in hotels, chalets, apartments

Transportation: Gateway Airport: Geneva (90 mi; 1½ hrs)

Closest Provincial City: Martigny (16 mi)

By Auto: Via Martigny to Sembrancher to LeChâble then to Verbier

By Train: Geneva to Martigny, change to Grand St. Bernard Express to Le Chable. Bus meets train

Best Deal: Winter package of 7 day's accommodation, 6 days of skiing

Other Information: Jumbo cable car, with 150-skier capacity, is largest in the country. Verbier has a very active apres-ski scene and many fine restaurants (60 in all) to please any palate

swissair SWITZERLAND

CRANS-MONTANA
TOURIST OFFICE:
Crans-Montana CH-3962
Telephone: (41) (27) 485 04 04
Fax: (41) (27) 485 04 60

Elevation: Village: 1,500 m (4,920 ft); Top: 3,000 m (9,840 ft)
Vertical: 1,500 m (4,920 ft)
Longest Run: 14 km (9 mi)
Terrain: 160 km (99 mi) of downhill runs; groomed trails will appeal mostly to intermediates, but there is adequate black terrain. 38% beginner, 50% intermediate, 12% advanced
Skiing Circus: Vast snowfields and a lot of tree skiing on lower levels are connected by a circus of lifts
Lifts: 41
Types: 1 Tram; 1 Funitel; 5 Gondolas; 4 Quads; 4 Doubles; 26 T-bars and J-bars
Lift Capacity: 41,000 p/h resort
Ski Season: December to April
Summer Skiing: 2 km on Plaine Morte glacier, which is 9,840 feet high
Cross Country: 50 km (24 mi); 30 km (18 mi) of skating tracks, 50 km (31 mi) of winter walking trails
Ski School: 200 instructors
Mountain Restaurants: 13
Other Winter Activities: Curling; fitness center; helicopter skiing; ice skating/natural artificial; indoor

LEUKERBAD*
TOURIST OFFICE:
CH 3954 Leukerbad, Switzerland
Telephone: (41) (27) 472 71 71
Fax: (41) (27) 472 71 51

Elevation: Village: 1,411 m (4,628 ft); Top: 2,700 m (8,856 ft)
Vertical: 1,289 m (4,228 ft)
Longest Run: 6.0 km (3.6 mi)
Terrain: 40 km (25 mi) of prepared slopes; 40% beginner, 50% intermediate, 10% advanced
Skiing Circus: None
Lifts: 17
Types: 2 Trams; 3 Gondolas, 3 Chairlifts (1 triple, 2 doubles); 9 T-bars
Lift Capacity: 11,000 p/h resort
Ski Season: December 10 - April 23
Summer Skiing: No
Cross Country: Yes, 8 km, 10 km, 15 km trails
Ski School: Swiss Ski School

VALAIS *(French speaking region)*
This is a major resort, with two side-by-side villages, offering many types of lodging. Skiing is on sunny slopes overlooking the Rhone River and facing mountains to the south.

swimming; squash; indoor tennis; mountaineering; paragliding; sauna; snowboarding; riding; ballooning; snowshoes; ski touring
Après-Ski: Bars, discos, cafes, casino, concerts
Shopping/Services: Full range of facilities, including elegant shops in chic Crans
Credit Cards: AE, DC, MC, VISA
Child Care: Kindergarten and kids' ski school
Lodging: 3,600 beds in 59 hotels; 36,400 in apartments
Transportation: Airports: Geneva (2½ hrs); Sion (½)
Closest Provincial City: Sierre
By Auto: Via Lausanne to Sion to Sierre on N-1, N-9, E-62
By Train: International train via Lausanne and Sion to Sierre. Postal bus or taxi up to resort. Also funicular.
Best Deal: "Ski Soleil" four-day package: lodging, half board, ski pass and lessons, from 452 to 781 SF, depending on season and hotel selected; also, ski and golf packages available
Other Information: Site of 1987 World Alpine Championship; Anzère resort is nearby

VALAIS *(German speaking region)*
Leukerbad is a year-round resort, noted since Roman times for its curative thermal waters. This spa town participates with Zermatt, Saas Fee, Crans Montana and Verbier in promoting the Valais canton as "The Matterhorn State."

Mountain Restaurants: Yes
Other Winter Activities: Curling; fitness center; hiking; ice skating/natural & artificial; indoor swimming; indoor tennis; mono-skiing; mountaineering; paragliding; snowboarding; sauna
Après-Ski: Folklore evenings, 3 bars, 2 discos
Shopping Services: Variety
Credit Cards: AE, DC, EC, VISA
Child Care: Ages 2-6 years, no nursery, kid's ski school
Lodging: 8,000 beds in hotels and apartments
Transportation: Gateway Airport: Geneva
Local Airport: Sion
Closest Provincial City: Sierre
By Auto from Airport: Via highway, 160 km (99 miles)
By Train: To Sion, transfer to postal bus or taxi

©Publishers Group International, 1998

SWITZERLAND

RIEDERALP
TOURIST OFFICE:
Riederalp CH-3987
Telephone: (41) (27) 927 13 65
Fax: (41) (27) 927 33 13

Elevation: Village: 1,930 m (6,330 ft);
Top: 2,335 m (7,659 ft)

Vertical: 405 m (1,329 ft) from Moosfluh peak to mid-mtn. village, but down to valley the drop is 1,576 m (5,169 ft)

Terrain: 100 km (62 mi) of prepared slopes in the region; Longest run is nearly five miles

Skiing Circus: Interconnected lifts allow long runs, including a long traverse along the glacier.

Lifts: 7 local, 27 in region, including aerial trams, gondolas, chairs and T-bars.

Lift Capacity: 8,000 p/h resort; 25,000 p/h region

Ski Season: December through April

Cross Country: 2 at Riederalp, several others, 13 km

Ski School: Several, 60 instructors. Ski kindergarten

Mountain Restaurants: In village and on slopes

Other Winter Activities: Helicopter skiing; ice skating/natural; night excursions on skis by torchlight; hiking; snowshoe walking; horse drawn sleighs; sledding; sports center and indoor swimming at Bettmeralp; walking routes; folklore evenings

SAAS-FEE
TOURIST OFFICE:
Saas-Fee CH-3906
Telephone: (41) (27) 958 18 58
Fax: (41) (27) 958 18 60

Elevation: Village: 1,800 m (5,904 ft);
Top: 3,600 m (11,808 ft)

Vertical: 1,800 m (5,904 ft)

Longest Run: 9 km (5.6 mi)

Terrain: 100 km (62 mi) of downhill runs that skirt the glacier and its crevasses. Several mountains make a bowl around the village; 25% beginner, 50% intermediate, 25% advanced

Skiing Circus: Mountains accessible to each other

Lifts: 26

Types: 2 Trams; 4 Gondolas; 1 Funicular (the famous underground "Metro Alpin"); 2 Chairlifts; 17 T-bars

Lift Capacity: 26,340 p/h resort

Ski Season: November through May

Summer Skiing: On glacier, end of June

Cross Country: 6 km (4 mi); 20 km (12 mi) of winter walking trails

Ski School: Downhill, X-C, telemark & snowboarding

Mountain Restaurants: 10, including the Mittelallalin, the highest revolving restaurant in the world

VALAIS (German speaking region)
Riederalp, a traffic-free village, is one of several mid-mountain resorts that sit on a sunny, south-facing terrace below the 23-km-long Aletsch glacier, Europe's largest. Riederalp, Bettmeralp and Fiescheralp overlook the Rhone Valley and are linked together by snowfields and lifts.

Apres-Ski: Restaurants, bars, discos, slide shows

Shopping/Services: 2 food stores, 3 sports shops

Lodging: 650 beds in hotels, from 1 to 4-star. Also 3,850 beds in chalets, holiday flats and group cntrs.

Transportation: Gateway Airports: Geneva (3 hrs), Zürich (3 1/2 hrs)

Closet Provincial City: Brig

By Auto: E-62 Motorway to Brig to Morel

By Train: International train to Brig; via Furka railway to Morel. Parking available in Morel. Ascend to Riederalp by gondola or cable car

Best Deal: Ski week packages, with half-board, lifts and lessons, in mid-December; January, mid-March and after Easter

Other Information: In addition to the awesome glacier, Riederalp has one of the highest pine forests in the alps. Switzerland's Nature Conservation Center is located here.
Area is acclaimed by Swiss and German visitors for its family-type slopes, but challenging off-piste opportunities exist, too. Some snowmaking, but high elevation assures long season

VALAIS (German speaking region)
Saas-Fee calls itself the "Pearl of the Alps." It offers great skiing and awesome scenery, including a fierce-looking glacier.

Other Winter Activities: Curling; fitness center; ice skating/natural; indoor swimming; mountaineering; sauna; sleigh riding; indoor tennis; Husky Power

Après-Ski: Bars, discos, concerts, cinema, museum

Shopping/Services: Sports, clothes, boutiques, butcher, photo, laundries, food, jewelry, hairdresser

Lodging: 2,500 hotel beds; 56 hotels; 4,700 other beds in chalets and apartments; 400 beds for groups; 4,000 other beds available in two nearby villages which are resorts themselves—Saas-Almagell and Saas-Grund

Transportation: Gateway Airport: Geneva (4¼ hrs)

Closest Provincial City: Visp (26 km)

By Auto: Motorway to Visp to Stalden to Saas-Fee. Must park at edge of town

By Train: International train to Brig; bus to Saas-Fee

Best Deal: Allalin Week, doing a variety of activities in the Blue Glacier World

Other Information: No cars allowed in Saas-Fee. Town is traffic free except for hotels' electric carts. Saas-Fee is noted for being starting point for week-long "High Route" adventure to Chamonix, France

SWITZERLAND

ZERMATT
TOURIST OFFICE:
Zermatt CH-3920
Telephone: (41) (27) 967 01 81
Fax: (41) (27) 967 01 85

VALAIS *(German speaking region)*
Zermatt is Switzerland's best-known ski resort and arguably the largest. This traffic-free village blends modern skiing with a tradition of mountaineering. Weathered old farmhouses stand among modern hotels and public buildings.

Elevation: Village: 1,620 m (5,314 ft); Top: 3,820 m (12,530 ft)

Vertical: 2,200 m (7,216 ft)

Longest Run: 15 km (9 mi)

Terrain: 3 major mountains: Sunnegga-Rothorn, Gornergrat-Stockhorn, and Schwarzsee-Trockener Steg-Klein Matterhorn. 246 km (153 mi) of prepared runs and almost immeasurable off-piste skiing; 27% beginner, 43% intermediate, 30% advanced

Skiing Circus: Best bet is to buy special ticket and ski over into Italy (Breuil-Cervinia) for lunch

Lifts: 74

Types: 15 Aerial Cableways, 1 rack railway, 1 underground railway; 7 Gondolas; 15 Chairlifts; 35 T-bars

Lift Capacity: 76,400 p/h in region

Ski Season: Skiing possible the whole year.

Summer Skiing: July-September on Theodul glacier; 26 km of runs; cableways & lifts operate 12 mos.

Cross Country: 10 km (6 mi); 60 km (37 mi) of ski hiking trails, 30 km (19 mi) of winter walking trails

Ski School: 175 instructors

Mountain Restaurants: 38

Other Winter Activities: Curling; fitness center; sauna; helicopter skiing; hiking; horse drawn sleigh; ice skating/natural/artificial; indoor swimming; squash; indoor tennis; mountaineering; paragliding; snowboarding; dog sled & sleigh riding; guided mountain expeditions; ice diving

Après-Ski: Bars, discos, cafes, 110 restaurants, museum, cinema, concerts, folklore evenings

Shopping/Services: Everything for skiers, hikers, climbers, sightseers—a wide variety of goods

Credit Cards: Cards accepted for lift tickets

Child Care: Kindergartens and baby sitting

Lodging: 6,500 hotel beds; 118 hotels; 7,000 apartment and chalet beds; youth hostel; Matterhorn hostel

Transportation: Gateway Airport: Geneva (160 mi)

Closest Provincial City: Brig (25 mi)

By Auto: Geneva-Visp-Täsch, where cars must be parked and skiers go the last 3 miles by train

By Train: International train to Brig or Visp, change to mountain railway to Zermatt; Heliport run by Air Zermatt

Other Information: Like all Swiss tourist offices, Zermatt's bureau is eager to assist. Exact dates on a Fax inquiry will get a quick response

Summer Skiing: July-September on Theodul glacier; 26 km of runs; cableways & lifts operate 12 months

The Matterhorn, the world's most dramatic rock, as viewed from Gornergrat across the glacier. Photo: Zermatt Tourist Office

©Publishers Group International, 1998

SWITZERLAND

ADELBODEN/LENK*
TOURIST OFFICE:
Adelboden CH-3715
Telephone: (41) (33) 673 80 80
Fax: (41) (33) 673 80 92

Elevation: Village: 1,350 m (4,428 ft); Top: 2,350 m (7,708 ft)

Vertical: 950 m (3,116 ft)

Longest Run: 6 km (3.7 mi)

Terrain: 166 km (103 mi) of prepared slopes; 46% beginner, 44% intermediate, 10% advanced

Skiing Circus: Several separate areas near Adelboden; many slopes across the mountains connect the villages

Lifts: 51

Types: 3 Trams; 8 Gondolas; 7 Chairlifts; 33 Surface

Lift Capacity: 39,930 p/h Lenk/Adelboden

Ski Season: December to April

Cross Country: 40 km (25 mi); 25 km (15 mi) of skating tracks

Ski School: Well-staffed schools in both villages

Mountain Restaurants: More than a dozen, most in wooden cabins

BERNESE OBERLAND *(German speaking region)*
These are two picturesque villages that jointly promote their ski region. Six miles apart as the crow flies, but connected by snowfields that billow over the mountains.

Other Winter Activities: Curling; ice skating/artificial; snowboarding; sleighriding; snowshoes; igloo sleeping

Après-Ski: Bars, discos, concerts, cinema

Credit Cards: AE, DC, MC, VISA

Child Care: Contact tourist office

Lodging: Adelboden: 1,454 hotel beds; 7,000 beds in chalets and apartments; Lenk: 4,860 beds

Transportation: Gateway Airport: Zürich

Closest Provincial City: Thun (24 mi)

By Auto: Bern-Thun-Spiez-Frutigen-Adelboden

By Train: Change in Bern, again in Frutigen to bus

Best Deal: Five all-day lessons and Adelboden-Lenk ski pass for 325 SF

Other Information: Adelboden has a World Cup race every year. Skiers may want to get brochures of both villages to compare surroundings and facilities

GSTAAD/SKI GSTAAD
TOURIST OFFICE:
Gstaad CH-3780
Telephone: (41) (33) 748 81 81
Fax: (41) (33) 748 81 83

Elevation: Village: 1,050 m (3,444 ft); Top: 3,000 m (9,840 ft)

Vertical: 1,950 m (6,396 ft)

Longest Run: 9 mi from the glacier down to Reusch, with a drop of more than a mile

Terrain: 85 km (53 mi) of local groomed runs, 250 km (155 mi) in region. Three areas around Gstaad—Eggli, Wispile and Wasserngrat; other villages have interconnected slopes and lifts. Good example: Schönried-Saanenmöser; 45% beginner, 35% intermediate, 20% advanced

Lifts: 69 in region

Lift Capacity: 50,000 p/h

Ski Season: December to Mid-April

Summer Skiing: On glacier Les Diablerets

Cross Country: 100 km (62 mi) classic; 40 km (25 mi) skating

Ski School: 4 schools with a total of 200 instructors

Other Winter Activities: Curling; fitness center; helicopter skiing; ice skating/natural; indoor swimming; indoor tennis; mountaineering; paragliding; snowboarding; sleigh riding; skeet; ballooning; riding school

BERNESE OBERLAND *(German speaking region)*
Fashionable Gstaad is the centerpiece of a region that also includes St. Stephan, Zweisimmen, Saanenmöser, Schönried, Gsteig, Lauenen, Saanen, Rougemont, Chateau d'Oex, and Glacier des Diablerets.

Après-Ski: Bars, discos, concerts, bridge, cinema, fine dining

Shopping/Services: Boutiques and elegant shops, but grocery stores, too

Lodging: 2,300 hotel beds; 6,000 beds in holiday flats & chalets

Transportation: Gateway Airport: Geneva; 2 hrs (149 km/92 mi)

Closest Provincial City: Thun; 55 km (34 mi)

By Auto: Montreux; 67 km (42 mi)

By Ski Bus: Geneva-Lausanne-Montreux-Gstaad

By Train: Same as auto

Heliport; Airport for business jets

Best Deal: All hotels have ski packages in January and March—breakfasts, lifts, lessons—from 555 SF for six nights

Other Information: This is a region where farming blends with tourism. It is also roughly the dividing line between German and French-speaking sections of the country. Tourist association operates for whole region

swissair

SWITZERLAND

GRINDELWALD
TOURIST CENTER:
Grindelwald CH-3818
Telephone: (41) (33) 854 12 12
Fax: (41) (33) 854 12 10

Elevation: Village: 1,034 m (3,392 ft); Top: 3,454 m (11,329 ft)

Vertical: 2,100 m (6,888 ft)

Longest Run: 15 km (9 mi)

Terrain: World famous runs, with 150 km (93 mi) of downhill in or near Grindelwald, and another 50 km (31 mi) in the region; 30% beginner, 50% intermediate, 20% advanced

Skiing Circus: The various ski areas connect or can be reached by short walks or quick bus or train rides

Lifts: 32 local; 49 in the Jungfrau Region

Types: Jungfrau region has 5 cable cars, 3 cogwheel trains, 2 gondolas, 12 chairs and numerous surface lifts—49 in all

Lift Capacity: 39,350 p/h in Jungfrau Region

Ski Season: December through April

Summer Skiing: Small lift on Jungfraujoch glacier

Cross Country: 34 km (21 mi); 7 km (4 mi) of skating tracks, 80 km (50 mi) of winter walking trails

Ski School: 80 instructors, all disciplines

Mountain Restaurants: 27, including glacier restaurant on Jungfrau

BERNESE OBERLAND *(German speaking region) Three of the most photographed mountains in Switzerland—the Eiger, Mönch and Jungfrau—are the spectacular backdrop for several major ski areas. Grindelwald is the largest of these. (See map and also refer to listings for Interlaken, Mürren and Wengen, all part of the Jungfrau region.)*

Other Winter Activities: Curling; helicopter skiing; ice skating/natural/artificial; mountaineering; paragliding; sauna; sleigh riding; snow rafting; sports center

Après-Ski: Bars, discos, concerts, folklore evenings

Shopping/Services: Many shops; 50 restaurants

Credit Cards: AE, DC, MC, VISA

Child Care: Ski nursery school; Tel.: 33 853 5200

Lodging: 2,900 hotel beds; 52 hotels; 6,000 chalet and apartment beds; 2,800 in camping and lodges/dorms

Transportation: Gateway Airport: Zürich, 195 km

Closest Provincial City: Interlaken (20 km)

By Auto: Zürich-Bern-Spiez-Interlaken-Grindelwald

By Train: Intercity to Bern and Interlaken, transfer to regional train to Grindelwald

Best Deal: 7 nights in one-star hotel, breakfast, regional ski pass, free entrance to sports center, reduced price in school, from 673 SF

Other Information: Jungfraujoch is reached by Europe's highest cog railway, which tunnels through the Eiger and the Mönch. Ice palace here is a "must see"

The Kleine Scheidegg station is a junction for skiers on the famous Lauberhorn run or sightseers going up the Jungfrau.

Photo: Fred McKinney

©Publishers Group International, 1998

SWITZERLAND   swissair

Wengen... "Let's have a bite, while waiting for the train."
Photo: Fred McKinney

WENGEN
TOURIST OFFICE:
Wengen CH-3823
Telephone: (41) (33) 855 14 14
Fax: (41) (33) 855 30 60

Elevation: Base/Village: 1,280 m (4,198 ft); Top: 2,970 m (9,741 ft)

Vertical: 1,690 m (5,543 ft)

Longest Run: 14 km (9 mi)

Terrain: 98 km (61 mi) of local downhill; 195 km (121 mi) with surrounding areas; 30% beginner, 50% intermediate, 20% advanced

Skiing Circus: Kleine Scheidegg, Lauberhorn, Männlichen and Allmend areas all interconnect

Lifts: 23 local; 49 in Jungfrau Region; See Grindelwald above for more details

Lift Capacity: 39,350 p/h in Jungfrau Region

Ski Season: December through April

Cross Country: 17 km (10.5 mi) in nearby Lauterbrunnen; 40 km (25 mi) of winter walking trails

Ski School: 60 instructors; cross country teachers on request

Mountain Restaurants: 7, some with overnight facilities

BERNESE OBERLAND (Jungfrau Region)
(German speaking region)
Long runs, with degrees of difficulty to please everyone, all within sight of the Eiger, Mönch, and Jungfrau mountain peaks, are some of the attractions of this complete resort.

Other Winter Activities: Curling; folklore evenings; ice skating/natural/artificial; mountaineering; paragliding; tobogganing; night skiing events

Après-Ski: Bars, discos, concerts, cafes, folklore evenings, museum

Shopping/Services: Variety of shops

Credit Cards: DC, MC, VISA

Child Care: Nursery: Holiday Kindergarten (ages 3-7); Day with lunch, 30 SF; Telephone Tourist office

Lodging: 2,200 hotel beds; 25 hotels; 2,500 apt. beds

Transportation: Gateway Airport: Zürich (3½ hrs)

Closest Provincial City: Interlaken (10 mi) (See Interlaken listing)

Regional train from Interlaken Ost, change in Lauterbrunnen; also ski bus from Interlaken

Best Deal: Bed and breakfast from 50-60 SF

Other Information: Traffic-free town—no cars allowed

SWITZERLAND

swissair

Jungfrau-Ski-Region

SWITZERLAND

MÜRREN
TOURIST OFFICE:
Mürren CH-3825
Telephone: (41) (33) 856 86 86
Fax: (41) (33) 856 86 96

BERNESE OBERLAND *(German speaking region)*
Mürren is a village on the edge of a cliff with picturesque hotels and chalets and the majestic peaks in full view—the Eiger, Mönch and Jungfrau.

Elevation: Base/Village: 1,650 m (5,412 ft); Top: 2,970 m (9,742 ft)

Vertical: 1,320 m (4,330 ft)

Longest Run: 16 km (10 mi)

Terrain: Challenging skiing under the Schilthorn, with a long run all the way down to Lauterbrunnen; 30% beginner, 50% intermediate, 20% advanced

Lifts: 49 in Jungfrau Region; 13 in Mürren

Types: 1 Tram; 2 Gondolas; 2 Funiculars; 4 Chairlifts; 4 T-bars

Lift Capacity: 6,780 resort; 39,350 p/h in Jungfrau region

Ski Season: December through April

Cross Country: 12 km (7.4 mi) course Stechelberg-Lauterbrunnen; 2 km course in Blumental

Ski School: All disciplines; 24 instructors

Mountain Restaurants: 7

Other Winter Activities: Curling; ice skating/artificial; indoor swimming; gym; squash; paragliding; snowboarding; sleigh riding; sports center; parallel slaloms at night; guest races; helicopter skiing.

Après-Ski: Bars, discos, fondue parties

Shopping/Services: Various small shops

Lodging: 11 hotels with 670 beds; two pensions with 110 beds

Transportation: Gateway Airport: Zürich; 2½ hrs (90 mi)

Closest Provincial City: Interlaken (11 mi)

By Auto: See Grindelwald listing and map

Other Information: Traffic free—no cars allowed. Revolving restaurant atop the Schilthorn will look familiar. The James Bond film, "On Her Majesty's Secret Service," was made here. Notice Lauterbrunnen on the Jungfrau map. It sits in the canyon below Mürren and Wengen, is closer to Interlaken. The village has 521 beds

The Schilthorn looms over Mürren.

Photo: Fred McKinney

SWITZERLAND

INTERLAKEN

INTERLAKEN TOURISM
Interlaken CH-3800
Telephone: (41) (33) 822 21 21
Fax: (41) (33) 826 53 75

Terrain: All the mountain statistics are really those of the entire Jungfrau Region. See listings for Grindelwald, Mürren and Wengen

Ski School: 4 schools, teaching all disciplines

Other Winter Activities: Snowboarding; telemark; monoskiing; mountaineering; ice canyoning; snowrafting; paragliding; hiking; ice skating/artificial; indoor swimming, tennis and indoor golf; horseback riding; carriage rides; coach excursions; bridge jumping; luge; toboggan; curling

Après-Ski: Bars, discos, cafes, folklore evenings, concerts, billiards, darts, cinema, casino

Shopping/Services: Complete variety

Credit Cards: AE, DC, MC, VISA

BERNESE OBERLAND *(German speaking region)*
Interlaken is a year-round resort and a major destination for skiers. It sits between two lakes, Brienzersee and Thunersee, but the skiing is 30 to 45 minutes away by train or ski bus. It is not ski in-ski out, but makes up for it with a wide range of attractions.

Child Care: Contact tourist office

Lodging: 4,500 hotel beds; 1,000 in apartments

Transportation: Gateway Airport: Zürich; 2½ hours (175 km/108 mi)

By Auto: Via Bern and Thun

By Train: Zürich-Olten-Bern-Interlaken

Ski Bus: Interlaken serves the various resorts

Best Deal: Rates in holiday apartments range from 30 to 50 SF per day per person, depending on degree of comfort

Other Information: Interlaken is popular with tour operators in the United States because of its size, convenience and attractive rates

MEIRINGEN/HASLIBERG

TOURIST OFFICE:
Meiringen/Haslital CH-3860
Telephone: (41) (33) 972 5050
Fax: (41) (33) 972 5055

Elevation: Village: 600 m (1,968 ft); Top: 2,433 m (7,980 ft)

Vertical: 1,833 m (6,012 ft)

Longest Run: 12 km (7.4 mi)

Terrain: 60 km (37 mi) of groomed runs; 30% beginner, 40% intermediate, 30% advanced

Lifts: 15

Types: 1 Tram; 3 Gondolas; 5 Chairlifts (2 quads, 3 doubles); 4 T-bars; 2 children lifts

Lift Capacity: 11,200 p/h resort

Ski Season: December-April

Cross Country: 40 km (25 mi); 10 km (6 mi) of winter walking trails

Ski School: Teaches all types of skiing, plus delta and paragliding, 30 instructors

Mountain Restaurants: 5

Other Winter Activities: Curling; ice skating/natural; indoor swimming; indoor tennis; mountaineering; paragliding; hang gliding; snowboarding

BERNESE OBERLAND *(German speaking region)*
This is a smaller resort, as far as accommodations go, but it need not apologize for its rugged terrain. Hot skiers and cool chamois like the mountains here.

Après-Ski: Bars, discos, cafes, folklore evenings, museum

Shopping/Services: Full range of facilities

Credit Cards: Accepted for passes or ski school

Lodging: 1,500 hotel beds; 40 hotels; 3,000 other beds

Transportation: Gateway Airport: Zürich (2 hrs)

Closest Major City: Luzern (40 mi)

By Auto: Zürich to Luzern to Brünig Pass

By Train: Via Luzern and Brünig

Best Deal: Half-board in 4-star hotel in high season for 150 SF a day

Other Information: Also Reichenbach Falls, famous for fictional struggle to the death by Sherlock Holmes and Professor Moriarty, but only seen in winter as a frozen string of ice

©Publishers Group International, 1998

SWITZERLAND

CENTRAL SWITZERLAND *(German speaking region)*
The major resort in Central Switzerland, Engelberg offers gentle skiing on one side of the valley. But on the other are challenging choices—down from imposing Mount Titlis, which has a revolving sight-seeing tram.

Après-Ski: Bars, discos, cafes, casino
Shopping/Services: Facilities of all types
Credit Cards: AE, DC, MC, VISA
Child Care: Possible in some hotels. Check with tourist office. Ski school kindergarten
Lodging: 2,000 hotel beds; 25 hotels; 5,000 other beds in chalets and apartments
Transportation: Gateway Airport: Zürich 100 km (2 hrs)
Closest Provincial City: Luzern (19 mi)
By Auto: A2 motorway to Stans-Süd to Engelberg
By Train: International train to Luzern, transfer to Stans-Engelberg railway
Other Information: Melchsee-Frutt, a smaller high altitude resort, is nearby; also, popular Luzern is a sightseeing bonus on a bad weather day. Mt. Titlis has the world's first rotating aerial tramway cabin, offering 360° panorama during the 5-minute ride

CENTRAL SWITZERLAND *(German speaking region)*
Andermatt is a health resort near the Furka, Oberalp and Gotthard passes. It is on the route of the famed Glacier Express.

Après-Ski: Bars, discos, cafes, folklore evenings
Shopping/Services: Standard shops
Credit Cards: AE, DC, MC, VISA
Child Care: Ski school with noon care
Lodging: 19 Hotels with 760 beds; 900 other beds
Transportation: Gateway airport: Zürich (117 km; 72 mi)
Closest Major City: Luzern (60 mi)
By Auto: Zürich-Luzern-Andermatt
By Train: Zürich-Zug-Schwyz-Altdorf-Andermatt
Best Deal: All inclusive ski week from 655 SF
Other Information: Site of biathlon and dogsled championships. Andermatt offers a regional lift ticket that also includes Sedrun and Disentis

---

(ft);

uns in all colors.
de of Titlis is almost
nowfields abound
mediate,

ular, 4 Chairlifts,

1
m (9 mi) of skating
ng trails
instructors

e skating/natural/
nis; sleigh riding;
enter

; Top:

ns on 23 slopes
beginner,

ifts, 6 T-bars

Ski Season: December through April
Cross Country: 28 km (17 mi); 10 km (6 mi) of skating tracks
Ski School: 20 instructors
Mountain Restaurants: 4
Other Winter Activities: Fitness rooms in various hotels; ice skating/natural; mountaineering; sleigh riding; paragliding; hanggliding; curling; hiking

---

Amazon.com
The best place to search, explore, and discover is just a click away.

And stay informed
Sign up for Amazon.com Delivers and get monthly e-mail recommendations on products that interest you the most.

Get it for less
Enjoy everyday savings of up to 50%.

Buy it fast
1-Click℠ Ordering makes shopping a snap.

Find it fast
Our All Products search function helps you locate a variety of products quickly and easily.

...We have what you want.

Books, Music, Videos, Toys & Games, E-cards, Auctions

With Earth's Biggest Selection...™

amazon.com

SWITZERLAND

DAVOS
TOURIST OFFICE:
Davos CH-7270
Telephone: (41) (81) 415 21 21
Fax: (41) (81) 415 21 00

Elevation: Village: 1,560 m (5,117 ft); Top: 2,844 m (9,328 ft)

Vertical: 1,284 m (4,212 ft)

Longest Run: 12 km (7.4 mi)

Terrain: 248 km (154 mi) of downhill runs locally; 320 km (198 mi) when terrain of nearby Klosters is added. From the Parsenn area and its wide snowfields, skiers can descend through steep and deep to small villages and to Klosters or cruise miles away and return by train; 30% beginner, 40% intermediate, 30% advanced

Lifts: 36 local, 52 with Klosters

Types: 8 Trams; 2 Gondolas; 2 Funiculars; 6 Chairlifts; 18 T-bars

Lift Capacity: 55,000 p/h in Davos-Klosters combined

Ski Season: December to April

Cross Country: 75 km (46 mi) in region, with 35 km (22 mi) of skating tracks; 84 km (52 mi) of winter walking trails

Ski School: 170 instructors

Mountain Restaurants: 27, ranging from cafeterias to mountain cabins, with outdoor decks

GRAUBÜNDEN *(German speaking region)*
Davos is a world-renowned resort, with ski areas on both sides of a high valley. Famous as a health resort for a century, it has become a major conference center. It is a sizable town of 13,000 inhabitants and quite cosmopolitan.

Other Winter Activities: Curling; hiking; horse drawn sleigh; ice skating/natural; ice skating/artificial; (natural ice rink is largest in Europe); paragliding; sauna; sleigh riding; sports center; riding; hang gliding; indoor swimming; indoor tennis

Après-Ski: Bars, discos, cafes, folklore evenings, concerts, cinema, several museums; sauna; casino

Shopping/Services: Many shops, all services

Credit Cards: AE, DC, VISA, MC

Child Care: Pinocchio Kindergarten; 30 SF/ ½ day

Lodging: 90 hotels; 23,000 beds in hotels and flats

Transportation: Gateway Airport: Zürich (2½ hrs)

By Auto: Zürich-Landquart-Davos on N-3

By Train: Rhaetian railway from Landquart (3¼ hrs

Best Deal: Special—7 nights, half-board, ski pass, ski school, from 1,087 SF, depending on hotel and week

Other Information: Town is divided in two parts—Davos Dorf and Davos Platz. This noted climatic resort was locale for Thomas Mann's "The Magic Mountain"

These cable cars are truly above the world in Davos.

Photo: Best of the Alps

SWITZERLAND

KLOSTERS
TOURIST OFFICE:
Klosters CH-7250
Telephone: (41) (81) 4 10 20 20
Fax: (41) (81) 4 10 20 10

GRAUBÜNDEN (German speaking region)
Klosters, a well-known resort near Davos, shares the snowfields of the Parsenn, but has other slopes on the Madrisa mountain

Elevation: Base/Village: 1,200 m (3,936 ft); Top: 2,844 m (9,328 ft)

Vertical: 1,644 m (5,392 ft)

Longest Run: 12 km (7.4 mi)

Terrain: 170 km (105 mi) of downhill runs, 315 km (195 mi) in region. Skiing on both sides of valley. Access to Parsenn, above Davos, by cable car to Gotschnagrat; 30% beginner, 40% intermediate, 30% advanced

Skiing Circus: Many interconnects on Parsenn side. On other side of valley is Madrisa, south-facing

Lifts: 32

Types: 3 Trams; 5 Gondolas; 10 Cableways; 5 Chairs; 9 T-bars

Lift Capacity: 16,190 p/h Resort; 55,000 p/h in Davos-Klosters combined (55 lifts)

Ski Season: December-April

Cross Country: 50 km (31 mi) of cross country and skating tracks; 30 km (19 mi) of winter walking trails. Back country adventure into Gargellen in Austria

Ski School: 150 instructors

Mountain Restaurants: 12; self-service, waiters, outdoor decks

Other Winter Activities: Curling; fitness center; horse drawn sleigh; ice skating/artifical; paragliding; hang gliding; sauna; sleigh riding; horseback; snowshoes; tubing; squash; indoor tennis

Après-Ski: Bars, discos, cafes, concerts

Shopping/Services: Support facillities of every type

Credit Cards: AE, VISA, MC

Child Care: Madrisa Day Care Center; Telephone: 422 23 33

Lodging: 2,000 beds in 30 hotels; 6,800 others

Transportation: Gateway Airport: Zürich (2½ hrs)
By Train: International train to Landquart, transfer to mountain railway (RhB)

Best Deal: Ski week package—7 days half-board, ski pass, from 930 SF in Jan. & Apr.—7 days from 1,200 SF in high season

Other Information: Klosters has been popular with celebrities, who consider it elegant but relaxed, but many families enjoy the variety of runs. (See also Davos)

Klosters and Davos share skiing terrain and a well-developed lift circuit.

Photo: Swiss National Tourist Office

SWITZERLAND

The railroad bridge between Chur and Arosa is an engineering marvel that has drawn "ahs" since 1912. Photo: Swiss National Tourist Office

AROSA*
TOURIST OFFICE:
Arosa CH-7050
Telephone: (41) (81) 378 70 20
Fax: (41) (81) 378 70 21

Elevation: Base: 1,800 m (5,904 ft); Top: 2,653 m (8,702 ft)

Vertical: 853 m (2,798 ft)

Terrain: Open snowfields on four mountains (Hörnli, Platterhorn, Weisshorn, Brüggerhorn), connected by circus of lifts; 31% beginner, 57% intermediate, 12% advanced

Lifts: 16

Types: 2 Funiculars; 1 Gondola; 7 Chairlifts; 6 T-bars

Lift Capacity: 21,700 p/h resort

Ski Season: Early December to late April

Cross Country: 25 km (15 mi); 3 km (2 mi) of skating tracks; 40 km (25 mi) of winter walking trails

Ski School: More than 100 instructors in various disciplines

Mountain Restaurants: 7

Other Winter Activities: Curling; fitness center; hiking; horse drawn sleigh; ice skating/natural; ice skating/artificial; indoor swimming; indoor tennis; paragliding; sauna; snowboarding; sleigh riding; indoor and outdoor golf; hang gliding; ballooning; torchlight skiing; citizen races

GRAUBÜNDEN *(German speaking region)*
Arosa is a health resort more than a mile high. Popular with celebrities through the years, it remains a favorite with skiers who seek cruising terrain and a lot of sun.

Après-Ski: Bars, discos, cafes, concerts, museum, billiards, chess, bowling, cinema, folklore evenings

Shopping/Services: Beauty center, fashionable shops

Credit Cards: Not accepted for ski school

Child Care: Ski nursery school. Contact tourist office

Lodging: Beds: 8,070; Nearly 5,000 beds are in 60 hotels, others are in chalets and apartments; hostel

Transportation: Gateway Airport: Zürich (3¼ hours)

Closest Provincial City: Chur (18 mi)

By Auto: Route N3 to N13 to Chur, then to Arosa. Road rises 4,330 ft, chains may be needed

By Train: International train to Chur, transfer to Rhaetian Railway (one hour ride)

Other Information: The village prides itself on its gastronomic achievements and a large number of events, including horse and greyhound races on frozen lake. Also special festivals. Free bus service. Traffic restrictions, particularly after midnight

©Publishers Group International, 1998

SWITZERLAND

DISENTIS/SEDRUN
TOURIST OFFICE:
Disentis CH-7180
Telephone: (41) (81) 920 30 20
Fax: (41) (81) 920 30 29

Elevation: Village: 1,150 m (3,772 ft); Top: 2,920 m (9,578 ft)

Vertical: 1,770 m (5,806 ft)

Longest Run: 12 km (7.4 mi)

Terrain: 110 km (68 mi) of pistes, 50% intermediate with more than a mile-high vertical. Parallel ridges with both groomed and off-piste areas are like giant fingers reaching down to the Rhine.

Lifts: 22

Types: 1 Tram; 4 Chairlifts (1 triple, 3 double); 17 Surface

Lift Capacity: 8,420 p/h region

Ski Season: December to April

Cross Country: 50 km (31 mi); 45 km (28 mi) of hiking and winter walking trails

Ski School: 70 instructors in two schools

Other Winter Activities: Curling; ice skating; indoor swimming; indoor tennis; snowboarding; sleigh riding; high altitude ski tours; golf on snow

GRAUBÜNDEN *(German speaking region)*
These villages, a half-dozen miles apart, share the same mountains and promote the same ski facilities. Located along the Rhine, near where the river has its source, they are now promoting themselves along with Andermatt

Après-Ski: Bars, discos, bowling, folk museum

Shopping/Services: Full range in both villages

Lodging: 9,000 beds in the two villages

Transportation: Gateway Airport: Zürich (3 hrs)
Closest Provincial City: Chur (38 mi)
By Auto: Routes N3 and N13 to Chur, proceed up the Rhine toward Andermatt
By Train: International trains from Zürich. Like Andermatt, Disentis is a stop on the Glacier Express.

Best Deal: Skiers can stay here for as low as 40 SF for bed and breakfast in low season

Other Information: Generally lower prices make this an attractive area for families. Popular with Belgians and Dutch, who tend to be more budget conscious

LENZERHEIDE/VALBELLA
TOURIST OFFICE:
Lenzerheide CH-7078
Telephone: (41) (81) 385 11 20
Fax: (41) (81) 385 11 21

Elevation: Village: 1,500 m (4,920 ft); Top: 2,865 m (9,397 ft)

Vertical: 1,365 m (4,477 ft)

Longest Run: 7 km (4.3 mi)

Terrain: 155 km (96 mi) of groomed downhill runs, plus many off-piste opportunities. Rothorn is 2,865 m high. Lower mountains across the valley, Piz Scalottas, Piz Danis and Stätzerhorn, are connected by lifts and many runs

Lifts: 36

Types: 2 Trams; 10 Chairlifts; 24 T-bars

Lift Capacity: 36,350 p/h resort

Ski Season: December to April

Cross Country: 50 km (31 mi); 20 km (12 mi) of skating tracks; 10 ski hiking trails; 80 km (50 mi) of winter walking trails

Ski School: 150 instructors

Mountain Restaurants: 16

Other Winter Activities: Curling; horse drawn sleigh; ice skating/natural; indoor swimming; indoor tennis;

GRAUBÜNDEN *(German speaking region)*
These two villages on opposite sides of the Heidsee Lake sit between imposing mountain ridges that appeal to skiers and sightseers.

squash; paragliding; hang gliding; snowboarding; sleigh riding; sports center; citizen races; ballooning; cinema

Après-Ski: Bars, discos, cafes, ski school socials

Shopping/Services: Both villages have all needed services and shops

Credit Cards: AE, DC, MC, VISA

Child Care: Ski nursery—check with tourist office

Lodging: 2,400 hotel beds; 32 hotels; 6,000 other beds in chalets and apartments

Transportation: Gateway Airport: Zürich (2½ hrs)
Closest Provincial City: Chur (10 miles) (30 minutes)
By Auto: Zürich to Chur on N-3 to Lenzerheide
By Train: International train to Chur, post bus to Lenzerheide resort

Best Deal: Bed and breakfast as low as 60 SF a day in pre-Christmas and January weeks

Other Information: Churs, capital city of Graubünden, has medieval charm and interesting sights—a good place to take a break

SWITZERLAND

FLIMS-LAAX-FALERA
TOURIST OFFICE: Flims CH-7018, Flims
Telephone: (41) (81) 920 92 00 Fax: (41) (81) 920 92 01
TOURIST OFFICE: Laax CH-7031
Telephone: (41) (81) 921 43 43 Fax: (41) (81) 921 65 65

Elevation: Village: 1,100 m (3,608 ft); Top: 3,000 m (9,840 ft)

Vertical: 1,900 m (6,232 ft)

Longest Run: 14 km (8.7 mi)

Terrain: 225 km (139 mi) of cleared downhill runs in the "White Arena." A wide array of lifts connects Crap Sogn Gion with other mountains La Siala and Cassons Grat. Wide variety, including glacier skiing; 29% beginner; 45% intermediate; 26% advanced

Lifts: 32

Types: 4 Trams; 3 Gondolas; 11 Chairlilfts; 14 Surface lifts

Lift Capacity: 41,200 p/h resort

Ski Season: End of October-Beginning of May

Cross Country: 60 km (37 mi); 21 km (13 mi) of skating tracks; 60 km (37 mi) of winter walking trails

Ski School: 150 instructors for all snowsports

Mountain Restaurants: 17, including restaurant at foot of Vorab glacier

Other Winter Activities: Curling; fitness center; horse drawn sleigh; ice skating/natural and artificial; indoor swimming; indoor tennis; mountaineering; paragliding; sauna; horse riding; ballooning; bowling

Après-Ski: Bars, discos, cafes, dining, concerts

Shopping/Services: Modest number of shops in Laax. Greater selection in Flims communities

Credit Cards: Not accepted in ski school

Child Care: Kid's Ski School: Ski Kindergarten

Lodging: 3,000 hotel beds; 7,800 beds in chalets, apartments, mountain huts and hostels

Transportation: Gateway Airport: Zürich (87 mi)

Closest Provincial City: Chur (19 mi)

By Auto: Routes N3 and N13 to Chur, then up to Flims

By Train: Train to Chur, then post bus to Flims or Laax

Best Deal: Special "White Weeks" for accommodations, 6 day pass and lessons, from 710 SF

Other Information: Chur, capital city of Graubünden, is blend of modern and medieval and a sightseeing adventure on a bad weather day
Characters of villages differ. Skiers may want to compare brochures of all of them

GRAUBÜNDEN (German speaking region)
Several villages comprise this major resort. Popular with Swiss and Germans, it is relatively close to the Zürich gateway.

SAMNAUN
TOURIST OFFICE:
Samnaun CH-7563

Telephone: (41) (81) 868 58 58 Fax: (41) (81) 868 56 52

Elevation: Village: 1,840 m (6,035 ft); Top: 2,872 m (9,420 ft)

Vertical: 1,032 m (3,385 ft)

Longest Run: 5 km (3 mi)

Terrain: 60 km (27 mi) of local downhill runs; 200 km (124 mi) when considered with Ischgl; 15% beginner, 65% intermediate, 20% advanced

Skiing Circus: Over to Ischgl, Austria and back

Lifts: 15 in Samnaun; 41 in both resorts; 27 T-bars; world's largest cable car (180 persons) has two floors

Lift Capacity: 9,600 p/h Samnaun; 43,000 p/h Samnaun-Ischgl

Ski Season: December to May

Cross Country: 10 km (6 mi); 10 km of walking trails

Ski School: 30 instructors, including a "carving" center

Mountain Restaurants: 12, from snacks to specialties

Other Winter Activities: Ice skating/natural; paragliding; snowboarding

Après-Ski: Bars, discos, folklore evenings, live shows

Shopping/Services: Duty free shops

Credit Cards: AE, DC, MC, VISA

Child Care: Possible at ski school or Panoramavest Alp Triola; Telephone: 8 68 52 13

Lodging: 1,103 hotel beds; 918 chalet/apartment beds

Transportation: Gateway Airport: Zürich (3 hrs)

Closest Provincial City: Scuol

By Auto: Zürich-Bregenz in Austria to Landeck to Samnaun

By Train: To Scuol in Switzerland or Landeck in Austria, then bus to Samnaun

Best Deal: Duty free shopping in Samnaun. A skier can stay in Samnaun in a bed & breakfast pension for as little as 50 SF

GRAUBÜNDEN (German speaking region)
Samnaun is another ski resort in Switzerland where a skier may want a passport in the parka. It connects across miles of snowfields with Ischgl in Austria. Part of the largest ski area in the eastern Alps, Samnaun is also a duty-free zone.

©Publishers Group International, 1998

SWITZERLAND

Skiing in the Swiss Alps can be way up there, but a lot of folks like to make tracks on the flat.

Photo: Swiss National Tourist Office

PONTRESINA
TOURIST OFFICE:
Pontresina CH-7504
Telephone: (41) (81) 838 8300
Fax: (41) (81) 838 8310

Elevation: Base: 1,800 m (5,904 ft); Top: 2,978 m (9,768 ft)

Vertical: 1,178 m (3,864 ft)

Terrain: Town itself is sheltered on a terrace facing southwest. Skiable mountains loom over it but skiers also visit Lagalb and Diavolezza south of town, in direction of Italy. High percentage of intermediate terrain.

Skiing Circus: See St. Moritz map for other possibilities; bus connections to other areas

Lifts: 60 in region, of many types and capacities

Lift Capacity: 65,000 p/h region

Ski Season: Early December to late April

Summer Skiing: On Diavolezza glacier

Cross Country: 150 km (93 mi) in region. Many of the scenic tracks and walking trails are near Pontresina

Ski School: 50 instructors

Mountain Restaurants: On Lagalb, Diavolezza, Alp Languard and many others in region

GRAUBÜNDEN
*(German speaking region—also Romansch and Italian)
Pontresina is a traditional Engadine village with narrow streets and medieval houses. A few miles southeast of St. Moritz, it is generally less expensive.*

Other Winter Activities: Ice skating/natural; curling horse drawn sleigh; indoor swimming; mountaineering; sleigh riding; snowshoe walking; ice hockey; more than 100 km of footpaths

Après-Ski: Bars, discos, cafes, concerts, cinema

Shopping/Services: Large variety of shops

Child Care: Kindergarten (Hotel Saratz)

Credit Cards: AE, DC, VISA and others accepted

Lodging: 2,200 hotel beds; 3,000 others in holiday flats and private rooms; youth hostel

Transportation: Gateway Airport: Zürich (3 hrs)

Closest Provincial City: St. Moritz (7 km)

By Auto: Via Chur and Julier Pass

By Train: Via Chur and Samedan

Best Deal: "Sunshine" or "Holiday" weeks run from 738 SF

Other Information: An acknowledged climatic resort

SWITZERLAND

SILVAPLANA
TOURIST OFFICE:
Silvaplana CH-7513
Telephone: (41) (81) 838 60 00
Fax: (41) (81) 838 60 09

GRAUBÜNDEN (German speaking region)
Silvaplana sits at foot of Julier Pass on an alpine lake. The Corvatsch mountain towers over the village. Almost a suburb of St. Moritz, this little village has an identity of its own.

Elevation: Village: 1,815 m (5,953 ft); Top: 3,303 m (10,834 ft)

Vertical: 1,488 m (4,881 ft)

Longest Run: 10 km (6 mi)

Terrain: Skiing on Corvatsch has combination of rugged and relaxing. Mountain has highest vertical in region

Skiing Circus: On lower elevations the snowfields are interconnected with lifts from Sils Maria

Lifts: 12 local; 60 in region; 2 Trams; 2 Chairlifts (1 h-s quad, 1 double); 8 Surface (4 T-bars, 4 others)

Lift Capacity: 1,000 p/h resort; 65,000 p/h in region

Ski Season: December to May

Ski School: All disciplines

Cross Country: 150 km (93 mi) in region

Mountain Restaurants: 3

Other Winter Activities: Curling; ice skating/natural; squash; indoor tennis; mountaineering; paragliding; snowboarding; sleigh riding; sports center

Shopping/Services: Limited, but St. Moritz is only 10-15 minutes away

Credit Cards: VISA, Eurochecks

Child Care: Contact tourist office

Lodging: 13 hotels; chalets & apts., 6,500 beds

Transportation: Gateway Airport: Zürich (3 hrs)
Closest Provincial City: St. Moritz (6 mi)
By Auto: Zürich-Chur-Thusis-Julier Pass-Silvaplana
By Train: Zürich-Chur-St. Moritz
Bus or taxi from St. Moritz to Silvaplana

Best Deal: Package deals between 805 and 1,460 SF, depending on hotel and week chosen

Other Information: Slopes above St. Moritz are nearby. Efficient bus service among areas

Where else but fashionable St. Moritz would you expect to see polo played in the snow?
Photo: Swiss National Tourist Office

SWITZERLAND

ST. MORITZ
TOURIST OFFICE:
St. Moritz CH-7500
Telephone: (41) (81) 837 33 33
Fax: (41) (81) 837 33 66

GRAUBÜNDEN *(German speaking region)*
This world-famous resort has hosted two Winter Olympics. It offers an acclaimed blend of good skiing and a lively apres-ski scene. St. Moritz is the hub of a ski region that includes Pontresina, Silvaplana and several small villages.

Elevation: Village: 1,860 m (6,101 ft); Top 3,027 m (9,929 ft)

Vertical: 1,167 m (3,828 ft)

Longest Run: 10 km (6 mi)

Terrain: 80 km (50 mi) of local downhill runs, 350 km (217 mi) in region. Corviglia and Piz Nair mountains offer smooth skiing, mostly above treeline. Glacier skiing and more challenge on Corvatsch above Silvaplana and Diavolezza and Lagalb; 10% beginner, 70% intermediate, 20% advanced

Lifts: 55 in region

Lift Capacity: 65,000 in region

Ski Season: December to end of April

Summer Skiing: On Diavolezza glacier, mid June & July

Cross Country: 150 km (93 mi); 60 km (37 mi) of skating tracks; 120 km (74 mi) of winter walking trails

Ski School: Large staffs in every community in the region, more than 400 instructors

Mountain Restaurants: 11 on Corviglia-Piz Nair slopes, from cafeteria to gourmet

Other Winter Activities: Curling; fitness center; horse drawn sleigh; ice skating/natural; indoor swimming; indoor tennis; squash; mountaineering; paragliding; sauna; snowboarding; bobsled; horse races; cricket on snow

Après-Ski: Bars, discos, cafes, fondue parties, art and folk museums, fine restaurants, casino, concerts

Shopping/Services: Fashionable shops abound; a credit card heaven

Child Care: Programs available at certain hotels
Kid's Ski School: Suretta Ski School; Other: Contact St. Moritz Tourist Office for information

Lodging: 5,580 hotel beds; 2,900 apt. beds

Transportation: Gateway Airport: Zürich (4 hrs; 206 km/128 mi)

By Auto: Via Chur and Julier Pass, also accessible from Milan via Maloja Pass

By Train: Via Chur

St. Moritz also has an airport

Best Deal: Tour operators put members of groups into standard class hotels for about 100 SF a day

Other Information: Well-organized bus and train systems make all region resorts readily accessible. Celebrities will be seen

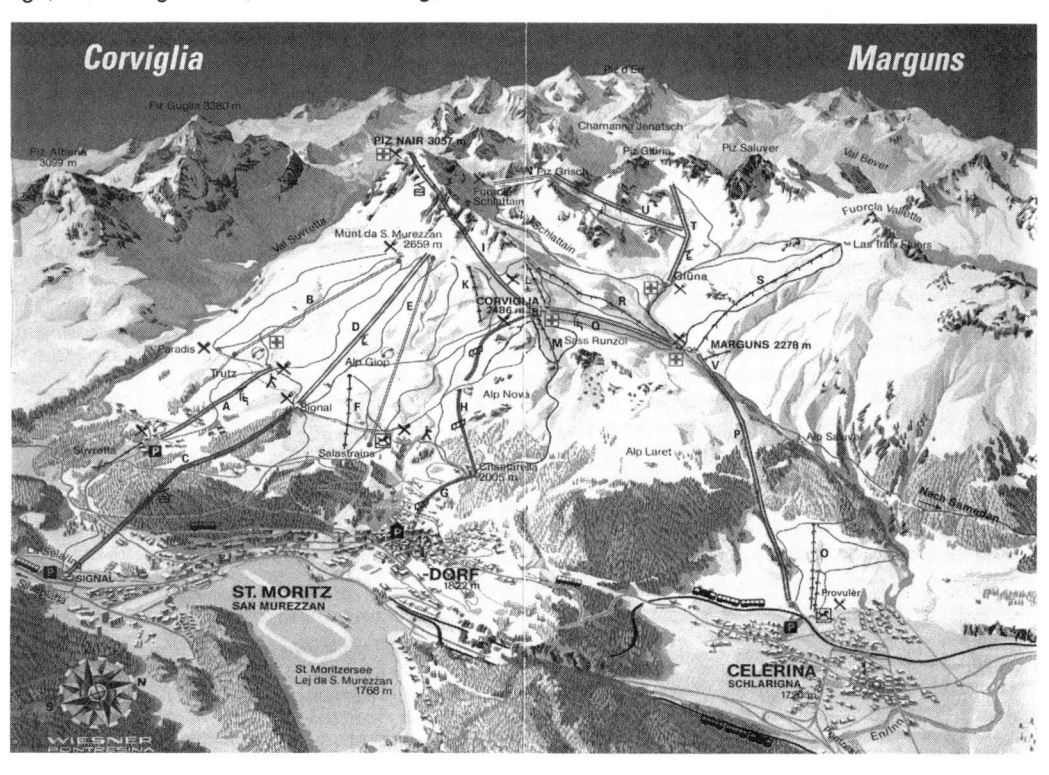

SWITZERLAND

TOGGENBURG
TOURIST OFFICE:
Toggenburg TVT
Wildhaus CH-9658
Telephone: (41) (71) 999 99 12 Fax: (41) (71) 999 99 13

Elevation: Village: 1,050 m (3,444 ft);
Top: 2,262 m (7,419 ft)

Vertical: 1,212 m (3,975 ft) at Unterwasser

Longest Run: 8 km (5 mi)

Terrain: 50 km (31 mi) of groomed slopes, many off-piste opportunities; trails colored for every level; 25% beginner, 50% intermediate, 25% advanced

Skiing Circus: Possible to yo-yo across the mountain, from Wildhaus to Alt St. Johann and back

Lifts: 20

Types: 1 Funicular; 1 Tram; 1 Gondola; 3 Chairs (1 quad, 1 triple, 1 double); 14 Surface lifts

Lift Capacity: 9,600 p/h resort

Ski Season: December-April

Cross Country: 40 km (24 mi); 5 km (3 mi) of ski hiking trails; 30 km (19 mi) of winter walking trails

Ski School: 60 instructors, including snowboarding

Mountain Restaurants: 6

Other Winter Activities: Curling; horse drawn sleigh; ice skating/natural; ice skating/artificial; indoor swimming; indoor tennis; sauna; snowboarding; sleigh riding; night skiing; bowling; hiking; squash

Après-Ski: Bars, pubs, discos, concerts, dairy alpine museum, raclette parties

Shopping/Services: Full range; also supermarket and a flea market

Credit Cards: AE, DC, MC, VISA

Child Care: Available at 5 SF/hr;
Telephone: (71) 999 17 22

Lodging: 1,400 hotel beds; 1,500 beds in chalets and apartments

Transportation: Gateway Airport: Zürich (1½ hrs)

Closest Major City: Feldkirch, Austria, or Vaduz, Liechtenstein

By Auto: Winterthur-Wil-Wattwil-Wildhaus

By Train: Change at Wil for Wil-Nesslau; change to bus

Best Deal: Special family packages, all inclusive for Mom or Dad from 670 SF and kids at half-price

MALBUN/STEG*
TOURIST OFFICE:
Malbun 9497
Triesenberg-Malbun, Liechtenstein
Telephone: (41) (75) 263 65 77 Fax: (41) (75) 263 73 44

Elevation: Base: 1,300 m (4,264 ft);
Top: 2,000 m (6560 ft)

Vertical: 700 m (2,296 ft)

Terrain: More than two thousand feet of vertical and 21 km of downhill runs on two facing mountains around the village

Lifts: 7

Types: 2 Chairlifts; 5 Surface

Lift Capacity: 6,600 p/h resort

Cross Country: Four loops at Steg, including easy and skating tracks. Also 1.7 km (1 mi) lighted

Other Winter Activities: Ice skating/natural; indoor swimming; sleigh riding; night skiing; snowboarding

EASTERN SWITZERLAND (German speaking region)
Three villages in eastern Switzerland, near the Principality of Liechtenstein, jointly promote their interconnected mountains. The villages are Wildhaus, Unterwasser and Alt St. Johann

PRINCIPALITY OF LIECHTENSTEIN
(German speaking region)
Malbun is a small ski area up a winding road from the capital city of Vaduz. Rarely a destination for American skiers, it would be a pleasant place to visit during a sightseeing trip to this romantic tiny nation.

Après-Ski: Bars, discos, restaurants

Shopping/Services: Limited, but made up for in Vaduz

Lodging: 700 beds nearby; additional facilities in Vaduz

Transportation: Gateway Airport: Zürich; 2 hrs (87 mi)

By Auto: Zürich-Rapperswil-Ziegelbrücke-Sargans-Vaduz

By Train: Zürich-Sargans-Buchs

Bus connection: Sargans-Buchs-Vaduz-Malbun

Best Deal: 7 days of lodging, half board, lift tickets for under 500 SF

Other Information: The principality has only 60 square miles, but it offers much to see

©Publishers Group International, 1998

SWISS ADVENTURES
by Ted Heck

In previous editions of *The Blue Book* I have written about a few experiences that have piled up in a half-century of skiing in the Swiss Alps. They are also pages in my mental scrapbook—such memories as getting lost in a whiteout on the Parsenn run in Davos . . . looking vainly for valuable pearls that a young woman lost in the snow of Saas-Fee . . . roller coasting down a mile-long chute with an instructor in St. Moritz.

Switzerland evokes images from everyone who has skied there: long runs through vast snowfields above the tree line, Rösti potatoes at lunch on the deck of a mountain restaurant, animated conversation in the lively après-ski scene.

Here are several other recollections that make some points that may be helpful to other skiers.

FUN WITH A RENTAL CAR

The Swiss rail system is one of the best in the world, offering a relaxed way to admire the stunning scenery. A Swiss train runs with the precision of a Swiss watch. Rail passes purchased ahead in the United States allow unlimited travel.

However, I usually have a companion and a lot of luggage and an itinerary so extensive that we most often rent a car, for its convenience and flexibility.

In a recent visit we picked up a car in southern Germany for a trip into Austria and Switzerland. The Avis rate was significantly cheaper in Germany, and we did not have to pay the extra charge tacked on at Swiss airports. But we paid about $30 on entering Switzerland for a special sticker allowing us to use the country's autobahns.

The car was no help to us in Flims-Laax in getting back and forth to the ski lifts. The elegant Park Hotels Waldhaus provided a shuttle. But our own car was handy in the après-ski scene for driving around in search of a restaurant with the right atmosphere. And it allowed us to take side trips to Disentis and Sedrun, smaller resorts farther up the Rhine Valley.

We moved from Flims, which is in the Graubünden canton of eastern Switzerland to Zermatt in the southern canton of Wallis—but not by car. Zermatt is a traffic free resort, with no private cars admitted. They must be parked up the road in Täsch. In Zermatt you hoof it or move about on ski buses, horse drawn sleighs or electric cart taxis.

The Oberalp and Furka passes on the direct route to Zermatt are closed to auto traffic in winter, but cars can be loaded on rail cars at the passes, a time-consuming and costly process. It was actually cheaper for us to leave the car at the Disentis train station near the Rhine River and take the famed Glacier Express for the 4½-hour trip to Zermatt. We lunched on the train and stared at spectacular mountains as we crossed many bridges and pierced many tunnels. I remarked to my special friend Connie that the rivers we followed, the Rhine and the Rhone, are generally associated with Germany and France, but both originate high in the Swiss Alps.

(Some years ago I spent two weeks following the Rhine from its source near the Oberalp pass all the way to its mouth at Rotterdam on the North Sea—hiking, biking, and whitewater rafting and traveling by car and Rhine cruise ship. I saw it grow from a trickle in the rocks to the estuary of the world's largest seaport.)

After several days of skiing with friends in Zermatt we made the return trip, left Zermatt in mid-morning, retrieved our car in Disentis, and arrived in Innsbruck, Austria, by dinner time.

The run to Cervenia under the mighty Matterhorn.   Photo: Best of the Alps

SWITZERLAND

THE RUN TO CERVINIA

There was no doubt it would be a great day. From our bedroom window in Zermatt, across snow-covered slate roofs of centuries old farm buildings, we could see the Matterhorn, glowing gold and orange in the morning sun.

We had not seen the landmark mountain on the first two days of our stopover in the charming village. The world's most distinctive rock had been hidden in the clouds. But today, all day, it reached into the clear blue sky, changing colors as the sun rose.

I have visited Zermatt many times, but it was the first for my friends Bob and Paul. I shared their childlike delight when we made the must-do run over the top of Zermatt down into Cervinia, Italy. They were glued to the window of the highest cable car in the Alps as it rose up the north face of the Klein Matterhorn.

The little Horn, several thousand feet shorter than its big brother, is across the way from it, on the far side of a skiable glacier. We passed other precipitous glaciers before entering the eye of the needle and dismounting for a long walk through a tunnel. Winds were fierce as we stepped into our skis, but a quick descent to the Plateau Rosa put us below the gusts.

Our first look at "the sunny side of the Alps" was at snowfields that billowed down to Cervinia. Scooped through them were several groomed, steep but wide trails, with the best snow I had seen in a six-week swing through Germany, Austria and Switzerland. It was the kind of snow that balloons every ego. We made long, arcing turns and also short cuts in the fall line, with lots of space to let the skis run while we shouted and sang. We covered about five miles and dropped nearly a mile in elevation, a vertical that exceeds anything in the U.S.

In Cervinia we had a leisurely lunch on a sunny terrace, where the waiter spoke lilting Italian instead of gutteral German, conducive to ordering spaghetti and ravioli.

Most folks who make this international day trip return to Switzerland right after lunch. Bob and Paul and I reached quick consensus for an encore and rode a gondola and chairlift back up near the top and reveled in another run.

Mountain restaurants play a prominent role in the alpine experience.
Photo: Adelboden Tourist Office

Coming out of the clouds amidst the dramatic Jungrau.
Photo: Fred McKinney

©Publishers Group International, 1998

SWITZERLAND

Back on the Swiss side of the border the snow had held up beautifully. Despite brilliant sunshine. the temperature had not climbed past the melting point. We skied most of the way down to Zermatt, taking a gondola only for the last leg to avoid late afternoon traffic.

After Connie and I left Zermatt, my friends had more adventures on the Gornergrat and Sunnegga mountains, which are other popular sections of this massive complex. And when they weren't skiing, they strolled along the traffic-free streets, browsed in shops, sampled restaurants, watched hockey games and curling matches and visited the museum that features the first climbing conquest of the Matterhorn in 1865.

Amade Perrig, director of the tourist office, says the focus of his efforts is to promote all these things. Not just the skiing, but the ambiance, the total experience. The synergism of Zermatt is what keeps the resort at the top of my list of favorite ski areas around the world.

VACATION HOME EXCHANGE

Several years ago I traded my house in Pennsylvania for a chalet in Bitsch, a tiny village near Brig, the main rail junction for trains coming down the Oberalp and Furka passes or coming eastward from the Geneva gateway. Our rustic retreat had a great view and was indeed private—halfway up a mountain on a narrow, winding road.

We made day trips to Zermatt and to the awesome glacier at Saas-Fee and to the sunny, south-facing slopes of Crans-Montana. Most of our skiing, however, was nearby on the terrain above us—on the Riederalp and Bettmeralp. These resorts are also traffic free, accessed by skiers in cable cars from the valley below. The extensive ski area adjoins Europe's longest glacier, the 14-mile-long Aletsch.

How does one find a place to keep house? Tourist offices deal primarily with hotels and pensions and apartments. But there are organizations that, for a fee, list and promote exchangeable houses. However, there is a two-way gamble in dealing with strangers. We found our chalet in Bitsch through networking. A Swiss friend of ours knew some folks in Basel, who wanted to come to Philadelphia. We struck a deal, but not for the same time. It was two years before they came to America to redeem their marker.

The idea worked so well that I keep mentioning it to skiers who just might have a friend with a place in the Alps. Connie and I have two houses, one of which can always be made available. If we lived in New York, we probably would get more offers than we could handle.

GRINDELWALD, AS IN "GREAT"

"Just two hours from the Zürich airport a skier is surrounded by some of the most spectacular scenery on the planet. In Grindelwald, in summer or winter, the mind has difficulty believing what the eye captures."

This is a quote from George Schissler, a fellow editor of this book. He is responsible for the section on France, but he was bowled over by Grindelwald when he detoured into Switzerland.

He wrote, "Of course, there are rugged peaks like the Eiger, Mönch and Jungfrau. There are glaciers and an abundance of snow. Europeans refer to their large resort complexes as circuses, because they enable skiers to travel on snow from one resort or village to another. The Jungfrau region is a three-ring circus, enabling skiers to move comfortably among the famous ski towns of Grindelwald, Wengen and Mürren and the hub city of Interlaken."

George describes some of his favorite runs, but then adds, "Grindelwald is more than skiing and scenery. It is shopping, dining, convenience, friendliness, music and elegance. For those who wish to be catered to for every wish and whim, there is the Grand Hotel Regina, the only five star hotel in the village.

"Grindelwald has all of the après-ski amenities a skier expects of a major resort. But one that I got a particular charge out of was Rodeling. We went up a twisting mountain road by bus. After a little liquid refreshment, we headed back down the road, each of us on a Rodel, much like a sled but with no steering mechanism. It has to be guided by your body and feet. Paul Revere's moonlit ride was probably easier."

Noted ski photographer Fred McKinney, whose photos have dressed up all editions of *The Blue Book*, skied with Schissler. He calls the Jungfrau railroad "one of the most unique mountain railroads in the world. The cog train serves skiers with some of the best skiing in Europe. The train climbs over 4,500 vertical feet, leaving skiers and riders gasping at the beauty of the mountain villages.

"One of the hardest decisions is picking which little village to ski to for lunch. No matter what choice is made, the first view is usually the local church steeple towering above the village. After lunch you select the train or tram to go back up an alp again for an afternoon of skiing. Soon come thoughts of the four o'clock tea and another wonderful Swiss experience."

OLYMPIC MUSEUM... A SWISS BONUS

Another non-skiing activity worth mentioning here in this Swiss spotlight is a visit to the Olympic Museum in Lausanne.

This beautiful city on the north shore of Lake Geneva is on the way to many ski resorts. Worth a stopover, it is headquarters of the Interna-

Car-free Murren.
Photo: Swiss National Tourist Office

SWITZERLAND

The Olympic Museum in Lausanne.

tional Olympic Committee and the site of a five-story museum. The Greek marble edifice is the world's most comprehensive repository of written, graphic and visual information on the Olympic Games. Art and artifacts illustrate the union of sport, art and culture.

The museum contains 15,000 volumes, more than 200,000 photographs and 7,000 hours of film and video. They trace the Games back to their origins at Olympia in Greece in 776 B.C. But primary focus is on the modern Games, which began in Athens in 1896. The most recent Summer and Winter Games are quickly added to the collections.

An afternoon in the museum is an emotional trip down memory lane. A century of images flash around in multi-media presentations. And everyone will find moments that cause goosebumps and thrills worth the $12 admission ticket.

All the heroes are here—those clad in shorts, like Jim Thorpe, Johnny Weismuller, Babe Didriksen, Jesse Owens, Florence Griffith-Joyner, and Carl Lewis.

Winter winners include Dick Button, Andrea Mead Lawrence, Gretchen Fraser, Jean-Claude Killy, the Mahre brothers, Bill Johnson, Tommy Moe and Picabo Street.

Not all the audio-visual material is devoted to winners and the joy of victory. The agony of defeat is captured often on the screens.

The museum pays tribute to Baron Pierre de Courbetin, the nobleman who reignited the Olympic flame before the turn of the 20th century. The father of the modern games is memorialized with a life-size wax figure. In addition to sports sculptures and Grecian urns with paintings of the earliest games, the museum features exhibitions of contemporary artists.

Lausanne, along with nearby Vevey and Montreux, are ripe with culture. They have rich literary and musical histories. Sampling some of them will corroborate our point of view that skiing in Europe has special rewards.

A DIFFERENT VIEW OF THE ALPS

During a summer vacation on the French Riviera, I had a rare opportunity to see my favorite mountains from the cockpit of a Swissair jet flying from Nice to Zürich. The pilot had invited me up front, after I had inquired about his route, in order to know which side of the plane to sit on. I saw peaks coming toward us and with the help of pilot and co-pilot was able to identify some of them.

Mountains do not look the same from 24,000 feet as they do when one is in touch with the snow. Some unkind beach type says they remind him of teeth ground down by a dentist before being capped. But to me they are majestic sentinels guarding a world of exhilarating adventure and indelible memories.

Skiers have a wide choice of some super runs above Grindelewald.
Photo: Fred McKinney

Three of The Blue Book *editors (l to r) Enzel, Muello & Schissler at the Schilthorn above Mürren.*
Photo: Fred McKinney

©Publishers Group International, 1998

SCANDINAVIA

©Publishers Group International, 1998

ICELAND	Page No.
Bláfjöll*	129
Hlídarfjall(Akureyri)*	129

NORWAY

Geilo	124
Hafjell	123
Hemsedal	124
Kvitfjell	123
Norefjell	125
Voss	125

SWEDEN	Page No.
Årefjällen	128
Bjursås*	126
Bydalen	127
Riksgränsen*	128
Sälen	126
Storlien*	127

*Areas marked with an asterisk in the text did not update their information for this edition.

SCANDINAVIA

by Bob Enzel

The Scandinavian countries of Norway, Sweden, Finland and Denmark have been home to cross country skiing, ice skating and ski jumping since the beginning of winter sports. While some downhill skiing is available in Finland and Denmark, most sportsmen participate in the Nordic sports.

Alpine skiers visiting Norway or Sweden won't find any mile-high vertical drops, jagged peaks or ski circuses that connect by ski terrain. What they will find, are excellent resorts that provide a variety of outdoor activities to singles and families. In a way, Sweden and Norway's world famous smorgasboard dining carries over into the variety of activities available. Both will amaze and satisfy even the most persnickity traveler.

NORWAY

The city of Lillehammer, a former headquarters of the Olympics, remains the focal point on a visit to the alpine venues of Kvitfjell and Hafjell. These two areas, 20 and 10 miles north of Lillehammer, have interesting statistics. Kvitfjell's nearly two-mile downhill course was described as "a skier's dream" by members of the U.S. Ski Team.

Norway has several alpine areas to visit. Two that are generally featured by SAS Airline are Geilo and Voss. Both are well-established resorts. Geilo is in the heart of Norway's mountains and Voss is in the center of Norway's fjord region. Geilo is the larger of the two and its lovely village setting makes it comfortable for families. In April, Geilo will hold the "Skarverennet," the world's largest cross-country race.

Hemsedal may be Northern Europe's largest ski resort in addition to being Norway's most popular winter recreation area. Norefjell is the closet resort to Oslo and was host to the sixth Winter Olympics in 1952. The largest descent in all of Scandinavia can be experienced at Norefjell. All these areas have a friendly après-ski scene that include live music and dancing, fondue, good drink and plenty of company.

SWEDEN

Sweden's Vasa Ski Race continues to celebrate the country's unification. The race starts in Salen, one of Sweden's more popular downhill areas. Also covered in the book are: Are, another well-known resort; and Storlien, a small area that has operated for seventy years and is host to the Swedish Royal family. Riksgransen, is located north of the 68th parallel, which means you can ski until mid-summer under the midnight sun. Lastly, Bydalen is a resort made up of four areas, known for its emphasis on family vacationing.

ICELAND

As a skiing lifestyle change of pace we've included a couple of areas in Iceland. However, Iceland does not package ski trips to Iceland, but it does allow a stop-over in Reykjavik in either or both directions on the flight to Luxembourg. Luxembourg can also be added as a layover in either or both directions. However, make the decision before leaving the U.S., as it is much less costly.

For more information, contact:

SCANDINAVIAN TOURISM, INC.
(212) 949-2333
Fax (212) 983-5260

ICELANDAIR TOUR DESK
(800) 223-5500

SWEDISH TRAVEL & TOURISM COUNCIL
(212) 885-9700
Fax (212) 885-9710
www.gosweden.org

SCANDINAVIAN AIRLINES (SAS TOUR DESK)
(201) 896-3600
(800) 221-2350

Other airlines that fly to Stockholm include,
Finnair (800) 950-5000
Icelandair (800) 223-5500
Delta (800) 241-4141
American Airlines (800) 433-7300

Rail information (800) 782-2424 or
(800) 438-7245

©Publishers Group International, 1998

NORWAY

HAFJELL (National Alpine Center)
TOURIST OFFICE:
2636 Oyer
Lillehammer, Norway
Telephone: (47) 61 27 79 50 Fax: (47) 61 27 70 50

Hafjell was one of the main venue sites for alpine events in the 1994 Olympics. Although Hafjell has been around since 1939 it was a long time developing into an alpine ski center. Along with Kvitfjell these two areas were featured as Lillehammer's alpine sites.

Elevation: Base/Village: 200 m (656 ft); Top: 1,050 m (3,445 ft)

Vertical: 850 m (2,789 ft)

Longest Run: 4.5 km (2.8 mi)

Terrain: Runs up to 3 miles; some above treeline; lower slopes are lighted until 8:30pm; snowmaking; groomed; 7 green, 7 blue, 5 red, 4 black runs; 1,062 acres

Skiing Circus: See "Best Deal"

Lifts: 9

Types: 3 Quads; 6 Surface (5 T-bars, 1 rope)

Lift Capacity: 12,500 p/h resort

Ski Season: Late-November-Mid-April

Summer Skiing: Galdhøgpiggen Summer Ski Centre

Cross Country: 450 km network of prepared trails

Ski School: Alpinsenter: (6 instructors) alpine, telemarking, snowboarding, cross country; 3-days 360 (NOK)

Mountain Restaurants: 3 Cafes

Other Winter Activities: Mono-skiing; sleigh riding; "rump racer"; tractor inner tubing

Après-Ski: Bars, discos, cafes, excursions

Shopping/Services: Variety of food available in Hafjell; Sports centre has rentals with full repair service shop

Credit Cards: Eurocard, VISA, MC, AE, DC

Child Care: Available in high season; nursery

Lodging: 4,000 beds; hotels and apartments

Transportation: Gateway Airport: Oslo/Gardernoer 160 km

Closest Provincial City: Lillehammer, 15 km (9 mi)

By Auto from airport: Rte. E6 Oslo to Hafjell, 2½ hrs

Ski Bus: Daily from Lillehammer and return; bus from Oslo on Saturday

By Train: From Oslo

Best Deal: TrollPass (Gausdal/Peer Gynt/Kvitfjell/Hafjell)

Other Information: During the 1994 Olympics, the following events were held at Hafjell: Men & Women's Combined Slalom; Men & Women's Giant Slalom; Men & Women's Slalom. Telephone: 61 27 70 78; Fax: 61 27 70 08

KVITFJELL
FÅVANG, NORWAY
Postboks 70, 2634 Fåvang, Norway
Area Telephone: (47) 61 28 2105
Fax: (47) 61 28 2315

Kvitfjell, Hafjell and the other Olympic venues are located in an area of Norway referred to as Troll Park, of which Lillehammer is at its center. The ski area lies in Ringebu which is an outstanding touring area. Kvitfjell was the site of the 1994 Olympic Men's & Women's Downhill; Downhill Combined & Super G. World Cup annually.

Elevation: Base/Village: 182 m (597 ft); Top 1,020 m (3,346 ft)

Vertical: 838 m (2,749 ft)

Longest Run: 3.5 km (2.2 mi)

Terrain: mostly advanced terrain; it sports a downhill run designed by former champion, Bernhardt Russi, and reportedly one of the world's toughest; 3 green, 7 blue, 5 red, 3 black runs

Skiing Circus: Trollpass (see Best Deal)

Lifts: 7

Types: 1 Chairlift (1 detachable quad); 6 Surface (2 T-bar, 3 platter, 1 rope)

Lift Capacity: 7,200 p/h resort

Ski Season: Mid-November-Mid-April

Summer Skiing: Galdhøgpiggen Summer Ski Cntr., 1½ hours from Kvitfjell

Cross Country: 400 km

Ski School: All categories of instruction

Mountain Restaurants: 4 on-mountain cafes

Other Winter Activities: Snowboarding halfpipe; telemarking; off-slope skiing

Shopping/Services: 5 km from Kvitfjell; Kindergarten, ski shop & rentals at area

Credit Cards: Eurocard, VISA, DC, AE

Lodging: Kvitfjell Hotel at midstation, 40 rooms, 20 w/ kitchen, 12 cabins; hotel at mid-station, 79 rooms, 6 cabins; Kvitfjell apartment, 12 rooms

Transportation: Gateway: Oslo (3 hrs via E6); Airport (2 hrs via E6)

Closest Provincial City: Lillehammer

By Bus from airport: Bus and train from Oslo to Hafjell-30 kms to Kvitfjell

By Train: Train stop is 50 meters from the chair lift; train travels directly from Oslo and the airport

Transportation between Hafjell and Kvitfjell

Best Deal: Troll-pass purchase allows use at 4 areas

NORWAY

GEILO
GEILO TOURISTKONTOR
N-3580 Geilo, Norway
Telephone: (47) 3209 5900 Fax: (47) 3209 5921

Elevation: Base/Village: 808 m (2,650 ft);
Top: 1,178 m (3,864 ft)

Vertical: 377 m (1,237 ft)

Longest Run: 2.0 km (1.2 mi)

Terrain: Night skiing on 2 slopes; 17 mi (28 km) of runs; snowmaking; 9 green, 5 blue, 13 red, 7 black runs

Lifts: 18

Types: 4 Chairlifts (3 quad, 1 doubles); 14 Surface (2 rope tows)

Lift Capacity: 21,000 p/h resort

Ski Season: November-May

Cross Country: 220 km (137 mi) of marked trails

Ski School: 3 ski schools: Per Bye (Tele: 3209 0650); Slaatta (Tele: 3209 1710); Vestlia (Tele: 3208 8340)

Mountain Restaurants: 7

Other Winter Activities: Fitness center; hiking; horse drawn sleigh; ice skating/natural; indoor swimming (hotels); snowboarding; movie; saunas; ice fishing; dog sledding; waterfall climbing; snowmobiling

Geilo (yea-low) remains one of Norway's most popular alpine resorts. It has a good variety of lodging and services, active après-ski with discos, live-music, and train & car day trips for non-skiers. The resort is open year round with lower summer rates attracting fisherman, hikers and boaters. Considered one of Norways better all-around resorts.

Après-Ski: Discos, cafes, pubs, restaurants

Shopping/Services: Cafeteria; 6 rental locations; well developed ski resort-one of Norway's largest

Child Care: Kid's Ski School: from age 3; Day nursery at the ski centers

Lodging: 5,000 beds; 1st class hotels, luxury cabins, camping cabins, boarding houses, chalets, pensions, 18-20 hotels and apartments

Transportation: Gateway Airport: Oslo, 152 mi (245 km); Bergen, 4 hrs; Dagali Airport 25 km

By Auto from airport: Highway 7 between Hønefoss and Bergen; Oslo 3½ hrs; Bergen 4 hrs

Ferry to Bergen, then (4) train departures

By Train: From Oslo (249 km) or Bergen (248 km)

Ski bus available next to skilifts and hotels

Best Deal: Lift pass Winterland ticket for 63 slopes, 41 lifts, 71 km of terrain-½ day to entire season; common ski pass Hemmsedal and Geilo

Other Information: Geilo booking (47) 3209 5940

HEMSEDAL
HEMSEDAL TOURIST OFFICE
N-3560
Hemsedal, Norway
Telephone: (47) 32-060156 Fax: (47) 32-060537

Elevation: Base/Village: 650 m (2,132 ft);
Top: 1,450 m (4,756 ft)

Vertical: 800 m (2,624 ft)

Longest Run: 6.0 km (3.7 mi)

Terrain: 40 km of terrain with 3.2 km lighted plus off-slope options; 30 runs; self-timer race course; 15 green, 11 blue, 8 red, 6 black runs; 2 mogul runs; night skiing

Lifts: 16

Types: 5 Chairlifts (4 quads, 1 triple); 11 T-bars

Lift Capacity: 24,700 p/h resort

Ski Season: Mid-November-Mid-May

Cross Country: 220 km of prepared slopes, valley & mountain area

Ski School: Yes, instruction in racing, snowboarding, telemarking; Tele: 32-062330 & 32-055300

Mountain Restaurants: 5 at lift area

Other Winter Activities: Indoor swimming; paragliding; sleigh riding; ice climbing; snow scootering; dog sleds; telemark; snowboard park w/2 halfpipes; tobogganing

Hemsedal hosted a World Cup Downhill in 1990. A favorite mountain for recreation activities and skiing because of slope grooming and its good ski conditions. Nightly dancing, active apré-ski, gift shops and sport shops, plus a full range of accommodations make this resort a popular duo with Geilo.

Shopping/Services: 8 restaurants, gift shop, sport shop, post office, drug store, gas station, medical; youth discotheque; conference facilities; mountain trips

Credit Cards: Diners Club/VISA/AE/Eurocard

Child Care: Available at the ski center: 3 mos. & up w/ free Kindergarten, Kid's Ski School: Trollia children's playground; Lighted nursery slopes; Tele: 32-055300

Lodging: 2 hotels, mountain lodge, guest house (218 rooms), 9 apartment sites (155 units), 5 chalets

Transportation: Gateway Airport: Oslo, 220 km (137 mi); Bergen, 330 km (206 mi), Gol 30 km

By Auto from airport: Highway 7 between Hønefoss and Bergen Highway 52

By Bus from airport: Hemsedal Tourist Office for info

By Ski Bus: Free ski bus

By Train: From Oslo to Gol, then transfer to bus

Best Deal: Two ski centers on one lift pass, Hemsedal and Solheisen; Special winter program

NORWAY

VOSS
VOSS TOURIST INFORMATION
HESTAVANGEN 10
5700 Voss, Norway
Telephone: (47) 56-520800 Fax: (47) 56-520801

Voss is located in the center of the fjord district and is base for excursions to 2 of Norway's largest fjords. Several World Cup competitions have been held here and its proximity to Bergen makes it a popular resort. In 1995 Voss hosted the Alpine World Cup for Juniors. Voss is a full service town with much to see and do.

Elevation: Base/Village: 57 m (187 ft); Top: 945 m (3,143 ft)

Vertical: 725 m (2,364 ft)

Longest Run: 6 km (3.7 mi)

Terrain: 40 kms of runs; 2 red, 5 blue, 1 green, & 3 black runs; night skiing Wednesday and Friday, 6pm-9pm

Skiing Circus: Combination of ski locations with town of Voss as the cental location

Lifts: 10

Types: 1 Cablecar; 4 Chairlifts (1 quad, 3 doubles, 1 single); 4 T-bars

Lift Capacity: 8,400 p/h resort

Ski Season: End-November-1st of May

Cross Country: 63 km; Touring on Mount Hangur; 8 lighted and 2 marked cross country trails

Ski School: All age groups; alpine, touring, telemark and snowboard; private and group at 3 locations

Mountain Restaurants: 3

Other Winter Activities: Ice fishing; hiking; ice skating/natural; heated pools; sauna; telemarking; movie; fjord tours; outdoor grill; bowling; squash; paragliding; snowboarding; fitness center

Après-Ski: Bars and restaurant dining

Shopping/Services: Museums, sightseeing (Knute Rockne Memorial); Full service town with 6 restaurants and 16 cafes; rentals

Lodging: 1,500 beds; 1st class hotels to camping cabins (4 hotels, several pensions, mountain lodges and apartments)

Transportation: Gateway Airport: Bergen

Closest Provincial City: Bergen, 101 km

By Auto from airport: Via E16 east, 115 km

By Train: On the main line between Oslo (5½ hrs) and Bergen (70 min)

NOREFJELL
NOREFJELL TURIST SERVICE AS
3536 Noresund Norway
Telephone: (47) 3215-0550 Fax: (47) 3215-0560

Norefjell was the venue for the downhill events during the 1952 Olympics. It is well established as an alpine skiing resort with a variety of terrain for all levels. Cross country enthusiasts will find well-marked and prepared trails. It's about 15 minutes to Lake Kroderen and has good surrounding scenery. Slopeside, lake view lodging, and apartments are all well established.

Elevation: Base/Village: 170 m (5,577 ft); Top: 1,460 m (4,790 ft)

Vertical: 1,010 m (3,313 ft)

Longest Run: 6 km (3.7 mi)

Terrain: 23 slopes; 24 km of trails; snowmaking; 4 green, 9 blue, 7 red, 3 black runs

Lifts: 11

Types: 3 Chairlifts (1 quad, 2 doubles); 8 Surface (6 T-bars, 2 platters)

Lift Capacity: 14,000 p/h resort

Ski Season: November-May 1

Cross Country: 120 km of marked trails; unlimited, mountains and woods

Ski School: 8 instructors; alpine; telemark, off-piste, powder, snowboard instruction; Tele: 32-149203

Mountain Restaurants: 5

Other Winter Activities: Mono-skiing; snowboarding; telemarking; horse drawn sleigh; indoor swimming; sauna; dog teams; snowshoeing; snowboarding

Après-Ski: 2 Bars, 2 discos, piano bar, 3 cafes, orchestra/dancing

Shopping/Services: Rentals; ski shop; grocery, service station; 30 minutes to Viksersund shopping center & home to the largest ski jump in Scandinavia

Credit Cards: VISA

Child Care: Available all ages

Lodging: 1,300 beds; 600 rooms; 1st class to mountain cabin; time-sharing or rentals available; On slope apartment units (time share or condo); Apartment-hotels; hotels; guest houses

Transportation: Gateway Airport: Oslo 100 km (62 mi)

Closest Provincial City: Hønefoss

By Auto from airport: Oslo to Hønefoss to Noresund to area

By Bus: Twice daily, Oslo to Norefjell-90 minute ride

Haglebu, 41 km; Geilo, 130 km; Viksersund, 30 km

SWEDEN

BJURSÅS SKI CENTER*

79021 Bjursås, Sweden
Telephone: (46) 23-63535 Fax: (46) 23-17796

DALARNA
Bjursås is located in the center of Dalarna, 20 km north of Falun.

Elevation: Base/Village:
Vertical: m (ft)
Terrain: Runs: 4 red, 3 green, 2 blue and 1 black
Longest Run: 1.3 km (0.8 mi)
Skiing Circus: None
Lifts: 6
Types: 4 T-bars, 2 others
Lift Capacity: 6,000 p/h resort
Ski Season: December-April
Summer Skiing: None
Cross Country: 2 km at area; 35 km nearby
Ski School: Yes

Other Winter Activities: Horse drawn sleigh; ice skating/natural; indoor swimming; sauna
Après-Ski: discos, bars, restaurants in Falun
Shopping/Services: Full variety in Falun
Credit Cards: VISA
Child Care: Kid's ski school; no nursery
Lodging: 20 rooms at resort
Transportation: Gateway Airports: Stockholm
Closest Provincial City: Falun, 20 km (12 m)
By Auto from Airport: Stockholm to Bjursås 250 km; Borlänge to Bjursås, 45 km (28 mi)
By Train: Stockholm to Falun

SÄLEN

SÄLEN TOURIST INFORMATION
Centrumhuset
S-78067 Sälen, Sweden
Telephone: (46) 280-20250 Fax: (46) 280-20580

Long ago established as a skiing region for both downhill and cross country, Sälen offers a variety of terrain. The town is well known for its Vasa Ski Race Week which comes at the First Sunday in March. There is a variety of lodging which along with the skiing is spread among several villages and 4 ski resorts. "Northern Europe largest ski resort."

Elevation: Base/Village: 4-600 m a.s.l. (2,000 ft); Top: 890 m (2,919 ft)
Terrain: 160 downhill runs; 140 km of runs; 60 green, 31 blue, 31 red, 31 black runs; off-piste skiing and halfpipes
Skiing Circus: Conglomerate of small villages and 4 ski areas: Kläppen; Lindvallen/Sälen Stugan/Högfjäll Shotellet; Tandåadalen/Hundfjället; Stöten
Lifts: 99
Types: 1 h-s 6-seat; 6 quad; 2 triple; 1 double; 89 surface lifts
Ski Season: Mid-November-End of April
Cross Country: 2.5 to 15 km long; some lighted; 200 km of marked trails
Ski School: At all 4 ski centers
Other Winter Activities: Dog and horse sleigh rides; snowmobile tours; snowscooter safari tours; ice-carting; paragliding; half & quarter pipes
Après-Ski: 40 restaurants, 10 dance/discos

Shopping Services: Full service town, i.e., doctor, supermarkets, gas stations, post office, cash machines
Credit Cards: AE, MC, VISA
Lodging: 50,000 beds; apartments; cottages, dorms, hotels, houses, hotel/apartments—mostly "self-catering"
Transportation: Gateway Airport: Stockholm (450 km)
Closest Provincial Village: Sälen
By Air: Domestic air service to Mora, plus air taxi for the last 100 km, (46) 250 30175, fax 250 30067
By Bus from Stockholm: 9 hours; daily buses from Mora
By Train: Daily connections to Mora or Malung, then bus to Sälen (46) 8 696 7540
By Auto: Stockholm to Sala to Falun to Mora to Sälen (426 km/265 mi); Avis (in Mora) (46) 250 16711
Other Information: An auto is convenient for village to village skiing

©Publishers Group International, 1998

SWEDEN

STORLIEN*
STORLIENS MOUNTAIN HOTEL
Box 47
83019 Storlien, Sweden
Telephone: (46) 647-70170 Fax: (46) 647-70446

Elevation: Base/Village: 640 m (2,100 ft); Top: 840 m (2,756 ft)
Vertical: 190 m (623 ft)
Terrain: 8 red, 4 green, 2 blue and 3 black runs
Longest Run: 1.5 km (0.9 mi)
Lifts: 7
Types: 5 T-bars and 2 platters
Lift Capacity: 5,500 p/h resort
Ski Season: Late Nov./early Dec.-May 1
Cross Country: 32 km of prepared terrain for skate or classical skiing; miles of unprepared but marked terrain
Ski School: Alpine, X-C, telemark, snowboarding
Mountain Restaurants: 1
Other Winter Activities: Ski tours; snowmobiles; indoor swimming; mountaineering; snowboarding; snowshoe tours; dog sleigh; reindeer sleigh; ice fishing

BYDALEN MOUNTAIN RESORTS
HALLENS TURISTBYRÅ, BYDALEN
5830 01 Hallen, Sweden

Telephone: (46) 643-320 11 Fax: (46) 643 320 96

Elevation: Base/Village: 600 m (1,968 ft); Top: 1,020 m (3,346 ft)
Vertical: 420 m (1,378 ft)
Terrain: Runs: 27 red, 4 green, 17 blue and 11 black, plus 2 snowboard parks and 2 halfpipes
Longest Run: 3.0 km (1.9 mi)
Skiing Circus: Between the 4 areas
Lifts: 15
Types: 12 T-bars, 3 platters
Lift Capacity: 11,000 p/h resort
Ski Season: Christmas-April 30; Nov./Dec. weekends dependent on snow conditions
Summer Skiing: None
Cross Country: 30 km; plus ungroomed, marked trails for hundreds of kilometers beginning in Bydalen
Ski School: Beginner to racing; snowboard & telemark
Mountain Restaurants: 5; one on slope at timberline—all accessible on skis
Other Winter Activities: Horse drawn sleigh; snowmobile safari; ice fishing; snowboarding; dog sleigh rides; haute route

NORTHERN SWEDEN
Small traditional ski resort by the Norwegian border in operation since 1924. The Swedish Royal Family has its winter chatet in Storlien on the hotel grounds.

Après-Ski: sauna, 4 bars, 2 discos, 4 cafes, live orchestra hotel entertainment; theme parties
Shopping/Services: Grocery, 3 clothing/sport shops
Credit Cards: Most major credit cards
Child Care: Nursery—SEK 50 p/h; kid's ski school, up to 12 years—cost depends on activity
Lodging: 520 beds; 197 rooms; 34 chalets, plus 38 beds in annex; approximately 1,000 at the resort
Transportation: Gateway Airports: Trondheim, Norway
Local Airport: Östersund—then bus to Storlien
Closest Provincial City: Trondheim, 100 km
By Auto from Airport: via E-14 70 km (44 mi)
By Train: From Trondheim Airport to Storlien, 70 km
Ski Bus: From Östersund
Best Deal: January 2 - Mid-February; Mid-April - May
Other Information: Close to Gulf stream with moderate temperature; T-shirt weather in April

JÄMTLAND COUNTY: ÅRE
Along a narrow valley there are 4 ski areas: Bydalen Höglekardalens, Gräftåvallen, and Falkfångerliften which comprise the second largest ski area in Jämtland. Typical of the area is a closeness to nature, open ski space and an active winter sports area for families.

Après-Ski: sauna, 4 bars, 1 disco, 1 ice bar, 3 cafes
Shopping/Services: Food stores, handicraft and Laplander art shop, 3 ski rental shops that sell snowboard equipment and ski accessories
Credit Cards: AE, DC, EC, MC, VISA
Child Care: Ages 4 and up; no nursery; kid's ski school
Lodging: All accommodations in cabins or apartments and all within walking distance to slopes; 600 beds
Transportation: Gateway Airports: Arlanda, Stockholm, 550 km (342 mi)
Local Airport: Östersund
Closest Provincial City: Östersund
By Auto from Airport: E14, then 321 south in winter, 50 km via Great Lake Ice Roads; in summer 80 km (50 mi)
By Train: Train to Östersund, then car or bus (bus service once a day)
Best Deal: Beginning Jan. (week 2-6). Low off season prices for lodging, lifts and ski school
Other Information: Snowmaking on 8 slopes

SWEDEN

ÅREFJÄLLEN
TOURIST INFORMATION
Årevägen 93, S-83013 ÅRE, Sweden

Telephone: (46) 647 17720 Fax: (46) 647 17712

Elevation: Base/Village: 400 m (1,312 ft); Top: 1,274 m (4,180 ft)

Vertical: 890 m (2,935 ft)

Longest Run: 6.5 km (4.0 mi)

Terrain: 91 kms of slopes, 108 ski runs; the lower slopes have snowmaking coverage; night skiing on a number of slopes; 18 green, 45 blue, 35 red, 5 black

Skiing Circus: By bus between towns

Lifts: 43

Types: 1 Cable car, 1 gondola, 7 chairs and 34 T-bars (1 quad chairlift)

Life Capacity: 53,200 p/h

Ski Season: Early-December-End of April

Summer Skiing: None

Cross Country: 2-15 km runs; 300 kms of marked trails; unlimited unmarked; 25 km groomed and lighted

Ski School: Everyday, all levels—alpine, snowboard, telemark, cross country

This is Sweden's most well known ski resort. It's located 100 km from Östersund and approximately 640 km from Stockholm. Åre and Duved are connected by ski buses. Duved is the quieter resort with a few restaurants; Åre offers more nightlife. Skiing for all levels, plus Sweden's only cable car.

Mountain Restaurants: 19 restaurants and cafes

Other Winter Activities: Ice fishing; dog sledding; para-gliding; hang-gliding; snowmobile touring; horseback riding

Après-Ski: 6 discos, 4 cafes, 30 restaurants

Credit Cards: AE, DC, MC, VISA

Lodging: 15,000 beds (3,800 in hotels and pensions); hotels, cottages, apartments and ski dorms

Transportation: Gateway Airport: Stockholm (620 km)

Closest Provincial City: Ostersund (100 km/62 mi)

By Air: Stockholm to Östersund, then transfer by taxi or bus - should be booked with air (reservations) ticket

By Train: Daily connections between Stockholm and Åre. The train stops in the village

By Auto: New number on the highway - E14

Other Information: Area has 100 snowguns

RIKSGRÄNSEN*

S-981 94 Riksgränsen, Sweden

Telephone: (46) 980 40080 Fax (46) 980 43125

Elevation: Base/Village: 500 m (1,640 ft); Top: 950 m (3,117 ft)

Vertical: 450 m (1,477 ft)

Longest Run: 3.5 km (2.0 mi)

Terrain: 19 runs; ski in the midnight sun until 1 am; above treeline; good off-slope variety; 6 green, 11 blue, 9 red, 6 black runs

Lifts: 6

Types: 2 Chairlifts (2 doubles); 4 Surface

Lift Capacity: 3,500 p/h resort

Ski Season: Mid-February-End of June

Cross Country: 2.5-5 km runs; 500 km of marked trails

Ski School: Traditional instruction; telemark; snowboarding; climbing and back country skiing available

Other Winter Activities: Guided ski trips (train return); helicopter skiing; ice fishing; hotel pool, sauna, solarium, Jacuzzi; mountaineering; snowmobile trips; fjord cruise; backpack country skiing; dog sled rides

Après-Ski: 1 Disco, hotel entertainment

Shopping/Services: 1 restaurant; food stores; rentals

LAPLAND
Riksgränsen is located 250 km north of the Arctic Circle making it one of the worlds most northerly ski resorts. Possibly the only ski area in the world where you can mid-summer ski in the midnight sun (from mid-May to the end of June). Obviously a unique experience, even for non-skiers.

Credit Cards: AE, DC, MC, VISA

Lodging: 330 apartment, 137 hotel beds in Riksgränsen, single, double, economy, suite or 2-6 bed apartments; restaurant, bar, gym, pool, sauna, sundry shop & conference facilities; Tele: (46) 980 40080 Fax (46) 980 43125 hotel

Transportation: Gateway Airport: Stockholm 1500 km (932 mi)

Closest Provincial City: Kiruna 130 km (81 mi)

By Auto from airport: Norkalott Highway from Kiruna

By air: Domestic flights Stockholm-Kiruna (90 min); air taxi or air bus transfers

By Train: Stockholm-Riksgranasen, 20 hours overnight; Special rate for trains leaving Friday evening with Saturday return

Best Deal: Hotel has special children rates: Ages 1-3 free; 4-7 free lifts and 50% lodging/meal discount; 8-12 50% lodging/meal discount

Other Information: Close to Norwegian Atlantic coast and the Gulf Stream which moderates temperature to 0°-15°C; 24 hours of sunshine May to August

©Publishers Group International, 1998

ICELAND

BLÁFJÖLL SKI AREA*
BLÁFJÖLL SKI AND RECREATION COMMITTEE
Bláfjöll, Iceland
Telephone: (354)1-52600 (Hafnarfjördur)
(354)1-76588 (Garoabaer/Kópavogur)

Under the administration of the Bláfjöll Ski Park Committee, which is comprised of 13 towns & counties, plus 2 sports clubs, Fram and Armann, 5 different areas of Bláfjöll have been connected. While the skiing is more for novice and intermediates, it does provide Reykjavik with a day area. Services are limited, but the area is only a half hour outside of town.

Vertical: 270 m (886 ft)

Terrain: Groomed beginner and intermediate terrain encompassing 5 different areas; all slopes are lit for night skiing

Skiing Circus: As above

Lifts: 11

Types: 2 Chairlifts (2 doubles); 9 Surface

Lift Capacity: 8,100 p/h

Ski Season: Mid-November—May

Summer Skiing: Glacier skiing at Vatnajokull, April-Oct.; Tele (354) 97-81503

Cross Country: 3, 5, and 10 km courses; 5 km trail is lit for night skiing

Mountain Restaurants: Service Center at midpoint in the area has hot snacks or brown bag acceptable; 2 other on-mountain huts have food service

Other Winter Activities: Hiking; hikers can take lift at Kongsgil for panoramic sightseeing

Shopping/Services: Restaurants, bars, services in Reykjavík; rentals, 1st aid, and food service at area

Transportation: Gateway Airport: Reykjavík

Closest provincial City: Reykjavík

By Ski Bus from airport: Daily buses from Reykjavík, Garoabaer, Hafnarfjördur and Kópavogur. Tele: (354) 1-22300; bus terminal near airport

Best Deal: Ski Iceland Package. For information and packages call AIT Agency (Icelandair representative) (800) 526-2358

Other Information: Weather conditions Tele: (354) 1-80111

HLÍDARFJALL (AKUREYRI)*
TOURIST OFFICE: Akureyri
82 Hafnarstraeti
Akureyri, Iceland
Telephone: (354)6-27733   Fax (354)461-2030

Hlídarfjall, in north Iceland is located in Akureyri the largest town outside Reykjavik. The mountain has beginner to upper intermediate terrain and lighted for night skiing. There is a ski lodge above Akureyri with sleeping bag accommodations for 60, or several hotels in town with bus service.

Elevation: Base/hotel: 500 m (1,640 ft); Top: 1,000 m (3,280 ft)

Vertical: 1,000 m (3,280 ft)

Longest Run: 2.5 km (1.5 mi)

Terrain: Wide open terrain, easy to advanced, off-slope skiing possible; groomed runs; open nights

Skiing Circus: None

Lifts: 4

Types: 1 Chairlift (1 double); 4 Surface (3 T-bars)

Lift Capacity: 2,680 p/h

Ski Season: Mid-December—End-April; Weekdays 1 pm-6:45 pm; Weekends 10 am-5 pm

Cross Country: Cross country and touring available

Ski School: Private and group lessons available 3 times daily; no children under 5 admitted to ski school; Monday-Friday

Mountain Restaurants: Self service cafeteria at Skidastadir Ski Lodge

Shopping/Services: Ski lodge has sitting room with TV for guests and rentals. At 700 m Stryta cabin has refreshments; all other services in town

Lodging: 4 hotels in Akureyri: KEA (354)6-22200; Akureyri (354)6-22525; Stefanía (354)6-26266; and Norjurland (354)6-22600

Transportation: Gateway Airport: Reykjavik

Closest Provincial City: Akureyri (4-5 mi; 7 km)

Bus from city 3 times daily

By Ski Bus from airport: Icelandair and the Nordurleio Bus Company operate daily services to Akureyri year round

Best Deal: Ski Iceland Package: See above listed information

ANDORRA
and the French Pyrénées

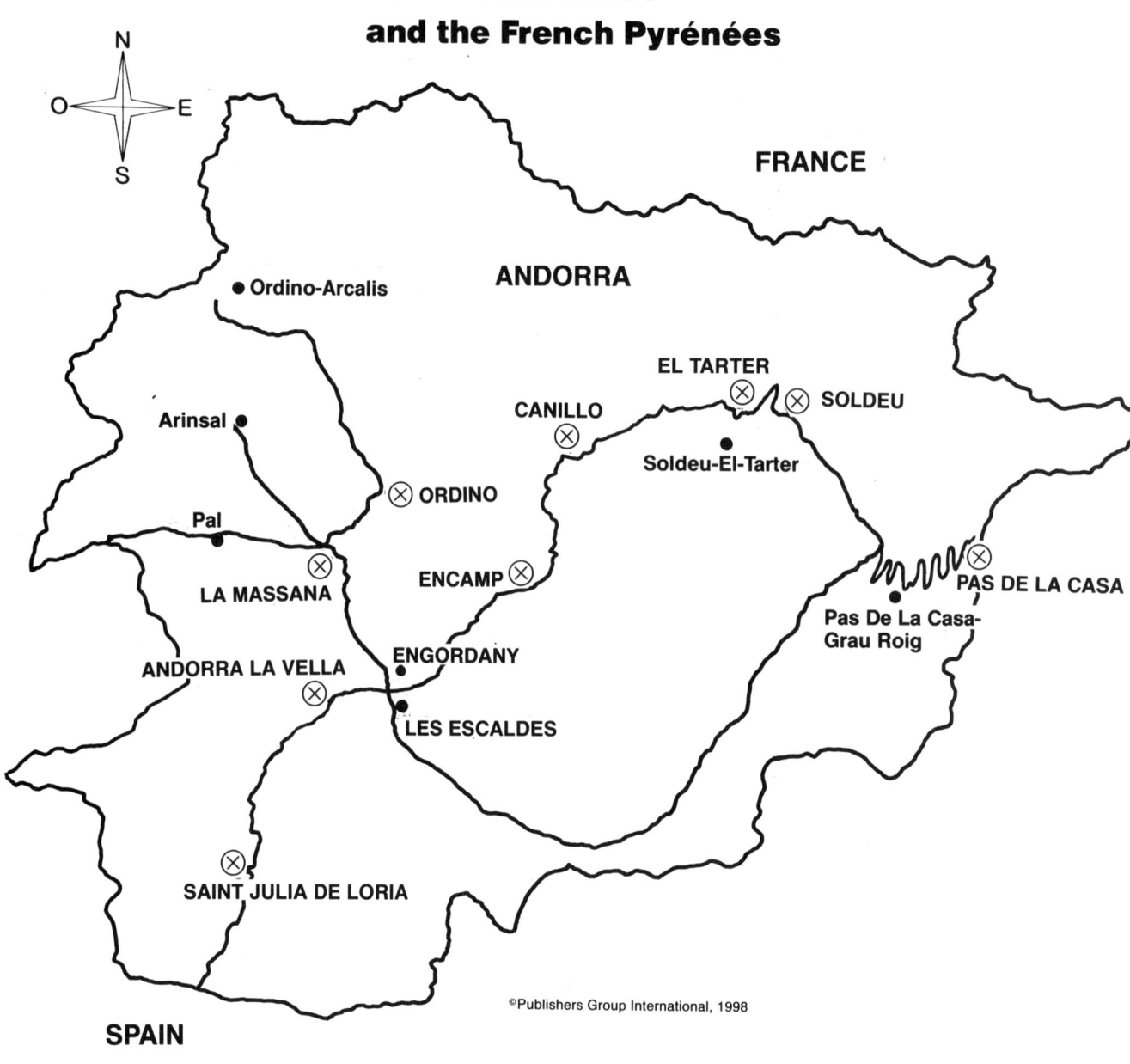

ANDORRA	Page No.	FRENCH PYRÉNÉES	Page No.
Arinsal	132	Les Angeles	134
Ordino-Arcalis	133	Luz Ardiden*	135
Pas de la Casa-Grau Roig	134	Saint Lary Soulan*	135
Pal	132		
Soldeu-El-Tarter	133		

*Areas marked with an asterisk in the text did not update their information for this edition.

SPAIN—ANDORRA THE PYRENEES

by Bob Enzel

The principality of Andorra was once known as a smuggler's refuge; safe because of it's size and location in the Pyrenees. Today this small, mountainous area nestled between northern Spain and southern France has a thriving economy thanks to agriculture, electric power and tourism.

Andorra's capital city, Andorra la Vella, is a tax-free-duty-free-great place to shop. Skiers get a double bonus vacationing in Andorra-great skiing and shopping.

Although Andorra is small and tucked away, it has not lost touch with modern civilization or shut out progress and growth. It has a literacy rate of 100% with many of its citizens fluent in four languages: the national language of Catalan, Spanish, French and distantly fourth, English.

Ski areas are scattered all along the Pyrenees from north central Spain to France with Andorra in between. Together, the three countries have over 30 ski resorts in the Pyrenees alone. This book contains all five of the Andorran areas but space constraints limited copy to three in France and three in Spain.

The resorts of Andorra offer a combined lift pass and are in close proximity to one another. Adorra's largest complex, Groi-Roig/Pas de la Casa, near the French border, is an internationally known area. Not too far away is the tax-free, VAT-free border town of Pas de la Casa.

- Andorra does not require a passport for entrance, but France and Spain might require one to re-enter.
- The Spanish currency is the Peseta and the French currency is the French Franc; both are equally accepted in Andorra.
- A visit to Andorra is no longer the visit back in time it once was, but Romanesque churches, stone chalets, ancient artifacts and an isolated mountain country of great beauty and charm should make it a top priority on every skier's to-do list. The three Pyrenees resorts of Spain summarized in this book are among the region's largest and most popular, The Spanish Pyrenees resorts are popular with skiers, even to the point of being crowded on weekends.

Included in this section is a resort that many consider Spain's finest, Sierra Nevada. Sierra Nevada is the southernmost ski area on the Iberian Peninsula. The Sierra Nevada mountain range is approximately 55 miles long with peaks over 11,000 feet. The ski resort base is at 7,000 feet and its top sits at 11,382 feet. The late season sun can crisp you quickly, so watch out. The drive up starts at 2,200 feet and a short time later, you are already climbing to 11,000 feet. At its base some 30 miles distant is a city not to be missed, Granada. This Moorish city's most famous attraction is the Alhambra Palace and gardens.

The three resorts of the French Pyrénées included in this book: Luz Ardiden, Saint Lary Soulan and Les Angles act as a sample representation of the region's twelve areas. There are others, such as Bareges and La Mongie that are also popular.

Bring your skis, a good tour-book and some walking shoes for shopping and we guarantee this will be a great adventure.

For more information, contact:

IBERIA AIRLINES
(800) 772-4642   (305) 267-7747
Fax (305) 267 1263

TOURIST OFFICE OF SPAIN
(212) 265-8822
(888) 657-7246
Fax (212) 265-8864

SKI ANDORRA
Plaça Rebés Núm 7
4a Planta
Andorra La Vella, Principat d'Andorra
(376) 86 43 89
Fax (376) 86 59 10
http://www.skiandorra.ad

ANDORRA

ARINSAL
TOURIST OFFICE—Estació d'Arinsal
Edifici Cresta—La Massana
Principat d'Andorra
Telephone: (376) 838438 Fax: (376) 838738

Elevation: Base/Village: 1,550 m (5,085 ft); Top: 2,560 m (8,397 ft)

Vertical: 1,010 m (3,313 ft)

Terrain: 21 trails on 741 acres encompassing 28 km (17 mi) of ski terrain; 2 green, 7 blue, 7 red, 5 black runs

Lifts: 14

Types: 4 Chairlifts (2 quads, 2 dbls); 9 Surface; 1 gondola

Lift Capacity: 13,000 p/h

Ski Season: December-April

Ski School: Located at the 1,950 m level; 60 instructors; private and group lessons Tele: 836135

Mountain Restaurants: 6 on-mountain including snack bars (2,100 m and 2,300 m)

Other Winter Activities: Snowboard park; heli-skiing

Après-Ski: Wide variety of live music, discos, bars and over 20 restaurants in Arinsal Village

Shopping/Services: At 1,950 m level: slalom stadium for competitions, ski shops, medical center and 4 bar-

PAL
TOURIST OFFICE: Estació de Pal
La Massana
Principat d'Andorra
Telephone: (376) 838438 Fax: (376) 838738

Elevation: Base/Village: 1,780 m (5,840 ft); Top: 2,358 m (7,736 ft)

Vertical: 578 m (1,896 ft)

Longest Run: 3.0 km (1.9 mi)

Terrain: Wooded runs, glades and open slopes; 20 mi (32 km) of terrain; 4 green, 4 blue, 12 red, 1 black; 4 ISF slalom runs

Lifts: 12

Types: 5 Chairlifts (4 quads, 1 double); 7 Surface

Lift Capacity: 13,500 p/h

Ski Season: December-April

Cross Country: No

Ski School: 80 instructors; Tele: (376) 836306

Mountain Restaurants: 5 bars and restaurants

Other Winter Activities: Mono-skiing

Après-Ski: Good variety in Arinsal Village (where many hotels for Pal skiing are situated)—live music, discos, bars and restaurants

PYRENEES MOUNTAINS (Language Catalán)
Arinsal sits just northwest of Andorra la Vella and La Massana. A base village with lodging, but the ski school, nursery and other activities are located at mid-station. The mountain's layout centers the skiing in a bowl with mostly red and black runs off the top, however, it can be skied by intermediate level skiers.

restaurants; at 1,550 m level: bar-restaurant, ski shops & rentals, lodging information

Child Care: Nursery and snow garden located at the 1,950 m base; from 1 to 8 years old

Lodging: 4,000 beds; 2,400 apartment beds; hotel and apartment lodging availability from central reservations (376) 838438 (at 1,550 m) in the Crest building, which also contains group reception

Transportation: Gateway Airport: Barcelona

Closest Provincial City: Andorra la Vella (11 km/7 mi)

By Auto from airport: Twice daily prebookable mini bus service from Barcelona airport—reservations (376) 838438 (See other Andorran areas for travel from France)

By Train: From Barcelona to Puigcerdà and then bus to La Seu d'Urgell, then 22 km to Andorra la Vella and on to La Massana

Other Information: Free parking available at 1,550 m level in car park and at 1,950 m level at Services building. Ski rental locations at both 1,550 m and 1,950 m levels; new gondola & quad lift

PYRENEES MOUNTAINS (Language Catalán)
Just outside the town of La Massana and about 8 miles from Andorra la Vella is Pal Ski Area. The principality's highest mountain peaks are nearby, yet despite this, the skiing is wooded. Sheltered runs on bad-weather days, cruising runs and panoramic views.

Shopping/Services: Five restaurants/snack bars at area; Après-ski, shopping and services in nearby Arinsal La Massana or Andorra la Vella

Child Care: Kindergarten and kid's ski school

Lodging: None at ski area; lodging is mainly in La Massana or Andorra la Vella. Central reservations (376) 838438 English speaking

Transportation: Gateway Airport: Barcelona, Spain

By Auto from airport: (See Arinsal)

By Train: From Barcelona to Puigcerdà and then bus to La Seu d'Urgell, then 22 km to Andorra La Vella and on to La Massana

Other Information: Area first opened for the 1982/83 season; extensive snowmaking; slalom course (see Pas de la Casa for language and currency); new high-speed quad and fixed-grip quad; Pal bus service for skiers in car park

ANDORRA

SOLDEU EL TARTER
El Tartar
Principality of Andorra
Telephone: (376) 851 777 Fax: (376) 851 337 and 851 151 El Tarter; 851 144 Soldeu

Elevation: Base/Vilage: 1,710 m (5,610 ft); Top: 2,560 m (8,398 ft)

Vertical: 850 m (2,789 ft)

Longest Run: 8.2 km (5.1 mi), Gall de Bosc

Terrain: 38 miles (62 km) of trails; 34 runs; 2 slalom slopes; glades and off slope skiing through the woods; 11 green, 5 blue, 8 red, 8 black runs

Skiing Circus: Inter-resort lift between Soldeu-El-Tartar and Pas de la Casa/Grau Roig

Lifts: 21

Types: 6 Chairlifts (3 doubles 3 quads); 1 cable car; 14 Platters

Lift Capacity: 21,000 p/h resort

Ski Season: Beginning December-End April

Cross Country: Soldeu 7 km; El Tarter 5 km

Ski School: 160 instructors in 2 schools (Soldeu & El Tarter); Kindergarten in both locations

Mountain Restaurants: 3 bars and restaurants

ORDINO-ARCALIS
Camp de neu Ordino Arcalis
Ed. La Font 1r pis Ordino
Principat d'Andorra
Telephone: (376) 836 963 Fax (376) 839 225

Elevation: Base/Village: 1,940 m (6,365 ft); Top: 2,600 m (8,530 ft)

Vertical: 660 m (2,165 ft)

Longest Run: 2.0 km (1.2 mi)

Terrain: 15 miles (24 km) of terrain, 6 green, 7 blue, 9 red, 2 black; 1 slalom run

Lifts: 12

Types: 4 Chairlifts (1 h-s qd, 2 quads, 1 triple); 8 Surface

Lift Capacity: 13,500 p/h

Ski Season: December-April

Cross Country: 6 to 12 km of runs

Ski School: 40 instructors; Tele: (376) 850 121; Group & private lessons; surf, X-C, slalom, telemark & racket lessons

Other Winter Activities: Mono-skiing; snowboarding; heliskiing

Après-Ski: Après-ski activities in Ordino, La Massana and Andorra la Vella

Shopping/Services: 2 Cafeterias, 4 cafe-bars, medical, 2 rentals and day nursery at base

PYRENEES MOUNTAINS *(Language Catalán)*
The villages of Soldeu and Sant Pere del Tarter in northeastern Andorra form the ski complex. This area offers a variety of terrain, above treeline to gladed runs. Off-slope tree skiing is plentiful, English is spoken by most of the instructors and there is a good choice of après-ski activity.

Other Winter Activities: Ice skating/artificial; indoor swimming (1 public/1 hotel); sports center; saunas; paragliding; hang-gliding; mono-skiing; mountaineering

Shopping/Services: Restaurants, 8 bars, 5 discos, 15 cafes, cafeterias, real estate office, medical facility; designer boutiques in Andorra la Vella

Child Care: 2 centers; Snowfield for children; Nursery

Lodging: Villages of Soldeu and El Tarter have 16 hotels with 1,200 beds and 75 apartments with 300 beds; lodging is in luxury condos in nearby Procasa Refuge or in traditional stone chalets at several locations

Transportation: Gateway Airport: Toulouse & Barcelona

Closest Provincial City: Andorra la Vella (17 km/11 mi)

By Auto from Airport: From Toulouse via L'Hospitalet; From Barcelona via the Cadí Tunnel. Bus parking & 2,000 car capacity in El Tarter

Other Information: Snowmaking covers 12 km of ski runs with 244 snowguns; magnetic ski pass card

PYRENEES MOUNTAINS *(Language Catalán)*
Arcalis, Andorra's newest ski area, is located in the far northwest corner of the principality. The closest lodging is in Ordino, but this inconvenience is offset somewhat by the historic character of the village. Encompasses two valleys, Arcalis and La Coma giving the area a long ski season.

Child Care: Nursery and kindergarten; Tele: (376) 864 121

Lodging: None at area—closest is in El Serrat (6 km) or Ordino (15 km); public transportation & parking available

Transportation: Gateway Airport: Barcelona, Spain (226 km/140 mi); 32 km from Spanish border

Closest Provincial City: Andorra la Vella (24 km/15 mi)

By Auto from airport: Barcelona to Andorra via Puigcerda and La Seu d'Urgell or to Igualada, Calaf, Ponts, and La Seu d'Urgell (see other Andorran ski areas for directions from France); French border 44 km

Best Deal: Andorra la Vella has every conceivable variety of duty free shops, and no sales or value-added taxes

Other Information: The official language of Andorra is Catalán, although Spanish and French are also common. Literacy rate is 100%. Modernized snowmaking; re-graded ski runs; refurbished La Coma restaurant

ANDORRA

PAS DE LA CASA-GRAU ROIG
TOURIST OFFICE: S.A.E.T.D.E.
Av. Carlemany, 46
Escaldes, Principat d'Andorra
Telephone: (376) 80.10.60 Fax: (376) 80.10.70

Elevation: Base/Village: 2,050 m (6,725 ft); Top: 2,640 m (8,659 ft)

Vertical: 550 m (1,804 ft)

Terrain: 63 mi. of runs: 49 runs: 8 green, 9 blue, 21 red, and 11 black; 1,484 skiable acres (601 hectares), wide open bowls; open for night skiing; 323 snowmaking guns

Skiing Circus: Grau Roig southern side and Pas de la Casa northern side

Lifts: 29

Types: 10 Chairlifts (1 h-s 6-passenger, 3 quads, 3 h-s quads, 3 doubles); 16 Surface; 3 Telebabies

Lift Capacity: 37,615 p/h resort

Ski Season: December-May

Cross Country: 13 km (9 mi) of prepared runs plus adjacent terrain is skiable

Ski School: 2: One in each area (150 instructors)

Mountain Restaurants: 4

Other Winter Activities: Mono-ski, snowpark; snowshoe, night skiing; sport center

LES ANGLES
OFFICE DU TOURISME
2, Avenue de l'Aude/BP18
66210 Les Angles, Pyrénées, France
Telephone: (33) 5 6804 3276 Fax: (33) 5 6830 9309

Elevation: Base/Village: 1,600 m (5,280 ft); Top: 2,400 m (7,920 ft)

Vertical: 2,640

Terrain: 40 km (24.5 mi) of trails; 255 snowmaking guns; snowboarding halfpipe, air space sowboard

Skiing Circus: None

Lifts: 26

Types: 2 Gondolas; 2 Chairlifts; 22 Surface lifts

Lift Capacity: 19,000 p/h resort

Ski Season: Year-round resort

Cross Country: 156 km of trails on 6 circuits

Ski School: Ecole du Ski Français alpine & XC

Other Winter Activities: Horseback riding; ice hockey; swimming; bowling; billiards; freestyle competitions; paragliding; climbing wall; scuba diving under ice; ice surfing

Après-Ski: Concerts, piano-bar, library, movies, January Festival du Raid; sauna; health salon

Shopping Services: Restaurants, bars, shops, local artifacts

PYRENEES MTNS (Language Catalán/French/Spanish) Pas de la Casa/Grau Roig (pronounced "roich") is the closest ski resort to the French border. Andorra's largest and most popular ski area comprises adjacent valleys with a growing base village. It has wide open bowls above treeline and is rated 75% intermediate to expert. Active après-ski and shopping.

Après-Ski: Many bars & discos, 40 restaurants, indoor swimming at hotel; Caldea thermal center 36 km

Shopping/Services: Good shopping in Pas de la Casa (no sales, duty or VAT); 2 medical facilities

Child Care: Municipal nursery & ski kindergarten in Pas de la Casa & one in Grau Roig, ages 12 mos.-3 yrs.

Lodging: Accommodations are best in Pas de la Casa on the border where après-ski is active. Other lodging is in Soldeu, Canillo, Escaldes, Andorra la Vella and Encamp. 9,000 beds; Reservations Tel.: (376) 801060

Transportation: Gateway Airport: Toulouse, France

Closest Provincial City: Encamp (10 mi)

By Auto: Toulouse-Blagnac Airport (165 km) - N20 Ax-les-Thermas-Pas de la Casa

By Train: To Ax-les-Thermes, L'Hospitalet or La Tour de Carol, then bus to Pas de la Casa

By Bus: Daily from Barcelona; regularly from Madrid

Other Information: Night skiing on "Font Negre"; FIS approved slalom stadium; snow park

PYRÉNÉES ORIENTALES
Authentic resort village with a focus toward children and families. Lakes, streams, forests and wild animals of the Pyrénées allow for an unspoiled vacation setting.

Credit Cards: Visa, Mastercard

Child Care: Kindergarten, 3 months & up

Lodging: 4 2-Star hotels; 1 1-Star hotel. Resort's newest hotel is Le Panoramic Residence Hotel w/2-6 person accommodations; apartments

Transportation: Gateway Airports: Perpignan/Rivesaltes "La Llabanere" 100 km

Closest Provincial City: Mont-Louis

By Auto:

Perpignan RN116 to Mont-Louis, north to Les Angles (92 km). Carcassonne south to AxAT to resort. From Spain, north thru the Cadi Tunnel

By Train: Latour de Carol and Mont-Louis/La Cabanasse (13 km) taxi

Other Information: Des Angles animal park covers 3,500 m circuit or 1,500 m. circuit (bears, warthogs . . . 12 species)

New this winter: 1 gondola (16 seats)

LUZ ARDIDEN
OFFICE DU TOURISME
65120 Luz-Saint-Sauveur, France
Telephone (33) 562 92 8160 Fax: (33) 562 92 8719

Elevation: Base/Village: 1,700 m (4,592 ft); Top: 2,450 m (1,476 ft)

Vertical: 750 m (2,460 ft)

Terrain: 45 km of slopes; 4 green, 10 blue, 14 red, 4 black runs; (80 in region)

Skiing Circus: Village of Aulian & Luz Ardiden resorts connect with Luz St.-Sauveur & Bederet

Lifts: 19 (60 in region with Ticket Toy)

Types: 6 Chairlifts; 13 Surface lifts

Lift Capacity: 14,000 p/h resort

Ski Season:

Summer Skiing: No

Cross Country: Yes, 5 km track

Ski School: Two ski schools

Other Winter Activities: Cross country; luge; hiking trails; mono-skiing; snowboarding; ice skating & other ice sports

HAUTES-PYRÉNÉES
Multiple activities geared to children of all ages and families. A resort in its natural wood and rock setting.

Après-Ski: Bars, restaurants

Shopping Services: Luz St.-Sauveur

Credit Cards: Unknown

Child Care: 18 mos. - 6 yrs. La Pitchounerie snow play garden; kindergarten

Lodging: For lodging information contact: Aulian et Bédéret; Luz St. Sauveur; or à Luz Ardiden

Transportation: Gateway Airports:
Paris to Tarbes-Ossun-Lourdes airport (75 km)
By Auto from Airport: See other Pyrénées areas
By Train: See other Pyrénées areas

Best Deal: Ticket Toy covers Gavárnie Gedre, Luz Ardiden, Barèges & Luz St.-Sauveur

Other Information: 1,000 parking spaces near the slopes

SAINT LARY SOULAN*
OFFICE DU TOURISME
37 rue Principale
6570 Saint-Larysoulan, France
Telephone: (33) 5 6239 5081 Fax: (33) 5 6239 5006

Elevation: Base/Village: 1,600 m (5,248 ft); Top: 2,450 m (8,036 ft)

Vertical: 850 m (2,788 ft)

Terrain: 38 runs: 10 green, 18 blue, 6 red & 4 black; bump skiing park; snowboard park; ski until 6:30 pm in February (Sunset skiing)

Skiing Circus: 2 linked skiing areas, 4 sectors: Pla D'Abet; Soum de Matte; Espiavbe; Vallon Du Portet

Lifts: 32

Types: Trams/Gondolas 3; Chairlifts 10 (including 4-seater); 19 Surface lifts

Lift Capacity: 25,000 p/h resort

Ski Season: Winter & summer mountain resort

Cross Country: Mountain lake circuit & 3 km mountain trail; 6 day lift pass

Ski School: Three ski schools: L'Ecole de Ski Français; Ski School Int'l; Ecole de Ski Snow-Fun

Other Winter Activities: Skating rink; tennis; omnisports gymnasium; paragliding; mountain biking; hiking; snowshoeing; snowboarding; cross country; climbing; swimming; horseback riding; rafting; kayaking; canyoning & hydrospeed; permanent bump skiing snowpark

HAUTES-PYRÉNÉES
Traditional village architecture of wood, stone & slate. Modern facilities favoring tourism but maintaining its old-world flavor. Close proximity & relationship with Spain. Home of Olympic Champion Isabelle Mir. Also, training site for the Spanish National Ski Team.

Après-Ski: Créperies, pubs, restaurants, health spa; National Pyrenean Park; sheep & goat farms

Shopping Services: In village of St.-Lary. Local Specialties . . . food & shopping

Child Care: Kid's program ages 5-12

Lodging: 23,000 beds, variety of accommodations in Saint Lary Village

Transportation: Gateway Airports:
Tarbes-Ossun-Lourdes Airport 80 km

Closest Provincial City: Spain 20 km thru the Bielsa Tunnel

By Auto: Rt A64 Bilbao-Bayonne to (RD 929)

Rt A64 from Toulouse to (RN 20; RN 117; RD 929)

Rt A10 Paris-Bordeaux to (RN 21 & RD 929)

By Train: TGV Atlantique connects Saint Lary with autocar SNCF

Best Deal: Altiplus-ski when & where you like; Altipass-allows cable car to village of St. Lary; Altikid-hosted kid's program for ages 5-12; free shuttle service

Other Information: 80 snowguns

SPAIN AND THE SPANISH PYRÉNÉES

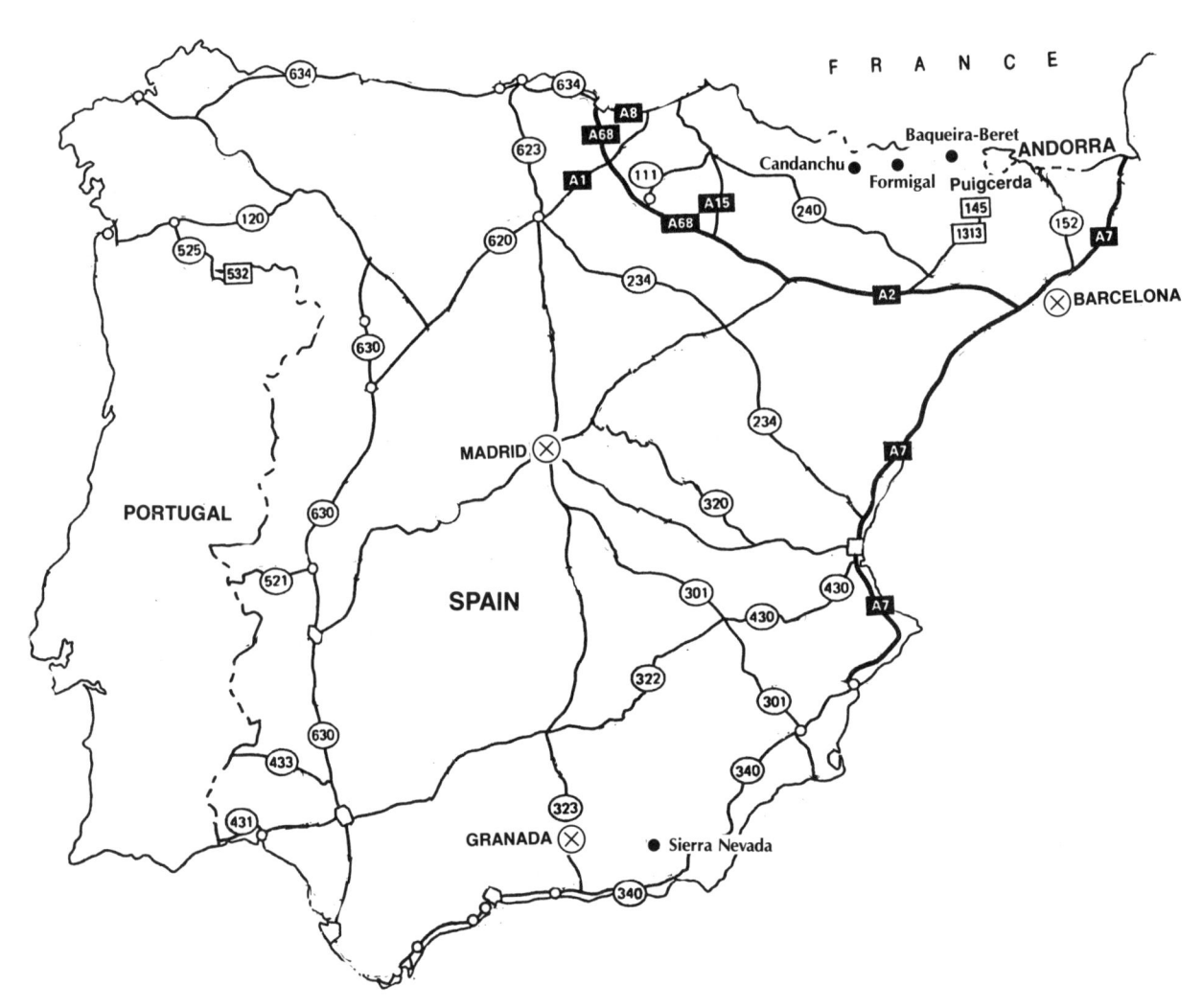

SPAIN	Page No.
Baqueria-Beret	137
Candanchu Winter Resort*	137
Formigal*	138
Sierra Nevada*	138

*Areas marked with an asterisk in the text did not update their information for this edition.

SPAIN

BAQUEIRA-BERET
P.O. Box 60
Vielha 25530, (Lerida) Spain
Telephone: (973) 64 44 55
Fax: (973) 64 58 84

Elevation: Base/Village: 1,500 m (4,921 ft); Top: 2,510 m (8,235 ft)

Vertical: 1,010 m (3,314 ft)

Terrain: Wide open terrain; slalom race area, 357 snowmaking guns; 1,863 acres (825 hectares) of runs; 47 runs: 3 green, 17 blue, 22 red, 5 black, plus 1 off-piste run

Lifts: 24

Types: 16 Chairlifts (1 6 person, 2 quad, 7 trpl, 6 dbl); 8 pomas

Lift Capacity: 30,968 p/h resort

Cross Country: 7 km circuit

Ski School: 200 Instructors; also snowboarding lessons and facilities

Other Winter Activities: Fitness center; bowling; helicopter skiing; mountain guide excursions; paragliding; sauna; snowboarding; squash; ice skating rink; indoor swimming pool

LERIDAN PYRENEES
This purpose built resort is set in the beautiful Arán valley near Romanesque churches, mountain lakes and the Algüestortes National Park. It has become one of Spain's popular ski resorts.

Après-Ski: Bars, discos, cafes, dancing, restaurants

Shopping Services: Rental shop, storage, first aid, bank, pharmacy, grocery, ski shop; Vielha nearby has a variety of activities and services

Child Care: 4 Kindergartens; play area; Telephone (73) 64 54 48

Lodging: 3,500 beds; 3 hotels with 600 beds, 125 chalets, and apartments

Transportation: Gateway Airport: Barcelona (340 km); Toulouse, FR (160 km north)

Closest Provincial City: Lerida (180 km); Vielha (14 km)

By Auto from Lerida: N-230 to Vielha, then C-142 east

CANDANCHU WINTER RESORT
22889 Candanchu
Huesca, Spain
Telephone: (974) 373192
Fax: (974) 373348 (Resort)

Elevation: Base/Village: 1,560 m (5,118 ft); Top: 2,400 m (7,874 ft)

Vertical: 840 m (2,756 ft)

Terrain: 53 km of prepared slopes, snowmaking, 54 main runs, slalom run; 9 green, 8 blue, 14 red, 17 black; 109 snowmaking guns. Snowboard halfpipe

Skiing Circus: None, but the Astun ski area with 10 lifts and 17 slopes is almost adjacent and Gourette, Artouste, La Pierre de Saint Martin in France are nearby

Lifts: 25

Types: 6 Chairlifts (1 quad, 3 triples, 2 doubles); 19 Surface

Lift Capacity: 21,000 p/h

Ski Season: December-May

Cross Country: 35 km circular track from Spain to France

Ski School: 85 Instructors; Telephone (34) (74) 373194

Après-Ski: Bars, cafeteria, restaurants, pubs, discotheque

ARGONESE PYRENEES
The winter resort of Candanchu sits on the French-Spanish border in the center of the Pyrenees. The city of Pau, France is about 60 km north (see Formigal description).

Shopping Services: Service station, grocery, gift shops, bank, photography, boutiques, dining variety

Child Care: Ski school for kids, play area, ages 3 months to 6 years; kindergarden from 6 months to 6 years

Lodging: In Candanchu Resort: 3 hotels, 1 aparthotel, 5 private houses, 1 hostel, 3 agency apartments for rent. In the Valley: 18 hotels, 3 aparthotels, private houses, 11 hostels, 6 agency apartments for rent

Transportation: Closest Provincial City: Jaca 28 km; Zaragoza (168 km); Pamplona 160 km

By Auto from Pamplona: N-240 to Jaca or from Huesca to Jaca, then N-330 north towards France

By Train: Canfranc, 6 km

Best Deal: Low season is first 3 weeks of December; January to 1st week in February and mid-March to Mid-April is medium rate season

SPAIN

FORMIGAL*
TOURIST OFFICE:
Valle de Ten
22640 Formigal (Huesca), Spain
Telephone: (34) (74) 48 81 26 Fax: (34) (74) 48 83 13

Elevation: Base: 1,510 m (4,954 ft); Top: 2,250 m (7,382 ft)

Vertical: 740 m (2,428 ft)

Longest Run: 3 5 mile runs

Terrain: Slalom course; 3 green, 8 blue, 15 red, 4 black

Skiing Circus: Panticosa ski area 10 km has 7 lifts and 14 slopes mostly blue & red

Lifts: 19

Types: 1 Gondola; 5 Chairlifts (1 quad, 1 triple, 1 double, 2 singles); 13 Surface

Lift Capacity: 14,800 p/h resort

Ski Season: December 1-Early May

Cross Country: Yes

Ski School: 53 instructors; Telephone: (974) 48 81 07

Mountain Restaurants: 3

ARAGONESE PYRÉNÉES
Located just about in the center of the Pyrénées Mountains, 8 km from the French border, Formigal shares the same valley with Panticosa ski resort. The surrounding region of El Serrablo has pre-Romanesque sites, Mozarab and Catalán-Lombard churches.

Other Winter Activities: Fitness center; indoor tennis; squash

Après-Ski: Bars, discos, cafes, dancing

Shopping Services: Grocery, photo shop, first aid, service station, dining, ski shop, storage, first aid, bank, pharmacy

Child Care: Kindergarten

Lodging: 18 Hotels and 4 apartments; 2 hostels

Transportation: Closest Provincial City: Huesca 89 km; Zaragoza 162 km; Pamplona 182 km

By Auto from Zaragoza: N-123 to Huesca; From Lerida, N-240 to Huesca then C-136 North to Sabiñánigo to Formigal

Best Deal: Low season: 1st 3 weeks of December and last week of April-May

SIERRA NEVADA*
TOURIST OFFICE:
Plaza de Pradollano, s/n
18196 Sierra Nevada (Granada), Spain
Telephone: (34) (58) 24 91 00 Fax: (34) (58) 24 91 22

Elevation: Base/Village: 2,100 m (6,890 ft); Top: 3,295 m (10,808 ft)

Vertical: 1,150 m (3,772 ft)

Longest Run: 5.9 km (3.6 mi)

Terrain: Wide open above treeline slopes with largest variety in the intermediate-high intermediate range; other runs are open and fast with some bowl skiing; off-slope, sun, high altitude skiing; 2 green, 11 blue, 5 red, 6 black

Lifts: 19

Types: 2 Gondolas; 10 Chairlifts (1 quad, 2 triples, 6 doubles); 7 Surface

Lift Capacity: 30,000 p/h resort

Ski Season: December - May

Ski School: Escuela Española de Esqui (34) (58) 48 01 68; Escuela International de Esqui (34) (58) 48 01 42; Escuela Oficial de Esqui (34) (58) 48 00 11

Cross Country: 2 circuits

Mountain Restaurants: 4

Other Winter Activities: Fitness center; indoor swimming; sauna; squash; snowboarding; paragliding; riding; indoor tennis

ANDALUSIA REGION
Located in Europe's southernmost mountain range with peaks to 11,000 feet. The peaks of the Sierra Nevada are covered with snow most of the year and are visible, even from the Costá del Sol on the Mediterranean Sea, as well as from nearby Granada, home of the Alhambra Palace.

Après-Ski: Bars, 2 discos, dining, dancing

Shopping Services: 14 restaurants, first aid, rentals, storage, bank, pharmacy, ski shops, conference facilities

Child Care: 3 kindergartens, 3 mos. - 4 years, telephone (34) (58) 24 91 00

Lodging: 5,000 beds in 4, 3 and 2-star hotels to family apartments

Transportation: Gateway Airport: Malaga (2½ hr drive); Granada airport (1½ hr. drive)

Closest Provincial City: Granada 30 km (18 mi); bus available to mountain

By Auto from Malaga: A-92 to Granada to ski resort

Bus: Daily bus to and from Granada to resort (departs 9am, return 5pm); driving time is one hour

Other Information: The road up to the resort is in good condition for the 9,000 ft. climb. Conditions Tele. (34) (58) 24 91 19

©Publishers Group International, 1998

SLOVENIA

SLOVENIA	Page No.
Bohinj (Kobla/Vogel)	143
Kranjska Gora	141
Krvavec	142
Kanin*	142
Rogla	144
Mariborsko Pohorje	144

SLOVENIA

by Ted Heck

A skier hunting for a bargain should move his sights several clicks to the east and consider the small country of Slovenia on the far end of the Alps.

Slovenia? Well, its resorts are not exactly on the tip of a namedropper's tongue, with names like Kranjska Gora, Kanin, Kobla, Rogla and Vogel. But they are real, they're good and the costs of a skiing vacation can be significantly lower than those in other alpine countries.

Few Americans can place Slovenia on a map, unless their ancestors were among turn-of-the-century immigrants. It is a tiny nation, only in existence since 1991, when it broke away from the old Yugoslavia. Half the size of Switzerland, it is tucked away in the northwest corner of the region where it meets Italy and Austria.

Slovenia has alpine charm of its own and fun-loving citizens who hold winter sports in esteem. Half of the mountainous country's two million people are skiers. We have selected only seven major resorts for detailed description here, but there are 47 ski centers in all.

The Slovenians were disappointed when the 2002 Winter Olympics were awarded to Salt Lake City. Their resort of Kranjska Gora has long been a major stop on the World Cup circuit. It was part of a troika, a unique three-country bid to host those Games. Nearby Tarvisio in Italy and Villach in Austria were the other ski centers who felt they offered adequate venues. A successful bid would have greatly increased awareness of Slovenia. However, the three countries are making another bid for 2006.

Skiing in Slovenia does not approach the proportions of, say France, which hosted the Olympics in 1992. The mountains are spectacular, but lower. Runs are shorter and lifts are not always state-of-the art.

But the upside is the price. A package deal in a good hotel in Kranjska Gora, for example, costs about $50 a day per person for a bed, breakfast and dinner. Lift tickets at some resorts cost as little as $15 to $20, rental skis $10. Lunch in a typical village inn is $10 for sausage, beer and dessert.

Other benefits include sightseeing attractions in the capital city of Ljubljana, a thriving commercial and cultural center. Slovenia is a country of big cities and little villages, of caves and castles, forests and mountains—and also a coastline. The western end of the country borders on the Adriatic Sea, not far from Trieste. On a non-skiing day, a day trip to Venice is possible.

As one comes down from the mountains and gets nearer the coast, vegetation becomes semi-topical. In picturesque villages such as Piran or the health resort of Portoroz, people stroll along the seawall in shirtsleeves.

Another benefit travelers notice quickly is the friendliness of the Slovenians. English is the second language they learn in school and many of them are comfortable conversing in it. Especially with Americans who have just discovered their country.

For more information, such as the winter sports brochure and package details, contact the Slovenian Tourist Office at 345 East 12th Street, New York City 10003. Telephone is (212) 358-9686. Fax is (212) 358-9025. Web page is www.touristboard.si and the E-mail address is slotouristboard@sloveniatravel.com.

Swissair has daily flights from the United States to Ljubljana, connecting through Zürich. Adria Airways is the Slovenian national carrier with daily flights to all major European cities and has code share arrangements with other carriers.

Swissair offers a brochure called "The Alpine Experience." It includes additional descriptions of major Swiss resorts, as well as popular resorts in Austria, France, Germany and Italy. The colorful brochure contains photos, trail maps, hotel listings and prices for package deals.

For a free copy of "The Alpine Experience" call 800-662-0021 or write to Swissair, P.O. Box 26028, Tampa, FL 33623-6028.

SLOVENIA

KRANJSKA GORA*
TOURIST OFFICE: Ticarjeva 2
4280 Kranjska Gora, Slovenia
Telephone: (386) (64) 881-768
FAX: (386) (64) 881-125

JULIAN ALPS
Probably the best known of Slovenian ski resorts, Kranjska Gora is a romantic alpine village. A frequent site of World Cup races, it is near the Austrian and Italian borders.

Elevation: Village: 810 m (2,656 ft)
Top: 1,623 m (5,323 ft)

Vertical: 813 m (2,667 ft)

Longest Run: 2.5 miles

Terrain: 30 km (19 mi) of downhill runs; 56% beginner, 25% intermediate, 19% advanced; snowmaking and night skiing

Lifts: 4 chairlifts, 16 surface

Lift Capacity: 16,256

Ski Season: Mid-December to end of March

Cross Country: 40 km (25 mi) of trails through forests and meadows

Ski School: 42 instructors on slopes and at certain hotels

Mountain Restaurants: Several at bases of slopes

Other Winter Activities: ice skating, curling, indoor tennis, indoor swimming, sauna

Après-Ski: Bars, restaurants, discos, nightclub, casino

Shopping/Services: Ski shops, food stores, general merchandise

Credit Cards: AE, DEC, MC, VISA

Child Care: Nursery (check with tourist office)

Lodging: 4,000 beds, half of them in 10 hotels

Transportation: Airport: Ljubljana (in Brnik, 1½ hours away)

Closest Provincial City: Jesenice (12 km) (7 mi)

By Auto: Motorway from Ljubljana to Kranj to Jesenice

Frequent bus service

Best Deal: Modest prices for accommodations, lift tickets and rentals

Other Information: International ski jumping competition at nearby Planica, which has six jumps, one 180 meters long; Elan ski factory between airport and resort has outlet store for equipment and clothing bargains

Different accents are heard in Kranjska Gora, a regular host of World Cup events.

Photo: Slovenia Tourism

SLOVENIA

KRVAVEC
INFORMATION: RTC Krvavec d.o.o.
Bleiweisova 2, 4000 Kranj, Slovenia
Telephone: (386) (64) 222-579
FAX: (386) (64) 221-829

Elevation: Base: 1,450 m (4,756 ft)
Top: 1,971 m (6,465 ft)
Vertical: 521 m (1709 ft)
Terrain: 25 km (15 mi) of maintained trails
Lifts: 1 cable car, 6 chairs, 6 surface
Beginners 20%, intermediate 60%, advanced 20%
Lift Capacity: 13,000 p/h
Ski Season: Mid-December to May
Cross Country: 6 km (4 mi) of trails
Ski School: Full range of instruction
Mountain Restaurants: 1 inn, three snackbars
Other Winter Activities: Ice skating/artificial; sledding

KAMNIK ALPS
In the foothills of these alps, the ski center is close to the Ljubljana airport in Brnik and only 32 km (20 mi) from the capital city.

Après-Ski: Night clubs, coffeehouses, fine dining, billiards
Credit Cards: AE, DC, MC, VISA
Child Care: Nursery
Lodging: 436 beds at Krvavec, but most skiers are day-trippers from Ljubljana and Kranj
Transportation: Airport: Ljubljana (10 km, 6 mi away)
Closest Provincial City: Kranj
Regular and ski bus service
Other Information: Krvavec has been honored as "the best organized ski center in Slovenia"

KANIN*
INFORMATION AGENCY: Hotel Bovec d.d.
5230 Bovec, Slovenia
Telephone: (386) (65) 86-022
FAX: (386) (65) 86-081

Elevation: Village of Bovec: 483 m (1,584 ft)
Top: 2,289 m (7,508 ft)
Vertical: At top snowfields, 700 m (2,296 ft)
Terrain: 14 km (9 mi), half in groomed slopes, half in open acreage for off-piste skiing; 10% beginner, 70% intermediate, 10% advanced
Lifts: 1 gondola, three chairs, two surface
Lift Capacity: 5,000 skiers p/h
Ski Season: November to May
Cross Country: 12 km (7 mi)
Ski School: 11 instructors for various disciplines
Mountain Restaurant: Prestreljenik lodge
Other Winter Activities: Ice skating, parasailing, hang gliding, sledding, hiking, indoor swimming, gym and fitness centers, sauna

JULIAN ALPS
The highest ski center in Slovenia, Kanin is situated in northwest corner, near the Italian border.

Après-Ski: Dining, disco, billiards, cultural activities, sightseeing
Shopping/Services: Full range of facilities in town of Bovec
Credit Cards: AE, DC, MC
Child Care: Nursery
Lodging: 2,510 beds in hotels, apartments and private homes
Transportation: Gateway Airport: Ljubljana (2½ hours)
Regular bus service from capital city to Bovec
Other Information: Among many sightseeing adventures is the war museum in the town of Kobarid. This region was featured in Hemingway's "A Farewell to Arms"

©Publishers Group International, 1998

SLOVENIA

BOHINJ (KOBLA/VOGEL)
TOURIST OFFICE: Ribčev laz 48
4265 Bohinjsko Jezero, Slovenia
Telephone (386) 64723-370
FAX: (386) (64) 723-330

JULIAN ALPS
Two major centers in the Bohinj glacial basin, Kobla is above the village of Bohinjska Bistrica and a beautiful alpine lake. Vogel is the other ski area accessible only by cable car.

Elevation (Kobla): Base: 552 m (1,811 ft)
Top: 1,480 m (4,854 ft)

Elevation (Vogel): Base: 569 m (1,861 ft)
Top: 1,800 m (5,886 ft)

Vertical (Kobla): 928 m (3,044 ft)

Vertical (Vogel): 1,231 m (4,025 ft)

Terrain (Kobla): 23 km (14 mi) of groomed slopes and trails; 20% beginner, 50% intermediate, 30% advanced; longest run 6 km (3.7 mi)

Terrain (Vogel): 35 km (22 mi) of manicured slopes winding through plenty of deep snow fields; 30% beginner, 50% intermediate, 20% advanced; longest run 8 km (5 mi)

Lifts (Kobla): 3 chairs, 3 surface

Lifts (Vogel): 1 cable car, 4 chairs, 4 surface

Lift (Kobla) Capacity: 5,700 skiers p/h

Lift (Vogel) Capacity: 5,700 p/h

Ski (Kobla) Season: Mid-December to the end of March

Ski (Vogel) Season: End of November to May

Cross Country: 35 km (22 mi), including a 10 km (6 mi) course along the lake, where FIS competitions are held

Ski School: Instructors for all winter activities

Moutain Restaurants: 5

Other Winter Activities: Waterfall ice climbing, ice skating on natural and artificial ice, parasailing, paragliding, gym, sauna, indoor swimming, sightseeing, hiking

Après-Ski: dining and many other activities down in town

Shopping/Services: Skiers' needs satisfied in Bistrica

Credit Cards: AE, MC, VISA

Child Care: Nursery

Lodging: 2,540 beds in Bistrica in hotels, apartments, and private homes

Transportation: Airport: Ljubljana 60 km (37 mi) 1½ hours

Closest Provincial City: Bled 25 km (15 mi)

Best Deal: A seven-day lift ticket costs only $120

Other Information: The city of Bled is a sightseer's delight

Mountains around stunning Lake Bled contain exciting ski resorts.

Photo: Slovenia Tourism

SLOVENIA

ROGLA*
INFORMATION: Unior Turizem
C, NA Rogla-15, 3214 Zrece, Slovenia
Telephone: (386) (63) 76280
FAX: (386) (63) 762-446

Elevation: Top: 1,517 m (4,961 ft)
Terrain: 10 km (6 mi) of downhill runs; 15% beginner, 75% intermediate, 10% advanced; longest run 1,400 m (4,592 ft)
Lifts: 2 double chairs, 11 surface
Lift Capacity: 13,000 skiers p/h
Ski Season: November to May
Cross Country: High plateau offers 30 km (19 mi) of cross country trails
Ski School: 6 instructors for all levels
Mountain Restaurants: 7, three of which are in Hotel Planja
Other Winter Activities: Hiking, sledding, squash, indoor tennis, indoor swimming, horseback riding, sightseeing
Après-Ski: Disco, cinema, usual spa amenities

POHORJE ALPS
An upside down resort, with lodging and facilities on top of the mountain.

Shopping/Services: In Zrece, 16 km (10 miles away)
Credit Cards: AE, MC, VISA
Child Care: Nursery
Lodging: Hotels and chalets on top of mountain have 249 beds, with more than 550 others in spa town of Zrece
Transportation: Airport: Ljubljana 115 km (71 mi) 2 hours
Closest Provincial City: Maribor
By Auto: Number 10 Motorway to Celje exit, north to Vojnik and Zrece
Bus: Regular bus service from Ljubljana via Celje and Zrece; local ski bus
Other Information: Rogla is a "company resort," owned and operated by Unior, a major equipment manufacturer in Zrece

MARIBORSKO POHORJE
INFO: Pohorska VZ Penjaca
2000 Maribor, Slovenia
Telephone: (386) (62) 631 850
FAX: (386) (62) 631 840

Elevation: Village: 325 m (1,066 ft)
Top: 1,347 m (4,418 ft)
Vertical: 1,022 m (3,352 ft)
Terrain: 60 km (37 mi) of downhill trails and slopes; 40% beginner, 35% intermediate, 25% advanced; snowmaking; night skiing
Lifts: 1 gondola, 2 chairlifts, 14 surface
Lift Capacity: 14,176 p/h
Ski Season: Mid-November to March
Cross Country: 20 km (12 mi) of trails
Ski School: All disciplines, including racing
Other Winter Activities: Hiking, ice skating, curling, indoor tennis, indoor swimming
Après-Ski: Sightseeing, exhibitions, cinema, theatre, fine restaurants, disco, nightclubs

POHORJE ALPS
Slovenia's largest ski area is in the northeastern part of the country. It is noted for hosting World Cup alpine races.

Shopping/Services: Maribor is Slovenia's second largest city and has everything a visitor could possibly need
Credit Cards: AE, MC, VISA
Child Care: Kindergarten
Lodging: 1,447 hotel beds
Transportation: Airport: Ljubljana 135 km (84 mi) 2½ hours
By auto on Motorway 10 from Ljubljana
By train from Ljubljana, 2 hours
Other Information: The Austrian and Hungarian borders are less than 30 miles away from Maribor, offering still other cultures to expore

RATES

ANDORRA
(Currency: Spanish Peseta and French Franc).).
(Rate as of 9/1/98: 149.8 SP per U.S.$;
5.9 FF per per U.S.$)

Ski Andorra Pass (5 ski resorts)
Lift Rates: (SP)
Low Season: 5 or 6 day rate, 14,150 (Mon. - Fri. only)
High Season: 5 or 6 day rate, 16,950

Arinsal
Lift Rates: (SP)
Adult: Low Season: 1 day rate, 2,600; 7 day rate, 13,650
High Season: 1 day rate, 3,150; 7 day rate, 16,550
Child: Low Season: 1 day rate, 2,000; 7 day rate, 10,500
High Season: 1 day rate, 2,400; 7 day rate, 12,600

Ski School:‡
Adult Group: 2 hour low 1,875; high 2,150
15 hour low 9,650; high 11,000

Ordino
Lift Rates: (SP)
Adult: Low Season: 1 day rate, 2,700; 7 day rate, 14,300
High Season: 1 day rate, 3,400; 7 day rate, 17,875
Child: Low Season: 1 day rate, 2,275; 7 day rate, 12,025
High Season: 1 day rate, 2,850; 7 day rate, 15,025

Ski School:‡
Adult Group: 2 hour low 1,875; high 2,150
15 hour low 9,650; high 11,000

Pal
Lift Rates: (SP)
Adult: Low Season: 1 day rate, 2,700; 7 day rate, 14,175
High Season: 1 day rate, 3,400; 7 day rate, 17,850
Child: Low Season: 1 day rate, 2,100; 7 day rate, 10,925
High Season: 1 day rate, 2,500; 7 day rate, 13,125

Ski School:‡
Adult Group: 2 hour low 1,875; high 2,150
15 hour low 9,650; high 11,000

Pas de la Casa—Grau Roig
Lift Rates: (FF)
Adult: Low Season: 1 day rate, 146; 6 day rate, 650
High Season: 1 day rate, 167; 6 day rate, 744
Child: Low Season: 1 day rate, 121; 6 day rate, 537
High Season: 1 day rate, 140; 7 day rate, 628

Ski School:
(5 days, 15 hours)
Adult High Season 497; Adult Low Season 400
Child (under 12) High season 421; Low Season 341

Soldeu
Lift Rates: (SP)
Adult: Low Season: 1 day rate, 3,200; 7 day rate, 15,575
High Season: 1 day rate, 3,700; 7 day rate, 18,900

‡—1997/98 rates
‡‡—1995/96 rates

Not all Areas Represented

Child: Low Season: 1 day rate, 2,600; 7 day rate, 13,650
High Season: 1 day rate, 3,200; 7 day rate, 15,750
Ski School:‡
Adult: 15 hour low 9,650; high 11,000

*1 through 7 day passes available at all resorts
Snow playground passes available 1 hour to 6 days

AUSTRIA
(Currency: Austrian Schilling).
(Rate as of 9/1/98: 12.4AS per U.S.$)

Altenmarkt/Zauchensee
Lift Rates:
Low Season: 6 day rate, 1,690; 7 day rate, 1,865
High Season: 6 day rate, 1,875; 7 day rate, 2,070

Ski School:
1 day rate, 500; 3 day rate, 1,300; 5 day rate, 1,500; Private instruction rates per hour approximately what one pays for 4 hrs. in a group

Rental Rates:
Adult: 1 day rate, 120; 6 day rate, 700
Child: 1 day rate, 90; 6 day rate, 500

Bad Kleinkirchheim/St. Oswald
Lift Rates:
Adult: 1 day rate, 350; 6 day rate, 1,740
Child: 1 day rate, 195; 6 day rate, 960
(Up to 14 day ski pass available)

Ski School:
Group: 1,200 (3 hours per day)
Private: 1,900 p/5½ hours; each add'l person 450 p/h

Rental Rates:
Adult skis: 1 day rate, 190; 6 day rate, 760
Adult boots: 1 day rate, 110; 6 day rate, 490
Child skis: 1 day rate, 130; 6 day rate, 310

Bad Gastein
Lift Rates:
Low Season: 2 day rate, 630/710; 6 day rate, 1,590/1,790
High Season: 2 day rate, 790; 6 day rate, 1,990

Ski School:
1 day rate, 520; 3 day rate, 1,350;
Private instruction approx. 470 per hr.

Ski Kindergarten:
½ day, 250; 1 day with lunch, 550; 6 day w/meals, 2,600

Brixental-Wilder Kaiser
Lift Rates:
High Season Adult: 1 day rate, 370; 6 day rate, 1,800
High Season Child: 1 day rate, 220; 6 day rate, 1,000
Low Season Adult: 1 day rate 290; 6 day rate 1,440
Low Season Child: 1 day rate 180; 6 day rate 800
(High season, Dec. 12, 1998 - Mar. 12, 1999; Low season, Mar. 13 - End of season)

Ski School:
Adult: 5 day rate, 1,390; 10 day rate, 2,200
Child: 5 day rate, 1,290; 10 day rate, 2,100

Rental Rates:
Adult: 1 day rate, 100; 7 day rate, 630 skis and boots
Child: 1 day rate, 70; 7 day rate, 441

Dachstein-Tauern Region
Lift Rates:
Adult: High Season: 1 day rate, 395; 6 day rate, 1,930; (Low season 1,795); 12 day rate, 3,165 (Low season 2,945)
Child: High Season: 1 day rate, 205; 6 day rate, 1,060; 12 day rate, 1,790

Ski School:
3 day rate, 1,050; 5 day rate, 1,250;
Private lessons about 465 per hour

Rental Rates:
Adult: 1 day rate, 210; 6 day rate, 1,000 skis and boots
Child: 1 day rate, 120; 6 day rate, 590

Galtür
Lift Rates:
Adult: 1 day rate, 345; 3 day rate, 900; 6 day rate, 1,625; 12 day rate, 2,745
Child: 1 day rate, 225; 3 day rate, 540; 6 day rate, 985; 12 day rate, 1,710 (lift rates for days 1-30 available) (special rates for seniors)

Ski School:
Adult or child: 1 day rate, 480; 3 day rate, 1,150; 6 day rate, 1,500; 10 day rate, 2,200

Rental Rates:
Adult skis and boots: 1 day rate, 200; 3 day rate, 575
Child skis and boots: 1 day rate, 90; 3 day rate, 270

Gurgl (Unter-Hoch-Obergurgl)
Lift Rates:
Adult High Season: 1 day rate, 440; 3 day rate, 1,210; 6 day rate, 2,160; 12 day rate, 3,300
Child High Season: 1 day rate, 290; 3 day rate, 770; 6 day rate, 1,320; 12 day rate, 2,040

Ski School:
Hochgurgl: 1 day rate, 570; 3 day rate, 1,270; 5 day rate, 1,540; (each add'l day @ 350)
Obergurgl: 1 day rate, 570; 3 day rate, 1,270; 5 day rate, 1,540 (each add'l day @ 270)

Rental Rates:
Skis and boots: 100-550 adult or child

High Montafon
Lift Rates:
Adult: 1 day rate, 415; 3 day rate, 1,120; 6 day rate, 1,990; 13 day rate, 3,515
Child: 1 day rate, 260; 3 day rate, 695; 6 day rate, 1,235; 13 day rate, 2,180 (lift rates for days 1-14 available)

Ski School:
Adult or child: 1 day rate, 510; 3 day rate, 1,300 (child 1,180); 5 day rate, 1,380 (child 1,310)

Innsbruck—Igls
Lift Rates: (Rates are the same all season.)
Adult: 1 day rate, 250-420 depending on area
Child: 1 day rate, 150-220 depending on area

Innsbruck Super Ski Pass (with Club Card)
4 out of 6 days: Adult 1,710; Child 1,150
5 out of 6 days: Adult 2,290; Child 1,550

Innsbruck Gletscher Ski Pass
Standard 3 days: Adult 1,190; Child 650
Standard 6 days: Adult 1,960; Child 1,180
With Club Card
Adult 3 day rate, 990; Child 3 day rate, 590

Adult 6 day rate, 1,780; Child 3 day rate, 1,070
3 out of 4 days: Adult 1,050; Child 630
3 out of 6 days: Adult, 1,120; Child 670

Ski School:
Adult or child: 1 day rate, 500; 2 day rate, 900; 3 day rate, 1,200; 5 day rate, 1,500

Rental Rates:
Adult skis, poles and boots: 1 day rate, 180; 3 day rate, 490; 5 day rate, 870; 6 day rate, 920
Child skis, poles and boots: 1 day rate, 100; 3 day rate, 270; 5 day rate, 450; 6 day rate, 500

Ischgl
Lift Rates:
Adult: 1 day rate, 395; 3 day rate, 1,080; 6 day rate, 1,970; 12 day rate, 3,260, high season
Child: 1 day rate, 275; 3 day rate, 690; 6 day rate, 1,275; 12 day rate, 1,900, high season

Ski School:
Adult or child (over 6): 1 day rate, 500; 3 day rate, 1,200; 6 day rate, 1,550
Ski Kindergarden (3-5 yrs.): 1 day rate, 500/lunch 580; ½ day 300

Rental Rates:
110-260 per day

Katschberg‡
Lift Rates:
Low Season: 1 day rate 320; 3 day rate 750; 6 day rate 1,320; 12 day rate 2,220
High Season: 1 day rate 320; 3 day rate 810; 6 day rate 1,450; 12 day rate 2,470

Ski School:
1 day 450; 3 day 1,200; 6 day 1,350

Rental Rates:
Skis & Boots 6 days, 1,200; 12 days 2,400

Kitzbühel
Lift Rates: (1-14 day rate available)
Low Season: 1 day rate, 390; 6 day rate, 1,820; 12 day rate, 3,050
High Season: 1 day rate, 420; 6 day rate, 1,980; 12 day rate, 3,310
(child and senior rates available)

Ski School:
1 day rate, 500; 6 day rate, 1,350

Rental Rates:
Skis: 1 day rate, 50-150; 6 day rate, 45-125 p/d; from 8 days, 95-150
Snowboard: 1 day rate, 180-350; 6 day rate, 880

Kirchberg in Tirol
Lift Rates:
Adult 1 day rate 390/420; 3 day rate 1,050/1,140; 6 day rate 1,820/1,980; 7 day rate 2,040/2,220; 14 day rate 3,340/3,630
Child: 1 day rate 210; 3 day rate 570; 6 day rate 990; 7 day rate 1,110; 14 day rate 1,815

Ski School:
Adult: 1 day 600; 3 day 1,400; 4 day 1,450; 5 day 1,500
Child: 1 day 550; 3 day 1,350; 4 day 1,400; 5 day 1,450

Rental Rates:
Adult 180 p/d; child 95 p/d; 8 days adult 1,340; child 660

Lech-Zürs
Lift Rates:
Adult: 1 day rate, 425-470; 3 day rate, 1,170-1,300;

7 day rate, 2,190-2,430; 13 day rate, 3,390-3,770
Child: 1 day rate, 255-280; 3 day rate, 700-780;
7 day rate, 1,320-1,460; 13 day rate, 2,060-2,260

Ski School:
Adult: 1 day rate, 500; 3 day rate, 1,000-1,100; 6 day rate, 1,390; 12 day rate, 2,370-2,640
(price reduction on 6-18 day rate for Arlberg resort guests)

Rental Rates:
Skis: 1 day rate, 190; 6 day rate, 1,110; 13 day rate, 2,150
Boots: 1 day rate, 100; 6 day rate, 580; 13 day rate, 1,175

Mayrhofen

Lift Rates:
Ski pass Mayrhofen adult from 1 to 3 days 1 day rate 350; 3 day rate 915
Zillertal Superskipass from 4 to 21 days; without glacier 6 day rate 1,690; 12 day rate 2,890. With glacier 6 day rate 2,010; 12 day rate 3,500

Ski School:
1 day rate, 600-630; 3 day rate, 1,250-1,300; 6 day rate, 1,450-1,490

Rental Rates:
Skis & Boots 6 day rate, 540-1,890

Neustift/Fulpmes Stubai Valley‡

Lift Rates:
Neustift im Stubital
Stubai Glacier
Oct. 24, 1998 - Jan. 9, 1999 & Jan. 31 - May 2, 1999
Adult: 1 day pass 420; 3 day pass 1,135; 6 day pass 1,845
Under 19: 1 day pass 275; 3 day pass 740; 6 day pass 1,200
Under 15: 1 day pass 210; 3 day pass 570; 6 day pass 925
Jan. 10 - 30, 1999
Adult: 1 day pass 370; 3 day pass 1,020; 6 day pass 1,660
Under 19: 1 day pass 245; 3 day pass 665; 6 day pass 1,080
Under 15: 1 day pass 185; 3 day pass 510; 6 day pass 830
Stubai Superski Pass (Minimum 4 days)
Dec. 19, 1998 - Jan. 9, 1999 & Jan. 31 - Apr. 8, 1999
Adult: 4 day pass 1,470; 6 day pass 2,040
Under 19: 4 day pass 1,180; 6 day pass 1,635
Under 15: 4 day pass 960; 6 day pass 1,330
Children under age 10 with their parents are free

Rental Rates:
Skis/Poles & Boots: per day rate, 100 adult; 80 child

Obertauern

Lift Rates:
Low Season Adult: 1 day rate, 380; 3 day rate, 1,005; 5 day rate, 1,445; 6 day rate, 1,640; 7 day rate, 1,835; 12 day rate, 2,650; 14 day rate, 2,995
High Season Adult: 1 day rate, 380; 3 day rate, 1,035; 5 day rate, 1,555; 6 day rate, 1,780; 7 day rate, 2,005; 12 day rate, 3,115; 14 day rate, 3,535
Low Season Child: 1 day rate, 195; 3 day rate, 550; 5 day rate, 770; 6 day rate, 870; 7 day rate, 970; 12 day rate, 1,450; 14 day rate, 1,640
High Season Child: 1 day rate, 195; 3 day rate, 570; 5 day rate, 920; 6 day rate, 1,080; 7 day rate, 1,235; 12 day rate, 1,895; 14 day rate, 2,190

Ski School:
Group: 1 day rate, 450-500; Private 450-480 p/h

Rental Rates:
Skis: 6 day rate, 600; 12 day rate, 850
Boots: 6 day rate, 350; 12 day rate, 550

Saalbach-Hinterglemm‡

Lift Rates: (1-21 day rate lift tickets available)
Low Season: 1 day rate, 380; 6 day rate, 1,650;
High Season: 1 day rate, 400; 6 day rate, 1,940

Ski School:
1 day rate, 520; Private instruction per hour is as much as 4 hrs. in a group

Rental Rates:
Skis: 1 day rate, 180; 3 day rate, 430; 6 day rate, 690

St. Anton am Arlberg

Lift Rates:*
Low Season Adult: 1 day rate, 425; 3 day rate, 1,170; 6 day rate, 2,100; 12 day rate, 3,490; 14 day rate, 3,850
High Season Adult: 1 day rate, 470; 3 day rate, 1,300; 6 day rate, 2,330; 12 day rate, 3,880; 14 day rate, 4,270
Low Season Child: 1 day rate, 255; 3 day rate, 700; 6 day rate, 1,260; 12 day rate, 2,090; 14 day rate, 2,310
High Season Child: 1 day rate, 280; 3 day rate, 780; 6 day rate, 1,400; 12 day rate, 2,330; 14 day rate, 2,560
*Approximate 8% discount on 6 day or more lift ticket rate for Arlberg area guests

Ski School:
Ski School Arlberg: 1 day rate, 545; 3 day rate, 1,290; 5 day rate, 1,580; 6 day rate, 1,640; 12 day rate, 3,100

Rental Rates:
Adult Skis & Boots: 1 day rate, 280/480; 3 day rate, 740-1,260; 6 day rate, 1,240-2,240
Child Skis & Boots: 1 day rate, 140; 3 day rate, 370; 6 day rate, 640

St. Johann im P./Alpendorf

Lift Rates:
Adult Main Season: 1 day rate, 380; 3 day rate, 1,050; 6 day rate, 1,875 until 12/23; Jan.-Feb. 3, 1,750
Child Main Season: 1 day rate, 210; 3 day rate, 890; 6 day rate, 1,030

Ski School:
Adult and Child: 1 day rate, 500; 3 day rate, 1,350; 4-6 day rate, 1,500
Advanced skiers 4-6 days, 1,500

Rental Rates:
Adult Skis & Boots: 1 day rate, 200
Child Skis & Boots: 1 day rate, 200

St. Johann in Tirol

Lift Rates:
Adult: Low Season: 3 day 830; 6 day 1,420; 12 day 2,390; child 3 day 415; 6 day 735
Adult: High Season: 3 day 925; 6 day 1,590; 12 day 2,595; child 3 day 480; 6 day 830
Schneewinkle Lift Rates:
Adult: Low Season: 3 day 910; 6 day 1,620
Adult: High Season: 3 day 1,010; 6 day 1,800
Child: Low Season: 3 day 495; 6 day 910
Child: High Season: 3 day 550; 6 day 1,000
Kitzbüheler Alps Lift Rates:
Adult: Low & High Season: 6 day 2,200
Child: Low & High Season: 6 day 1,100

Ski School:
1 day 550-680; 3 day 1,180; 6 day 1,390-1,450

Rental Rates:
Skis & Boots 6 day 1,800

Seefeld (3-21 day rates available)

Lift Rates:
Low Season: 3 day rate, 890; 6 day rate, 1,640; 12 day rate, 2,630 (after 14th of March)
High Season: 3 day rate, 990; 6 day rate, 1,825; 12 day rate, 2,925

Ski School:
Adult: 1 day rate, 540; 3 day rate, 1,300; 6 day rate, 1,520 (4 hours per day)

Rental Rates:
Skis 6-day 600-800; 12-day 1,200
Boots 6-day 240-420; 12 day 480-840
Cross Country: Skis, poles, and boots; Toboggan (sled); Snowboard; Monoski; "Big Foot" available

Sölden/Ötztal Arena
Lift Rates:
Adult Low Season: ½ day 320; 1 day rate, 410; 3 day rate, 1,050; 6 day rate, 2,110
Adult High Season: ½ day 340; 1 day rate, 460; 6 day rate, 2,180;
Child: ½ day 180; 1 day rate, 290; 6 day rate, 1,210

Ski & Snowboard School (4 hours per day):
Sölden/Hochsölden: 1 day rate 500; 3 day rate 1,150; 6 day rate 1,600
Total Vacancia: 1 day rate 500; 3 day rate 1,140; 6 day rate 1,590
Ötztal 2000: 1 day rate 590; 3 day rate 1,490; 6 day rate 1,990
Ski Nursery/Children's Ski School: Sölden/Hochsölden/Total Vacancia: 1 day rate 470; 3 day rate 1,070; 6 day rate 1,520
Ötztal 2000: 1 day rate 590; 3 day rate, 1,290; 6 day rate 2,040

Rental Rates:
Adult: skis 110-270 p/d; boots 60-110 p/d; set 170-480 p/d
Child: skis 60-110 p/d; boots 40-90 p/d; set 180-370 p/d

Zell Am See/Kaprun
Lift Rates:
Low Season: 1 day rate, 380; 6 day rate, 1,840
High Season: 1 day rate, 420; 6 day rate, 1,990

Ski School:
1 day rate, 550; 3 day rate 1,350-1,400; 6 day rate, 1,450-1,600; Private instruction 2,200 per 4 hrs.

Rental Rates:
6 day rate: 750-1,250 including skis, boots & poles

FRANCE
(Currency: French Franc).
(Rate as of 9/1/98: 5.9FF per U.S.$)

Alpe d'Huez
Lift Rates:
Adult: 1 day 191; 2 day 377; 6 day 1,010, these rates are in effect week days and weekends

Avoriaz
Lift Rates:
Portes du Soliel - Adult: 1 day rate, 199; 3 day rate 531; 6 day rate, 909; 12 day rate, 1,502
Child: 1 day rate 131; 3 day rate 349; 6 day rate 598

Ski School:
Group: Approx. 450 for six ½ day lessons
Private: 2½ hrs. 450; Full day, 1,150

Chamonix-Mont-Blanc
Lift Rates:
Adult: 2 day rate, 420; 6 day rate, 960; 9 day rate, 1,280; 12 day rate, 1,580
Child: 4-11 yrs: 2 day rate, 294; 6 days, 672; 9 days 896; 12 days 1,106
(1-13 day rates available)

Child (12-15/Adult over 60) 2 days 357; 6 days 815; 9 days 1,088, 12 days 1,343

Chamrousse‡
Lift Rates:
Adult: 1 day rate, 125; 6 day rate, 618; 7 day rate 700
Children under 5 and adults over 70 ski free

Ski School:
Group (2½ hr lesson) 95; Private (1 hr.) 165
Child: 1 day rate, 180; 3 day rate, 470; 5 day rate, 720

Rental Rates:
Adult: 100 p/1 day
Child: 70 p/1 day

Courchevel
Lift Rates:
Adult: 1 day rate, 188; 6 day rate, 897
Child: 1 day rate, 141; 6 day rate, 673 (10-16 yrs)
Adult 3 Vallèes' Ticket: 1 day rate, 225; 6 day rate, 1,100;
Child 3 Vallèes' Ticket: 1 day rate, 169; 6 day rate, 825 (also applies to adults age 60+); under 5 ski free

Ski School:
Private: 1,350-1,600 - 1 Day
Group: Morning lesson, 160; afternoon lessons, 120

Rental Rates:
Adult Skis: 1 day rate, 62-134; Boots: 1 day rate, 41-72
Child Skis: 1 day rate, 30-68; Boots: 1 day rate, 26

Flaine‡
Lift Rates:
Adult: 1 day rate, 175; 3 day rate, 480; 6 day rate, 840

Ski School:
Adult: 1 day rate, 95; 6 day rate, 460; 12 day rate, 700 (Group lesson 2 hours)
Child: 1 day rate, 85; 6 day rate, 410; 12 day rate, 550

Rental Rates:
Adult Skis & Boots: 1 day rate, 75-180; 6 day rate, 320-850
Child Skis & Boots: 1 day rate, 40-90; 6 day rate, 195-460

La Plagne
Lift Rates:
Low Season: 1 day rate, 165; 2 day rate, 305; 6 day rate, 770; 12 day rate, 1,300
High Season: 1 day rate, 219; 2 day rate, 400; 6 day rate, 1,025; 14 day rate, 1,885

Ski School:
Adult: 6 day rate, 875;
6½ day lessons 520 high & low season

Rental Rates:
Skis: 6 day rate, 464; 12 day rate, 880

Le Grand-Bornand
Lift Rates:
Adult: 6 day rate, 652 - Espace Aravis, 825

Le Collet D'Allevard
Lift Rates:
Adult: 1 day rate 94 (weekdays) 112 (weekends); 6 day rate 348
Night skiing Tues. & Fri. 55
Group lesson (2 hrs.) 76
Private lesson (1 hr.) 160

Les Arcs
Lift Rates:
Adult: 1 day rate, 215; 3 day rate, 560; 6 day rate, 1,015; 14 day rate, 1,885

Child (−14 or adult +60): 1 day rate, 185; 3 day rate, 480; 6 day rate, 865; 14 day rate, 1,600
Free ski pass for children under 7 yrs (official document req.)

Ski School:
Rates quoted at approx. 800 p/p per week

Rental Rates:
Rentals starting at 400 per week at 16 ski shops

Les 2 Alpes‡

Lift Rates: (1-6 day rate available)
Adult: 1 day rate, 178; 3 day rate, 495; 6 day rate, 890
Child: 1 day rate, 138; 3 day rate, 386; 6 day rate, 668
Access to all lifts free of charge for children under 4 years of age and Adults over 75 years

Ski School:
Adult: 1 day rate, 120; 1 week mornings, 700; afternoons, 590, 6 days; afternoons, 5 days 540
Child: 1 day rate, 100; 1 week mornings, 585, afternoons, 510, 6 days; afternoons, 470, 5 days

Rental Rates:
Adult Skis, poles & boots: 1 day rate, 70-200; 6 day rate, 350-1,100
Child Skis, poles & boots: 1 day rate, 50-95; 6 day rate, 240-600
Snowboard & boots: 1 day rate 140-195; 6 day rate 700-1,100

Les Menuires

Lift Rates:
1 day rate, 186; 2 day rate, 365; 6 day rate, 900; 13 day rate, 1,585

Ski School:
Adult: 6 consecutive mornings, 750; 6 consecutive afternoons, 590; 1 week morning and afternoon, 930
Child: 6 consecutive mornings, 665; 6 consecutive afternoons, 510; 1 week morning and afternoon, 800

Rental Rates:
Skis & Boots: From 518 to 1,100 for adults for 6 days; child 235-385

Les 7 Laux

Lift Rates:
Adult: 1 day rate 133; 2 day rate 242; 6 day rate 654

Ski School:
Group lesson (2 hrs.) 425 (6 days 2¼ hrs)
Private lesson (1 hr.) 865 1 hr x 6 days for 1 person; 960 for 2 persons 1 hr x 6 days

Megeve

Lift Rates:
Adult: 2 day rate, 306-340; 3 day rate, 432-480; 6 day rate, 756-840; 12 day rate, 1,350-1500 (low and high season)
Child: 2 day rate, 204-238; 3 day rate, 288-336; 6 day rate, 504-590; 12 day rate, 900-1,050
(This ticket also includes free access to resort's "shuttle buses and all Evasion Mont Blanc lifts.")

Ski School:
Adult: 1 hr./1 or 2 persons-private lessons, 195; 15 hrs. of lessons; 660 in high season 10 hrs. of lessons 460 FF in high season
Child: 10-12 hrs. of lessons 460-486; 22 hrs. of lessons and test 765 (high season only)

Rental Rates:
Adult/Reg. Rate: 1 day rate, 85; 3 day rate, 250; 6 day rate, 470; 12 day rate, 850
Adult/Top of Line: 1 day rate, 165; 3 day rate, 470; 6 day rate, 920; 12 day rate, 1,630
Child: 1 day rate, 60; 3 day rate, 180; 6 day rate, 340

Meribel

Lift Rates:
Adult: 3 day rate, 526; 6 day rate, 897; 14 day rate, 1,685
Child (5-16 yrs.): 3 day rate, 342-396; 6 day rate, 583-673; 14 day rate, 1,095/1,263.
(Passport photo required - available on site)

3 Valley Ski Pass (covers 5 resorts, 200 lifts):
Adult: 3-day 645; 6-day 1,100; 14 day 2,055
Child/Sr. (5 − +60): 3 day 420-489; 6 day 715-825; 14 day 2,055

Ski School:
12 hr 30 instruction 520-620
Off piste guides: 1 day 280; 5 days 1,150

Rental Rates:
Skis & Boots: 1 day 83 to 195; 6 days 456-1,105

Morzine

Lift Rates:
High Season: Adult: 1 day rate, 148; 3 day rate, 408; 6 day rate, 741; 14 day rate, 1,429

Ski School:
6 × ½ day rate: Adult: 545
Child: 460. Private lesson: 1,630

Rental Rates:
Skis: 6 day rate, 409
Boots: 6 day rate, 203

Peisey Vallandry

Lift Rates:
Adult: 1 day rate, 175; 2 day rate, 400; 6 day rate, 1,015
Child: 1 day rate, 185; 2 day rate, 340; 6 day rate, 865
(1-14 day rates available)

Ski School:
Group ½ hour 100; 6 days 2½ hours per day - Adult 540, child 450

Serre-Chevalier

Lift Rates: (No Low or High Season)
Adult: 1 day rate 180; 6 day rate 900; 7 day rate 990
Child (6-12 yrs): 1 day rate 120; 6 day rate 600; 7 day rate 655

Ski School: (Full day)
Adult: 770
Child: 695

Rental Rates:
Adult: 1 day rate 40-85; 7 day rate 260-550
Child: 1 day rate 40; 7 day rate 200

Saint Pierre De Chartreuse

Lift Rates:
Adult: Half day 73; Full day 95; 2 day 156; 6 day rate 525

Ski School:
Group Rate: 105 (2 hrs.); Private Rate: 160 (1 hr.)

Tignes

Lift Rates:
Adult: 1 day rate, 200; 3 day rate, 565; 6 day rate, 1,025
Child: 1 day rate, 160; 3 day rate, 400; 6 day rate, 715 (5-12 years)
(Reduced rate for age 60+ and free under 5 and over 70)

Rental Rates:
Skis: 1 day rate, 350/620
Boots: 6 day rate, 190/260

Val d'Isere

Lift Rates: (1-21 day rates available)

Adult: 1 day rate, 217; 3 day rate, 555; 6 day rate, 1,005
Child: 1 day rate, 158; 3 day rate, 395; 6 day rate, 705

Ski School:‡
Adult: 1 day rate, 206; 6 day rate, 1,030
Child: 1 day rate, 153; 6 day rate, 765

Rental Rates:
Average daily rate for skis, boots, poles 104 FF. 6 days 490 FF

Val Thorens
Lift Rates: Adult 6 day rates range from 770 FF to 910 FF.
Child: 6 day w/meal from 1,350 to 1,700 FF and 590 FF to 830 FF w/o meal.
Trois Vallées 1 day rate 215; 3 day rate 607; 6 day rate 1,035; 12 day rate 1,712
Child 5-15 yrs./Adult Over 60: 1 day rate 120; 3 day rate 305; 6 day rate 540; 12 day rate 930
Trois Vallées 1 day rate 161; 3 day rate 455; 6 day rate 776; 12 day rate 1,284

Ski School:
Adult: 6 days/3 hours morning, 675; 6 days/2½ hours afternoon, 560
Adult: 1 hour private lesson, 180

Rental Rates:
Skis: 1 day rate, 65-106; 6 day rate, 355-636; 12 day rate, 806-1,273
Boots: 1 day rate, 26-39; 6 day rate, 315-342; 12 day rate, 437-552

Vars‡
Lift Rates:
Adult: 1 day rate, 145; 2 day rate, 280; 3 day rate 410; 6 day rate, 780; 7 day rate, 870
Child: 1 day rate, 130; 2 day rate, 240; 3 day rate 360; 6 day rate, 670; 7 day rate, 740

Ski School:
Adult and Child:
2 h/day: 100; 2 h/day - 6 days 430;
2 h/day - 6 days (Feb. & Mar.) 470;
2 h/day - 6 days (Jan.) 340

Villard de Lans
Lift Rates:
Low Season Adult: 1 day rate, 105; 6 day rate, 535
High Season Adult: 1 day rate, 124; 6 day rate, 635; 10 day rate, 920
Low Season Child: 1 day rate, 70; 6 day rate, 428
High Season Child: 1 day rate, 99; 6 day rate, 508; 10 day rate, 736

Ski School:
Adult: 2 hours, 90; 6 day, 2 hours per day, 460; 6 day, 4 hours per day, 690
Child: 2 hours, 80; 6 day, 2 hours per day, 390; 6 day, 4 hours per day, 610

Rental Rates:
Adult Skis & Boots: 1 day rate, 60-145; 6 day rate, 250-695
Child Skis & Boots: 1 day rate, 45-85; 6 day rate, 180-410

GERMANY
(Currency: Deutsch Mark).
(Rate as of 9/1/98: 1.76GDM per U.S.$)

Berchtesgaden Land‡
Lift Rates:
Adult: 1 day rate, 35; 6 day rate, 195
Child: 1 day rate, 20; 6 day rate, 140
Day pass includes Oberau, Rossfeld, Zinken & Bad Dürrnberg

Ski School:
All: 5 day rate, 150
Private: 30-50 per hour; each add'l person, 10

Garmisch-Partenkirchen
Lift Rates:
Adult: 1 day Zugspitze: 61, 1 day Garmisch-Partenkirchen Ski area without Zugspitze: 48, 3 days complete ski area (Happy Ski Card): 141
Child: 1 day Zugspitze: 37, 1 day Garmisch-Partenkirchen Ski area without Zugspitze: 31, 3 days complete Ski area (Happy Ski Card): 90
The Happy Ski Card is available from 3-21 days.

Ski School: (Average)
Adult: 1 day (3 hours) 60, 3 days (à 3 hours) 150, 5 days (à 3 hours) 190
Child: 1 day (3 hours) 55, 5 days (à 3 hours) 185, 5 days (à 6 hours, meals included) 345
Skikindergarten: ½ day (9-12:30 or 13-16:30) 9, (12-16:30) 10, 1 day (9-16:30) 15, 5 days 60, meal 5 (per day)

Rental Rates: (Average)
Adult Skis, Boots and Poles: 1 day 32, 2 days 60, 5 days 130
Child Skis, Boots and Poles: 1 day 22, 5 days 80

Oberstdorf
Lift Rates:
High Season: Dec.-Jan. 10; Jan. 30-Apr. 10
Adult: 1 day rate, 57; 2 day rate, 111; 5 day rate, 228; 7 day rate, 284; 10 day rate, 356; 12 day rate, 397
Child: 1 day rate, 40; 2 day rate, 80; 5 day rate, 164; 7 day rate, 204; 10 day rate, 256; 12 day rate, 287

Low Season: Jan. 11-Jan. 29
Adult: 1 day rate, 55; 2 day rate, 104; 5 day rate, 213; 7 day rate, 264; 10 day rate, 331; 12 day rate, 370
Child: 1 day rate, 36; 2 day rate, 73; 5 day rate, 149; 7 day rate, 185; 10 day rate, 232; 12 day rate, 259

Ski School:
Adult or Child: 1 day rate, 50; 2 day rate, 90; 5 day rate, 180 (Average rates between several ski schools)
Private: ½ day 110; 1 day, 200

Rental Rates:‡
Adult Skis from 10-15 p/d, 40-80 p/w; Boots 5-9 p/d, 30-40 p/w
Child Skis from 7 p/d, 40 p/w; Boots from 4 p/d, 20 p/w

Reit im Winkl/Winklmoos-Alm/Steinplatte
Lift Rates:‡
Adult: 1 day rate, 48; 3 day rate, 126; 6 day rate, 220; 7 day rate, 248; 12 day rate, 348; 14 day rate, 370
Child: 1 day rate, 29; 3 day rate, 75; 6 day rate, 132; 7 day rate, 146; 12 day rate, 206; 14 day rate, 230

Ski School:
Adult or Child: 5 day rate, 160; 10 day rate, 290

Rental Rates:
Adult Skis & Boots: 1 day rate, 19; 10 day rate, 129
Child Skis & Boots: 1 day rate, 15; 10 day rate, 103

Voss
Lift Rates:
Adult: 1 day rate, 200; 3 day rate, 490; 6 day rate, 790; 7 day rate, 840; 60 p/d thereafter
Child: 1 day rate, 155; 3 day rate, 390; 6 day rate, 660; 7 day rate, 700; 50 p/d thereafter

Ski School:
  Private: 250 p/50 minutes
  450 p/100 minutes
  Group: 1 day 150; 3 days 400; 6 days 700 (2 hours per day)

Rental Rates:
  Adult: 1 day rate, 170; 3 day rate, 300; 6 day rate, 420;
    40 p/d thereafter
  Child: 1 day rate, 130; 3 day rate, 230; 6 day rate, 330;
    30 p/d thereafter

ITALY

(Currency: Italian Lira).
(Rate as of 9/1/98: 1,741.IL per U.S.$)

Altopiano Di Asiago 7 Comuni‡‡
Lift Rates:
  1 day rate, 33,000; 6 day rate, 80,000 (Asiago card)
  Holiday Season: 1 day rate, 35,000; 6 day rate, 195,000

Ski School:
  Low Season: 6 day rate, 130,000 (*50,000)
  (*White Weeks - 2 hours daily/group of 25)

Bormio
Lift Rates:
  Low Season: 1 day rate, 46,000; 2 day rate, 88,000; 6 day rate, 225,000; 14 day rate, 355,000
  High Season: 1 day rate, 49,000; 2 day rate, 95,000; 6 day rate, 250,000; 14 day rate, 400,000
  Child and over 65: 6 day rate, 160,000/Low; 175,000/High

Ski School:
  6 day rate, 150,000 p/2½ hrs.

Rental Rates:
  Skis & Boots: 6 day rate, 70,000; 12 day rate, 105,000

Claviere-Cesana Torinese‡
Lift Rates:
  *Low Season: 6 day rate, 165,000; 13 day rate, 240,000
  *High Season: 6 day rate, 180,000; 13 day rate, 255,000
  *Milky-Way Pass - (6 Resorts)

Ski School:
  Adult 6 day rate, 130,000
    (Six Consecutive Days - 3 hours daily)

Rental Rates:
  Skis & Boots: 6 day rate, 60,000

Cortina d'Ampezzo‡
Lift Rates:
  Low Season: 1 day rate, 45,000;
    6 day rate, 221,000; 13 day rate, 384,000
  High Season: 1 day rate, 51,000
    6 day rate, 255,000; 13 day rate, 441,000
  Children discount: −30 Percent from the 2nd day

Ski School:
  Private - Low season 1 hour, 1 person: 52,000 + 16,000 each additional person; High season 62,000 + 20,000 for each additional person; Group Lesson: 1 day rate, 60,000; 6 day rate, 270,000 (Six consecutive Ski School days)

Rental Rates:
  Ski/Binding: Adult 1 day 15-30,000; Child 1 day 10-20,000
  Boots: Adult 6 day rate, 35,000; Adult 13 day rate, 55,000;
    Child 6 day rate, 25,000; Child 13 day rate, 35,000

Courmayeur Mont-Blanc
  High Season: (12/5-12/8/98; 12/26/98-1/6/99; 4/1/99-4/6/99)
    - 53,000-1 day
  Low Season: 12/9-12/24/98; 1/7/99-3/31/99; 4/7-4/13/99-
    except on Saturdays, Sundays & Holidays) - 50,000 1 day
    1 day 40,000 - 4/12-4/25/99

Lift Rates:
  Low Season: 1 day rate, 50,000; 6 day rate, 230,000
  High Season: 1 day rate, 53,000; 6 day rate, 265,000
  A one week Courmayeur ski pass is good for several days of skiing at Chamonix, Pila & Megève

Ski School:
  Group Lessons: 6 day rate, Low Season: 195,000
  High Season: 210,000

Rental Rates:
  Skis: 6 day rate, 70,000
  Boots: 6 day rate, 47,000

Dolomite Superski Pass
Lift Rates:
  High Season: Dec. 24-Jan. 6; Jan. 31-Mar. 13
  Adult: 1 day rate, 59,000; 6 day rate, 291,000;
    10 day rate, 415,000
  Child: 1 day rate, 51,000; 6 day rate, 204,000;
    10 day rate, 290,000

  Low Season: Jan. 7-Jan. 30, Mar. 14-Apr. 11
  Adult: 1 day rate, 51,000; 6 day rate, 253,000;
    10 day rate, 361,000
  Child: 1 day rate, 46,000; 6 day rate, 177,000;
    10 day rate, 253,000
  (Other rates from 1-21 days)

Gressoney
Lift Rates:
  Low Season: 6 day rate, 195,000
  High Season: 6 day rate, 243,000

Ski School:
  Adult 6 day rate, 160,000 (12 hours), 190,000
    (15 hours) - Six Consecutive Days

Rental Rates:
  Rental of: Skis, boots, and skates

La Thuile‡
Lift Rates:
  Low Season: 6 day rate, 190,000
  High Season: 6 day rate, 215,000

Ski School:
  Adult 6 day rate, 155,000 (Six days - 1 hour daily)

Rental Rates:
  Rental of: Skis, boots, skates, sleds

Limone Piemonte‡
Lift Rates:
  Low Season: 6 day rate, 170,000; 13 day rate, 280,000
  High Season: 6 day rate, 190,000; 13 day rate, 305,000

Ski School:
  Adult 6 day rate, 120,000-200,000
    (Six consecutive days - 2 hours daily)

Rental Rates:
  Adult Ski/Bindings: 6 day rate, 32,000; 13 day rate, 48,500
  Child Ski/Bindings: 6 day rate, 24,000; 13 day rate, 35,500
  Adult Boots: 6 day rate, 20,000; 13 day rate, 27,000
  Child Boots: 6 day rate, 15,000; 13 day rate, 22,000

Livigno
Lift Rates:
  Low Season/Adult: 1 day rate, 46,000; 2 day rate, 87,000;
    6 day rate, 225,000; 14 day rate, 355,000

High Season/Adult: 1 day rate, 50,000; 2 day rate, 96,000; 6 day rate, 250,000 (Ski Circus—6 day minimum); 14 day rate, 400,000
Low Season/Child: 1 day rate, 36,000; 2 day rate, 68,000; 6 day rate, 160,000; 14 day rate, 255,000
High Season/Child: 1 day rate, 42,000; 2 day rate, 70,000; 6 day rate, 175,000; 14 day rate, 280,000
Photo is needed for ski passes valid more than 5 days.

Ski School:
Low Season/Adult: 43,000 per person per hour + 8,000 for every other person
High Season/Adult: 47,000 per person per hour, + 8,000 for every other person
Group lesson 6 day rate/2 hours per day: Low Season, 110,000; High Season, 125,000

Rental Rates:
6 day rate, Approx. 64,000; 12 day rate, 100,000

Macugnaga‡‡

Lift Rates:
Low Season: 6 day rate, 130,000; 13 day rate, 240,000
High Season: 6 day rate, 160,000; 13 day rate, 320,000

Ski School:
Adult: 35,000 per person, per hour - 5,000 for each additional person

Rental Rates:
Ski/Binding: Adult 6 day rate, 48,000; Child 6 day rate, 38,000; Adult 13 day rate, 71,000; Child 13 day rate, 56,000
Boots: Adult 6 day rate, 27,000; Child 6 day rate, 22,000; Adult 13 day rate, 41,000; Child 13 day rate, 33,000

Monte Bondone

Lift Rates:
Low Season: Adult 1 day rate, 30/35,000; 6 day rate, 137,000; 7 day rate, 148,000
High Season: Adult 1 day rate, 35/37,500; 6 day rate, 152/170,000; 7 day rate, 163/182,000
(Child: 20% discount, low and high season)

Ski School:
All: 1 day, 1 hour, 45,000 p/p; 6 days, 12 hours, 140/150,000

Pila

Lift Rates:
Low Season: 6 day rate, 211,000; 7 day rate, 238,000
High Season: 6 day rate, 242,000; 7 day rate, 276,000

Ski School:
5-day rate - 4 hours daily 185,000/without ski pass
5-day rate - 4 hours daily 195,000/without ski pass

Rental Rates:
Rental of: Skis, boots, sleds

Sauze d'Oulx‡

Lift Rates:
Low Season: 6 day rate, 210,000*; 10 day rate, 310,000*
High Season: 6 day rate, 230,000*; 10 day rate, 342,000*
*Lavia Lattea Pass - "Milky Way" 1 day 44,000

Ski School:
Six (6) Consecutive days - 3 Hours Daily
Low Season: 160,000; High Season: 180,000

Sestriere‡

Lift Rates:
*Low Season: 6 day rate, 210,000; 7 day rate, 230,000
*High Season: 6 day rate, 230,000; 7 day rate, 257,000
*'Milky Way' Pass - (6 Resorts)
Child: Under age 8 free if accompanied by a paid adult for the same time period

Ski School:
Adult/Child: 6 day rate, 190,000
(Six consecutive days - 3 hours daily)
Private: 49,000 p/h, p/p - each additional person 7,000

Rental Rates:
Adult: 1 day skis 13,000, boots 7,000
Child: 1 day skis 8,000, boots 6,000
Adult: 6 day skis 60,000, boots 30,000
Child: 6 day skis 36,000; boots 20,000

Val Di Fassa‡

Lift Rates:
Dolomite Super Ski Pass
Low Season: 1 day rate, 47,000; 3 day rate 132,000; 6 day rate, 233,000; 12 day rate, 381,000
High Season: 1 day rate, 54,000; 3 day rate, 152,000; 6 day rate, 268,000; 12 day rate, 438,000
Ski Pass Fassa: High Season Adult
6 day rate, 231,000; 14 day rate, 421,000
Child 30% less
Ski Pass TreValli: High Season Adult 1 day rate, 43,000; 6 day rate, 225,000; 14 day rate, 406,000
Child 30% less

Ski School:
1 hour for 1 person 42,000; 5 days, 3 hours per day, 140,000-155,000

Rental Rates:
Skis & Boots: 1 day, 15,000-20,000; 6 days, 70,000-100,000

Val Di Fiemme

Lift Rates:
Adult Low Season: 1 day rate, 42,000; 6 day rate, 214,000; 10 day rate, 305,000
Child Low Season: 1 day rate, 30,000; 6 day rate, 150,000; 10 day rate, 213,000
Adult High Season: 1 day rate, 47,000; 6 day rate, 246,000; 10 day rate, 350,000
Child High Season: 1 day rate, 34,000; 6 day rate, 172,000; 10 day rate, 245,000
(Rates for adults and children available for 1-14 days)

Ski School:
Adult or Child: 1 day, 1 hour per person, 45,000
For 10 hours weekly in groups of 10 persons, 140,000 per person
Special rates for children: 50% less when both parents take a lesson

Rental Rates:
Adult or Child: Skis and boots, 1 day 18,000; groups of 10-20 persons, 1 week 50,000

Val Gardena

Lift Rates:
Low Season: Adult 1 day rate, 47,000;
Adult 6 day rate, 231,000; Child 6 day rate, 162,000
High Season: Adult 1 day rate, 54,000;
Adult 6 day rate, 266,000; Child 6 day rate, 186,000

Ski School:
Low Season: 6 day rate, 215,000
High Season: 6 day rate, 230,000
Private Lesson - For 1 hour/1 person is 50,000 Low Season, 54,000 High Season

Rental Rates:
Adult Skis & Boots: 32,000 per day
Child Skis & Boots: 18,000-21,000 per day

NORWAY

(Currency: Norwegian Krone).
(Rate as of 9/1/98: 7.81 NOK per U.S.$)

Geilo

Lift Rates:
Adult: 1 day rate, 220; 6 day rate, 860
Child: 1 day rate, 160; 6 day rate, 645
Under 7: Free
Hourly rate: Adult: 2 hours, 135
Child: 2 hours, 100

Ski School:
Class: 1 day rate, 180; 2 day rate, 340; 3 day rate, 485; 4 day rate, 615; 5 day rate, 740 p/p

Rental Rates:
Adult: 6 day rate, 525
Child: 6 day rate, 390

Hafjell (National Alpine Center)

(All rate information is the same as Kvitfjell)

Hemsedal‡

Lift Rates:
Adult: 1 day rate, 220; 3 day rate, 550; 5 day rate, 790; 6 day rate, 890; 8 day rate, 1,065; 9-21 days + 75 p/d
Youth: Discounted rates; Children age 0-7: free

Ski School:
Group: Age 6 & over: 410 p/h
Youth: Discounted rates
Children: Age 0-7 free
Private: 240 p/50 minutes; 440 p/100 minutes
Snowboard or Telemark: 160 p/lesson

Rental Rates:
Adult: 6 day rate, 480; 12 day rate, 670
Child: 6 day rate, 380

Kvitfjell‡

Lift Rates: (Trollpass)
Adult: 1 day rate, 185; 2 day rate, 345; 3 day rate, 480; 4 day rate, 590; 5 day rate, 690; 6 day rate, 785; 7 day rate, 875
Child (7-15): 1 day rate, 140; 2 day rate, 250; 3 day rate, 350; 4 day rate, 440; 5 day rate, 520; 6 day rate, 590; 7 day rate, 655
Under age 7: Free
Options: Night skiing 4 of 7 days; Punchcard (chairlift 2 punches/T-bar 1 punch)

Ski School:‡‡
Group: (2) 250; (3) 300; (4) 350 minimum 6 persons per class of 2, 3 or 4 lessons
Private: (1) 250; (2) 160; (3) 130; (4) 120; (5) 110 per person, 45 minute lesson

Rental Rates: complete
Adult: 1 day rate, 165; 2 day rate, 260; 3 day rate, 320; 4 day rate, 375; 5 day rate, 430; 6 day rate, 480 (50 p/d thereafter)
Snowboard or Monoski: 1 day rate, 250, 2 day rate, 350; 3 day rate, 430; 4 day rate, 500; 5 day rate, 570; 6 day rate, 620 (50 p/d thereafter)

Norefjell

Lift Rates: (Child 7-9; Youth 10-15; Adult 16 & over)
Adult: 1 day rate, 220; 2 day rate, 400; 3 day rate, 550; 4 day rate, 670; 5 day rate 780; 6 day rate 880; 7 day rate 980; 8-14 days +90
Youth: 1 day rate 180; 2 day 320; 3 day 440; 4 day 550; 5 day 650; 6 day 740; 7 day 830; 8-14 days +80
Child: 1 day rate, 150; 2 day rate, 280; 3 day rate 390; 4 day rate, 480; 5 day rate, 560; 6 day rate 630; 7 day rate 700; 8-14 days +70

Ski School:
Private lesson, per person: (1) 280; (2) 190; (3) 140; (4) 110; (5) 90; (6) 80; 50 minutes p/lesson

Rental Rates:
Skis, Boots, Poles: 1 day rate, 180; 2 day rate, 280; 3 day 320; 5 day rate, 420; 6 day rate, 460
Cross country skis/boots/poles; Telemark skis/boots/poles, and Snowboards available for rent

SPAIN

(Currency: Spanish Peseta).
(Rate as of 9/1/98: 149.8SP per U.S.$)

Candanchu‡

Life Rates:
Low Season: 1 day rate 3,200; 3 day rate 8,500; 5 day rate 9,250 (Monday-Friday)
High Season: 1 day rate 3,200; 3 day rate 8,500; 5 day rate 10,250 (Monday-Friday)

Rental Rates:
Skis and Boots: 6 day rate 7,000

SWEDEN

(Currency: Swedish Krona).
(Rate as of 9/1/98: 8.07SKR per U.S.$)

Bjursås‡

Lift Rates:
Adult: 1 day rate, 160; 7 day rate, 730
Child: 1 day rate, 130; 7 day rate, 580

Ski School:
Adult: 150 per hour
Child: 120 per hour

Rental Rates:
Adult Skis & Boots: 1 day rate, 160; 7 day rate, 550
Child Skis & Boots: 1 day rate, 140; 7 day rate, 430

Bydalen

Lift Rates:
Adult: 1 day rate, 165; 7 day rate, 880
Child: 1 day rate, 125; 7 day rate, 660
Children under 8 free
(Family rates Available)

Ski School:
Adult: 1 day rate, 165; 3 day rate, 375; 5 day rate, 445
Child: 1 day rate, 145; 3 day rate, 325; 5 day rate, 395

Rental Rates:
Adult Skis & Boots: 1 day rate, 140; 2 day rate, 245; 3 day rate, 320; 7 day rate, 460
Child Skis & Boots: 1 day rate, 115; 2 day rate, 200; 3 day rate, 265; 7 day rate, 385

Sälen

Lift Rates:
Adult: 1 day rate, 200; 2 day rate, 390; 3 day rate, 580; 6 day rate, 840; 7 day rate 870
Children age 8-15 reduced rates; under 8 with helmet - free

Ski School:
Adult: 4 day (1.5 hour p/d) 490

Rental Rates:
Adult Skis 4 day 420

SWITZERLAND

(Currency: Swiss Franc).
(Rate as of 9/1/98: 1.441F per U.S.$)

Adelboden/Lenk
Lift Rates:
Adult: 1 day rate, 46; 6 day rate, 204
Child: 1 day rate, −40%; 6 day rate, −40%
Ski School:
½ day rate, 29; 6 day, 150
Rental Rates:
Adult: 1 day rate, 28; 6 day rate, 105

Andermatt
Lift Rates:
Adult: 1 day rate, 50; 6 day rate, 187
Child: 1 day rate, 34; 6 day rate, 125
Ski School:
1 day rate, 55; 5½ day rate, 160
Rental Rates:
Adult: 1 day rate, 50; 6 day rate, 180

Arosa
Lift Rates:
Adult: 1 day rate, 52; 6 day rate, 219
Child: −50% adult rate
Senior citizen discounts
Ski School:
Adult: ½ day rate, 29; 5 day rate, 185
Child: ½ day rate, 25; 5 day rate, 165
One day private lesson, with lunch, 275
Rental Rates:
Adult: 1 day rate, 43

Champery
Lift Rates (Portes du Soleil region):
Adult: 1 day rate, 49; 6 day rate, 224
Child: 1 day rate, 32; 6 day rate, 148
Ski School:
Adult: ½ day rate, 30; 5½ day rate, 120
Rental Rates:
Adult: 1 day rate, 28; 6 day rate, 105

Crans-Montana
Lift Rates:
Adult: 1 day rate, 56; 6 day rate, 265
Child: 1 day rate, 34; 6 day rate, 160
Ski School:
½ day rate, 37; 6½ day rate, 155
Rental Rates:
Adult: 7 day rate, 173
Child: 7 day rate, 95

Davos
Lift Rates:
Adult: 1 day rate, 52; 6 day rate, 265
Child: 1 or 6 day rate, less 40%
Ski School:
½ day rate, 30; 5 half days, 120; Private lesson 270/day
Rental Rates:
Adult: 1 day rate, 28

Disentis/Sedrun
Lift Rates:
Adult: 1 day rate, 43; 6 day rate, 199
Child: 1 day rate, 33; 6 day rate, 139
Ski School:
½ day rate, 26; 5 day rate, 155; Private lesson 210 p/day

Engelberg
Lift Rates:
Adult: 1 day rate, 48; 6 day rate, 214
Child: 1 day rate, 29; 6 day rate, 123
Ski School:
1 day rate, 84; 5 day rate, 358; (includes lift tickets); Private lesson 230 p/day
Rental Rates:
Adult: 1 day rate, 43; 6 day rate, 157

Flims-Laax-Falera
Lift Rates:
Adult: 1 day rate, 55; 6 day rate, 270
Child: 1 day rate, 27; 6 day rate, 135
Ski School:
1 day rate, 50; 5 day rate, 175
Rental Rates:
Adult: 1 day rate, 28

Grindelwald
Lift Rates:
Adult: 1 day rate, 50; 6 day rate, 244
Child: 1 day rate, 25; 6 day rate, 122
Ski School:
½ day rate, 32; 5 day rate, 192; Private, 288 p/day
Rental Rates:
Adult: 1 day rate, 50; 6 day rate, 180

Gstaad
Lift Rates:
Adult: 1 day rate, 46; 6 day rate, 233
Child: 1 day rate, 28; 6 day rate, 140
Ski School:
1 day rate, 50; 6 day rate, 205; Private, 260 p/day
Rental Rates:
Adult: 1 day rate, 38; 6 day rate, 130

Interlaken
Lift Rates:
Adult: 1 day rate, 69; 6 day rate, 265
(rate includes ski bus)
Ski School:
½ day rate, 37; 5 day rate, 205; Private lesson, 240 p/day
Rental Rates:
Adult: 1 day rate, 45

Klosters
Lift Rates:
Adult: 2 day rate, 115; 6 day rate, 265
Child: 2 day rate, 69; 6 day rate, 155
*Gotschna/Parsenn - Regional pass includes Davos
Ski School:
½ day rate, 35; 6 half day rate, 160; Private Lesson, 250 p/day
Rental Rates:
Adult: 1 day rate, 28; 6 day rate, 105

Lenzerheide/Valbella
Lift Rates:
Adult: 1 day rate, 48; 6 day rate, 226
Ski School:
½ day rate, 30; 5½ day rate, 140

©Publishers Group International, 1998

Rental Rates:
Adult: 1 day rate, 28; 6 day rate, 105

Les Diablerets
Lift Rates:
Adult: 1 day rate, 42; 6 day rate, 210

Ski School:
½ day rate, 26; 5½ day rate, 115; Private, 220 p/day

Rental Rates:
Adult: 1 day rate, 45; 6 day rate, 189

Leysin
Lift Rates:
Adult: 1 day rate, 34; 6 day rate, 170
Child: 1 day rate, 21; 6 day rate, 102

Ski School:
Adult: ½ day rate, 26; 6½ day rate, 130
Child: ½ day rate, 23; 6 day rate, 115

Meiringen-Hasliberg
Lift Rates:
Adult: 1 day rate, 46; 6 day rate, 191
Child: 1 day rate, 30; 6 day rate, 124

Ski School:
Adult: day rate, 40; 5 day rate, 145
Child: 1 day rate, 36; 5 day rate, 130
Private lesson, 1 hour, 55; 2 hours, 105; 5 hours, 240

Rental Rates:
Adult: 1 day rate, 38

Mürren
Lift Rates:
Adult: 1 day rate, 52; 7 day rate, 227
Child: 1 day rate, 26; 7 day rate, 114

Ski School:
½ day rate, 30; 6½ day rate, 130; Private lesson, 250 p/day

Pontresina
Lift Rates:
Adult: 1 day rate, 54; 7 day rate, 300
Child: 1 day rate, 42; 7 day rate, 150

Ski School:
1 day rate, 44; 6 days, 220; Private lesson, 240 p/day

Rental Rates:
Adult: 1 day rate, 28

Riederalp
Lift Rates:
Adult: 1 day rate, 35; 6 day rate, 169
Child: 1 day rate, 21; 6 day rate, 102

Ski School:
1 day rate, 38; 5 day rate, 150

Rental Rates:
Adult: 1 day rate, 38; 6 day rate, 130

Saas Fee
Lift Rates:
Adult: 1 day rate, 58; 6 day rate, 270
Child: 1 day rate, 33; 6 day rate, 150

Ski School:
1 day rate, 44; 6 day rate, 165

St. Moritz
Lift Rates:
Adult: 1 day rate, 50; 6 day rate, 258
Child: 1 day rate, 34; 6 day rate, 129

Ski School:
1 day rate, 60; 6 day rate, 230

Rental Rates:
Adult: 1 day rate, 43; 6 day rate, 157

Samnaun
Lift Rates:
Adult: 2 day rate, 87; 6 day rate, 225
Child: 2 day rate, 57; 6 day rate, 140

Ski School:
1 day rate, 54; 5 day rate, 161

Rental Rates:
Adult: 1 day rate, 28; 6 day rate, 105

Silvaplana
Lift Rates: (Region Ski Pass)
Adult: 1 day rate, 50; 5 day rate, 222
Child: 1 day rate, 35; 5 day rate, 111

Ski School:
½ day rate, 40; 6 day rate, 200; Private, 260 p/day

Rental Rates: (Skis & Boots)
Adult: 1 day rate, 57; 6 day rate, 207

Toggenburg
Lift Rates:
Adult: 1 day rate, 42; 6 day rate, 184
Child: 1 day rate, 29; 6 day rate 129

Ski School:
Adult: ½ day rate, 30; 6½ day rate, 120
Child: ½ day rate, 25; 6 day rate, 105

Verbier
Lift Rates:
Adult: 1 day rate, 56; 6 day rate, 282
Child: 1 or 6 day rate, less 40%

Ski School:
6½ day rate, 128

Rental Rates:
Adult 6 day rate, 157; Child 6 day rate, 64

Villars
Lift Rates:
Adult: 1 day rate, 42; 6 day rate, 210

Ski School:
½ day rate, 22; 6½ day rate, 100; Private lesson, 260 p/day

Rental Rates:
Adult: 1 day rate, 28; 6 day rate, 105

Wengen
Lift Rates:
Adult: 1 day rate, 52; 6 day rate, 244

Ski School:
1 day rate, 43; 6 day rate, 204

Rental Rates:
Adult: 1 day rate, 28

Zermatt
Lift Rates:
Adult: 1 day rate, 60; 6 day rate, 292
Child: 1 day rate, 35; 6 day rate, 146

Ski School:
Private lesson, 270 p/day; 6 day group rate, 215

Rental Rates:
Adult 6 day rate, 157-207

‡—1997/98 rates
‡‡—1995/96 rates

Not all Areas Represented

INDEX

ANDORRA
Arinsal, 132
Ordino-Arcalis, 133
Pal, 132
Pas de la Casa-Grau Roig, 134
Soldeu-El Tarter, 133

AUSTRIA
(C = Carinthia; Sa = Salzburg;
St = Styria;
T = Tirol; V = Vorarlberg)
Alpbach (T), 11
Alpendorf (Sa), 20
Altenmarkt (Sa), 20
Axamer Lizum (T), 14
Bad Gastein (Sa), 19
Bad Hofgastein (Sa), 19
Bad Kleinkirchheim (C), 22
Brandnertal (V), 4
Brixen im Thale (T), 16
Dachstein (St), 21
Dorfgastein (Sa), 19
Eben (Sa), 20
Ellmau (T), 15
Europa Sport Region (Kaprun, Zell am See) (Sa), 19
Filzmoos (Sa), 20
Flachau (Sa), 20
Fulpmes (T), 12
Galtür (T), 9
Gargellen (V), 4
Gaschurn (V), 4
Gastein Valley (Badgastein, Bad Hofgastein, Dorfgastein, Sportgastein) (Sa), 19
Gerlos, 15
Going (T), 16
Gurgl (T), 11
High Montafon (St. Gallenkirch, Gortipohl, Silvretta Nova) (V), 5
Hinterglemm (Sa), 18
Hintertux (T), 15
Hochgurgl (T), 11
Hopfgarten-Itter (T), 15
Hungerburg (T), 14
Igls (T), 14
Innsbruck Area (Axamer Lizum, Hungerburg, Igls, Tulfes) (T), 14
Ischgl (T), 9
Kaprun (Sa), 19
Katschberg (C), 22
Kirchberg (T), 16
Kitzbühel (T), 17
Kleinarl (Sa), 20
Lech am Arlberg (V), 8
Leogang (Sa), 18
Mandling (St), 19
Mayrhofen (T), 15
Mutters (T), 14
Montafon Valley (Gargellen, Gaschurn, Partenen, Schruns, Tschagguns) (V), 4
Neustift (T), 12
Obergurgl (T), 11
Obertauern (Sa), 21
Ötz Valley (Hochgurgl, Obergurgl, Sölden) (T), 10
Partenen (V), 4
Pichl (St), 20
Radstadt (Sa), 20
Ramsau (St), 20
Rohrmoos (St), 19
Saalbach (T), 18
Salzburg Sport World (Altenmarkt, Eben, Filzmoos, Flachau, Kleinarl, Radstadt, St. Johann im Pongau, Wagrain) (Sa), 20
St. Anton am Arlberg (T), 7
St. Christoph (T), 7
St. Gallenkirch (V), 5
St. Johann im Pongau (Sa), 20
St. Johann in Tyrol (T), 18
St. Oswald (C), 22
Scheffau (T), 17
Schladming (St), 21
Schruns (V), 4
Seefeld (T), 10
Silvretta Nova (V), 5
Sölden (T), 10
Sportgastein (Sa), 19
Stubai (T), 12
Stuben am Arlberg (T), 7
Tauern (St), 21
Tschagguns (V), 4
Tulfes (T), 14
Wagrain (Sa), 20
Westendorf (T), 16
Wilder Kaiser (T), 16
Zauchensee (Sa), 20
Zell am See (Sa), 19
Zell am Ziller (T), 15
Zillertal (T), 15
Zürs am Arlberg (V), 8

FRANCE
Alpe d'Huez, 49
Autrans, 51
Avoriaz, 30
Chamonix, 36
Chamrousse, 50
Courchevel, 47
Flaine, 35
La Clusaz, 32
La Plagne, 42
Lans en Vercors, 54
Le Grand Bornand, 32
Les Angles, 134
Les 7 Laux, 52
Les Arcs, 40
Les 2 Alpes, 50
Les Menuires, 43
Les Portes du Soleil (Les Gets, Morzine, Avoriaz, Châtel, St. Jean D'Aulps, Chapelle D'Abondance), 31 (Switzerland, 96)
Les Trois Vallées (Courchevel, Les Menuires, Meribél, Mottaret/Val Thorens), 43-47
Luz Ardiden, 135
Megève, 33
Méribel, 44
Mont Blanc, 36
Morzine, 30
Mottaret, 44
Peisey Vallandry, 41
Saint Gervaise Mont Blanc, 34
Saint Lary Soulan, 135
Saint Pierre de Chartreus, 52
Serre Chevalier-Briançon, 53
Tignes, 39
Val d'Isère, 48
Valmorel, 49
Val Thorens, 46
Vars, 54
Villard de Lans, 53

GERMANY
Berchtesgadener Land (Götschen, Jenner, Loipi, Rossfeld, Hochschwarzeck), 64
Garmisch-Partenkirchen, 61
Götschen, 64
Hochschwarzeck, 64
Jenner, 64
Loipi, 64
Oberammergau, 62
Oberstdorf, 63
Reit im Winkl, 64
Rossfeld, 64
Steinplatte, 64
Winklmoos, 64

©Publishers Group International, 1998

ICELAND
Bláfjöll, 129
Hlídargjall (Akureyri), 129

ITALY
(Regions: F = Friuli-Venezia; L = Lombardia; P = Piemonte; T = Trentino-Alto Adige; Va—Valle d'Aosta; Ve = Veneto)
Alpe Siusi-Sciliar (T), 79
Altopiani di Asiago (Ve), 77
Arabba (Ve), 77
Ayas (Va), 68
Bardonecchia (P), 72
Bormio (L), 76
Cervinia (Va), 70
Cesano Torinese (P), 75
Claviere (P), 75
Cortina d'Ampezzo (Ve), 78
Courmayeur (Va), 69
Folgárida (T), 80
Gressoney (Va), 71
La Thuile (Va), 70
Limone Piemonte (P), 73
Livigno (L), 75
Macugnaga (P), 74
Madonna di Campiglio (T), 81
Marillèva (T), 81
Monte Bondone (T), 80
Piancavallo (F), 86
Pila (Va), 71
S. Caterina Valfurva (L), 76
Sauze d'Oulx (P), 74
Selva (T), 85
Sestrière (P), 73
Solda Tra Foi (T), 82
Val Di Fassa (T), 83
Val Di Fiemme (T), 83
Val Gardena (T), 85
Val Senales (T), 84
Val Tourenche (Va), 70

LIECHTENSTEIN
Malbun/Steg, 116

NORWAY
Geilo, 124
Hafjell, 123
Hemsedal, 124
Kvitfjell, 123
Lillehammer (Hafjell, Kvitjell), 123
Norefjell, 125
Voss, 125

SLOVENIA
Kanin, 142
Kobla, 143
Kranjska Gora, 141
Krvavec, 142
Mariborsko, 144
Rogla, 144
Vogel, 143

SPAIN
Baqueira-Beret, 137
Candanchu, 137
Formigal, 138
Sierra Nevada, 138

SWEDEN
Årefjällen, 128
Bjursås, 126
Bydalen, 127
Riksgränsen, 128
Sälen, 126
Storlien, 127

SWITZERLAND
Adelboden, 101
Alt St. Johann, 116
Andermatt, 107
Anzère, 96
Arosa, 110
Bettmeralp, 99
Champery, 96
Champoussin, 96
Chateau-d'Oex, 94
Crans-Montana, 98
Davos, 108
Disentis, 111
Engelberg, 107
Flims, 112
Falera, 112
Grindelwald, 102
Gstaad, 101
Interlaken, 106
Klosters, 109
Laax, 112
Lenk, 101
Lenzerheide, 111
Leukerbad, 98
Leysin, 95
Les Diablerets, 94
Les Portes du Soleil (Champery, Champoussin, Planachaux, Morgins, Val D'Illiez, Les Crosets, Torgon), 96 (France, 31)
Meiringen, 106
Mürren, 105
Planachaux, 96
Pontresina, 113
Riederalp, 99
St. Moritz, 115
Saanenland, 101
Samnaun, 112
Saas-Fee, 99
Sedrun, 111
Silvaplana, 114
Toggenburg, 116
Unterwasser, 116
Verbier, 97
Villars, 95
Wengen, 103
Wildhaus, 116
Zermatt, 100

INSTEAD OF THE SAME SKI TRIP AS EVERY
TOM, DICK AND HARRY,
TAKE THE SAME SKI TRIP AS EVERY
PIERRE, HANS AND ANTONIO.

ALPINE EXPERIENCE. SKI, SLEEP, FLY EUROPE STARTING AT $774. This year, while the Joneses and the Smiths snowplow the Rockies, you can schuss a glacier or even ski from one country to another – for the same price. From only $774*per person, choose from 90 hotels, 17 resorts in Switzerland, Italy, France, Austria and Germany. Including round-trip Economy Class air, 7 nights accommodations, transfers, breakfast daily and often dinner. Plus, the undying admiration of every average Joe. Call your travel agent or **1-800-662-0021**, ext. 34 for a free Alpine Experience brochure.

swissair +
the refreshing airline
www.swissair.com

*Package costs are per person based on double occupancy and airfare from New York, Newark or Boston. Surcharges from other gateways apply. Fees, taxes and airport charges of up to $53 not included. Price of $774 is for destination Kitzbuehel. Certain conditions and restrictions apply.

Partner in the Delta Air Lines, Midwest Express Airlines and US Airways frequent flyer programs.

The White Book of Ski Areas, U.S. & Canada, 1998/99
AND
The Blue Book of European Ski Resorts, 1999–2000

The perfect birthday or holiday gift for that skier in your life. They'll appreciate your thoughtfulness every time they open the book. Or, get an extra copy for the home, office or car.

The White Book of Ski Areas, U.S. & Canada, 1998/99

AND

The Blue Book of European Ski Resorts, 1999–2000

☐ Send me a copy of the 23rd edition of The White Book/U.S.
☐ Send me a copy of the 5th edition of The Blue Book/Europe

The White Book of Ski Areas: _____ (Number of copies) × $21.95 = $ _____
The Blue Book of European Resorts: _____ (Number of copies) × $18.95 = $ _____
Shipping (Add $4.00 for 1st copy and $2.00 per copy thereafter. Canadian orders please add $2.00 additional per copy) $ _____

Make check or money order payable to: InterSki Services.
TOTAL ENCLOSED OR TO BE CHARGED $ _____

Method of payment ☐ Check ☐ Money Order ☐ Visa ☐ Master Card
Credit Card Account Number and Expiration Date

[ ][ ][ ][ ][ ][ ][ ][ ][ ][ ][ ][ ][ ][ ][ ][ ] [ ][ ] [ ][ ]
                                                    Month   Year

SIGNATURE _____
NAME _____ DAY / MONTH / YEAR
ADDRESS _____
CITY / STATE _____ ZIP / POSTAL CODE
(_____) _____
DAYTIME TELEPHONE

The White Book of Ski Areas, U.S. & Canada, 1998/99

AND

The Blue Book of European Ski Resorts, 1999–2000

☐ Send me a copy of the 23rd edition of The White Book/U.S.
☐ Send me a copy of the 5th edition of The Blue Book/Europe

The White Book of Ski Areas: _____ (Number of copies) × $21.95 = $ _____
The Blue Book of European Resorts: _____ (Number of copies) × $18.95 = $ _____
Shipping (Add $4.00 for 1st copy and $2.00 per copy thereafter. Canadian orders please add $2.00 additional per copy) $ _____

Make check or money order payable to: InterSki Services.
TOTAL ENCLOSED OR TO BE CHARGED $ _____

Method of payment ☐ Check ☐ Money Order ☐ Visa ☐ Master Card
Credit Card Account Number and Expiration Date

[ ][ ][ ][ ][ ][ ][ ][ ][ ][ ][ ][ ][ ][ ][ ][ ] [ ][ ] [ ][ ]
                                                    Month   Year

SIGNATURE _____
NAME _____ DAY / MONTH / YEAR
ADDRESS _____
CITY / STATE _____ ZIP / POSTAL CODE
(_____) _____
DAYTIME TELEPHONE

**Please place in an envelope
and return to:**

Publishers Group International, Inc.

The Blue Book of European Ski Resorts
P.O. Box 3775
Washington, D.C. 20007

**Please place in an envelope
and return to:**

Publishers Group International, Inc.

The Blue Book of European Ski Resorts
P.O. Box 3775
Washington, D.C. 20007

The White Book of Ski Areas, U.S. & Canada, 1998/99
AND
The Blue Book of European Ski Resorts, 1999–2000

The perfect birthday or holiday gift for that skier in your life. They'll appreciate your thoughtfulness every time they open the book. Or, get an extra copy for the home, office or car.

The White Book of Ski Areas, U.S. & Canada, 1998/99

AND

The Blue Book of European Ski Resorts, 1999–2000

☐ Send me a copy of the 23rd edition of The White Book/U.S.
☐ Send me a copy of the 5th edition of The Blue Book/Europe

The White Book of Ski Areas: _____ × $21.95 = $ _____
                              Number of copies

The Blue Book of European Resorts: _____ × $18.95 = $ _____
                                    Number of copies

Shipping (Add $4.00 for 1st copy and $2.00 per copy thereafter. Canadian orders please add $2.00 additional per copy) $ _____

Make check or money order payable to: **TOTAL ENCLOSED**
InterSki Services.   **OR TO BE CHARGED** $ _____

Method of payment ☐ Check ☐ Money Order ☐ Visa ☐ Master Card
Credit Card Account Number and Expiration Date

[ ][ ][ ][ ][ ][ ][ ][ ][ ][ ][ ][ ][ ][ ][ ][ ]   [ ][ ] [ ][ ]
                                                    Month   Year

_____
SIGNATURE

_____   _____
NAME   DAY / MONTH / YEAR

_____
ADDRESS

_____   _____
CITY / STATE   ZIP / POSTAL CODE

( )_____
DAYTIME TELEPHONE

The White Book of Ski Areas, U.S. & Canada, 1998/99

AND

The Blue Book of European Ski Resorts, 1999–2000

☐ Send me a copy of the 23rd edition of The White Book/U.S.
☐ Send me a copy of the 5th edition of The Blue Book/Europe

The White Book of Ski Areas: _____ × $21.95 = $ _____
                              Number of copies

The Blue Book of European Resorts: _____ × $18.95 = $ _____
                                    Number of copies

Shipping (Add $4.00 for 1st copy and $2.00 per copy thereafter. Canadian orders please add $2.00 additional per copy) $ _____

Make check or money order payable to: **TOTAL ENCLOSED**
InterSki Services.   **OR TO BE CHARGED** $ _____

Method of payment ☐ Check ☐ Money Order ☐ Visa ☐ Master Card
Credit Card Account Number and Expiration Date

[ ][ ][ ][ ][ ][ ][ ][ ][ ][ ][ ][ ][ ][ ][ ][ ]   [ ][ ] [ ][ ]
                                                    Month   Year

_____
SIGNATURE

_____   _____
NAME   DAY / MONTH / YEAR

_____
ADDRESS

_____   _____
CITY / STATE   ZIP / POSTAL CODE

( )_____
DAYTIME TELEPHONE

**Please place in an envelope
and return to:**

Publishers Group International, Inc.

The Blue Book of European Ski Resorts
P.O. Box 3775
Washington, D.C. 20007

**Please place in an envelope
and return to:**

Publishers Group International, Inc.

The Blue Book of European Ski Resorts
P.O. Box 3775
Washington, D.C. 20007